Founding Grammars

ROSEMARIE OSTLER

Founding Grammars

HOW EARLY AMERICA'S
WAR OVER WORDS SHAPED
TODAY'S LANGUAGE

ST. MARTIN'S PRESS ✹ NEW YORK

FOUNDING GRAMMARS. Copyright © 2015 by Rosemarie Ostler. All rights reserved. Printed in the United States of America. For information, address St. Martin's Press, 175 Fifth Avenue, New York, N.Y. 10010.

www.stmartins.com

The Library of Congress Cataloging-in-Publication Data is available upon request.

ISBN 978-1-250-04612-3 (hardcover)
ISBN 978-1-4668-4628-9 (e-book)

St. Martin's Press books may be purchased for educational, business, or promotional use. For information on bulk purchases, please contact the Macmillan Corporate and Premium Sales Department at 1-800-221-7945, extension 5442, or write to specialmarkets@macmillan.com.

First Edition: May 2015

10 9 8 7 6 5 4 3 2 1

Contents

Acknowledgments   *vii*

Preface   *1*

1. Grammar for a New Country   *5*

2. Grammar for Different Classes of Learners   *41*

3. The Value of Grammar   *79*

4. Rational Grammar   *111*

5. Grammar and Gentility   *143*

6. The Science of Grammar   *175*

7. Grammar for a New Century   *209*

8. The Persistence of Grammar   *243*

Notes   *271*

Bibliography   *291*

Index   *297*

Acknowledgments

Big thanks go to the following people: my excellent editor at St. Martin's, Daniela Rapp, for helping me produce the best book possible; my wonderful agent, Janet Rosen of Sheree Bykofsky Associates, for her support and professional know-how over the years; my critique group, Mary-Kate Mackey, Deanna Larson, Kelly O'Brien, and Sophia Bennett, for their enthusiasm and sharp editing skills; and, as always, my husband, Jeff Ostler, for his support and valuable input as I was writing this book.

Founding Grammars

Preface

What's your pet usage peeve? Do you grind your teeth when someone starts a sentence with *hopefully*? Does it drive you crazy when someone says *between you and I*? We all have intense feelings about language use, and nearly everyone has a few usage gripes. These can range from the purely grammatical, such as substituting *me* for *I*, to spelling errors like writing *it's* instead of *its*. We've all been exposed to the standard rules at some time or another—"Don't split an infinitive"; "never end a sentence with a preposition"; "use *whom* in objective case"; "avoid double negatives."

Never mind that these rules are seldom followed and may be impossible to apply consistently. (Try using subject pronouns after every instance of the verb *to be*. *It is I* might be okay, but how does *It couldn't have been we* sound?) Never mind that some of them don't make sense for English. (Infinitives, for example, are already "split," since they consist of two words—*to* plus a verb. There's no reason not to boldly insert an adverb in between.) These well-worn axioms are woven into the culture. Once they get a grip on us, it's hard to break free.

Every so often, language scholars will point out the pitfalls of trying to follow arbitrary grammar rules from earlier centuries. Their well-meaning interventions never fail to trigger red-hot outbursts from purists. Blog posts that touch even indirectly on style issues draw huge numbers of angry comments. People who've learned the traditional rules don't want to be told that those rules are confused or don't really matter. A command of the standard grammar rules is one hallmark of a good education and has been for centuries. For many people it's more than that—it's a sign of civic virtue.

Our fascination with grammar is nothing new. Americans have been passionate about grammar and linguistic style since the earliest days of the republic. The question of which linguistic model the new country should follow was energetically debated in the early United States. On one side were those who still saw England as the source of superior speech habits. Although they could imagine polishing and improving the language, they weren't interested in making any radical changes. They preferred to stick with the tried and true, including imported British grammar books.

On the other side—a much smaller group—were the linguistic freethinkers who wanted to see Americans develop their own speech standards based on their own natural idiom. Famous dictionary author Noah Webster was among the first to champion this side. His alternative grammar writings encouraged Americans to blaze their own linguistic path. Webster's challenges to his grammatical enemies—and their furious retorts—were the first of those explosive clashes that seem to be an inevitable feature of any grammar discussion.

No matter which side you were on in the late eighteenth century, grammar books were big business. They provided the foundation of a solid education. Children learned how to read and spell from the lists of letters and syllables in the first chapters of the book. Those who were lucky enough to attend school for more than a year or two progressed to more advanced lessons. Older students spent a large part of the school day memorizing parts of speech and usage rules, and meticulously dissecting sentences into their component parts. The carefully chosen readings, either at the back of the book or in a separate volume, were meant to do more than teach language skills. They turned children's thoughts toward righteous living. Just studying a grammar book was in itself considered a step in the direction of goodness.

Plenty of adults in early America memorized grammar books, too. In the new country, opportunities for self-betterment were greater than ever before, but a command of standard English was a necessary first step. That meant mastering the contents of one of the popular grammar texts. Because they were cheaper and more available than other books, they were an educational lifeline for anyone too poor, too geographically isolated, or too old to take advantage of formal schooling.

Early grammar books are exotic items today. They are filled with antiquated prose, obscure quotations, and elevated passages from long-forgotten volumes. With their ornate typefaces, they are sometimes a struggle to read. Yet in some ways grammar books are oddly familiar. Most of the rules that people think about when they hear the words "correct grammar" can be found in these books, often with their wording virtually unchanged. The double negatives rule—"two negatives make a positive"—has come down to us over the centuries very much as it appeared in 1770s grammar books.

Old-fashioned grammar books held a powerful cultural sway until recent decades. As late as the mid-twentieth century, they were an important part of many people's education. We used them in the small parochial school that I attended in the 1960s. Like schoolchildren of previous centuries, we worked our way straight through the books, memorizing and reciting everything in our path, including the inspirational poems that the authors inserted to break up the lists of verb forms and usage rules.

(Longfellow's "Excelsior" is one example that stands out in my recollection.) By the time we graduated, my classmates and I had the rules down cold. I'm guessing that most of us still do.

People these days no longer learn grammar by memorizing a book. Few schoolchildren study grammar as a distinct subject, and in any case, rote memorization as a teaching tool has gone out of style. The books still matter though. Their rules—and their point of view—continue to color how we think about language. Ask anyone for a grammar rule and the odds are that you'll be told not to end a sentence with a preposition or split an infinitive. Grammar advice, both in print and online, remains a booming business. Many people still believe that being able to hit all the grammar marks reveals something positive about their intelligence, social class, and character. Even if we realize that speech styles change over time, we can't help feeling jarred when writers or our conversational partners violate familiar shibboleths, such as saying *like* when it should be *as* or using *I* instead of *me* after a preposition.

The terms of the grammar debate have changed remarkably little since the late eighteenth century. There are some signs, however, that the gulf between the two sides may be narrowing. One is the more flexible attitude of many style advisors toward common usages. Another is the increased number of linguists and other language professionals writing about usage in terms that nonspecialists can follow. Whichever side of the debate you're on, understanding how we got to this place is sure to give you a better appreciation of your own and other people's approach to language use.

1.

Grammar for a New Country

On the evening of October 19, 1785, thirty people braved the rainy Baltimore weather to attend the first of five lectures on the English language. The cautious ones had paid a quarter for a ticket to this one event. The more committed had spent seven shillings sixpence (equal to a dollar) for the whole series. The lectures were to take place in the First Presbyterian Church, a plain brick building on Fayette Street. Although the building was small—only fifty pews—the audience didn't begin to fill it. The speaker, a young visitor to Baltimore named Noah Webster, was not well enough known to draw a big crowd.[1]

This evening would be Webster's first experience as a public lecturer. An unsuccessful lawyer and itinerant schoolmaster, the twenty-six-year-old native of Hartford, Connecticut, had recently launched a new career—author of grammar and spelling books. Webster's three-part *Grammatical Institute of the English Language* featured a speller, a grammar, and a reader, the three subjects typically taught under the broad heading of "grammar" in early American schools. They were the first books of their kind written by an American, for Americans.

Although the speller was on its way to becoming popular, the grammar had not come close to replacing the available British versions. Webster hoped to change that. He had been on the road since May, crisscrossing the Eastern Seaboard from New York to

South Carolina. In every town he visited, he distributed his books to schools, left stacks of them with booksellers, advertised them in newspapers, and talked about them to anyone who might be interested. The American language was Webster's passion. He believed strongly that Americans deserved language books designed expressly for them.[2]

Webster also wanted protection from book printers who might pirate his work. As he traveled, he registered his books in the few states that guaranteed copyright, and petitioned legislators in other states to pass copyright laws. Catching the legislatures in session often meant loitering in one place for weeks. He had traveled from Baltimore to Charleston in late June only to find South Carolina's legislature out of session, so he returned to Baltimore to wait until it reconvened.

While he waited, he kept busy. There was plenty to do in this bustling harbor town. Almost daily, Webster breakfasted or took tea with new acquaintances, or simply strolled through town with them. At least twice, he went down to the harbor and boarded ships that had recently arrived from exotic places like China and India. He joined the First Presbyterian Church and became friends with its young pastor, Dr. Patrick Allison. With Allison's approval, he started a singing school at the church and gave music lessons during the week. He began studying French.

The English language and grammar were still Webster's main concern. One week in late August when he had fewer social engagements than usual, he decided to occupy himself by putting his ideas on paper. Over the next month, he wrote steadily. By early October he had finished five "dissertations"—essays outlining his theories about language, and especially about American English. Over cups of tea, he read them to Allison, who liked them well enough to agree that Webster could use the church for a series of lectures.

Public lectures were a popular form of entertainment in the

eighteenth century. Webster attended several during his book-selling trip, mainly on scientific subjects. Americans of the time believed that most leisure activities should be aimed at self-improvement. As citizens of a new democracy, they also considered it their duty to stay well informed. Besides providing an evening out, lectures were a way to keep up with the latest scientific discoveries and cultural trends. Writers, inventors, preachers, and speakers of all kinds took to the traveling lecture circuit to make money and spread their ideas.

No doubt part of Webster's plan was to earn a little money. He was currently surviving on the edge of poverty, and traveling was expensive. At least as important, though, was his desire to influence the way Americans used and thought about their language. The announcement advertising the lectures promised a "general history of the English language," but Webster's real aim was more radical.[3] He wanted to convince his audience to take a bold new approach to grammar—a uniquely American approach.

Some of those waiting in the sparsely filled pews that October evening may have been fellow church members. Others would have been drawn there no matter what the topic, simply as a way to fill an evening. Grammar was an especially compelling issue, though, for anyone who cared about education or self-betterment. Schoolchildren spent much of their class time memorizing and reciting grammar rules, but the books were important for adults, too, especially those who lacked formal schooling. People who wanted to advance in life needed a command of educated-sounding English. That meant poring over and memorizing standard grammar texts. Grammar books were prized possessions in the late eighteenth century. Quite a few households owned only two volumes—the Bible and a grammar book.

Webster started his talk promptly at 7:00 p.m. Tall, angular, and square-jawed, with an erect posture and curling auburn hair, he would have made an imposing figure. He was not a polished speaker. Some of his listeners later remarked on his high-pitched voice and stiff gestures. He spoke in an overbearing style that to many came off as arrogant, but it was really the intensity of fierce commitment and confidence in his own point of view.

Webster began with boilerplate remarks on the value of language study and on the "purity, strength, and elegance" of English in particular. This type of commentary was typical among eighteenth-century language scholars. Soon, however, he was expounding more original ideas.[4]

He spoke of the political desirability of achieving a uniform speech standard for the whole country. This idea was not new in itself—others had suggested it. Webster had an unusual perspective on it though. "As an independent nation," he told his listeners, "our honor requires us to have a system of our own, in language as well as government." The mother country, he argued, was too far away to act as a model. Besides, it was no longer appropriate for Americans to follow the old world's lead.

In Great Britain, the speech habits of royalty and the upper classes were the preferred model, but Webster thought it was absurd to base a country's linguistic standards on the speech of one group, especially as their usage was bound to change over time. That would be "like fixing a lighthouse on a floating island." Instead, Webster believed that Americans should set their own standards. "The rules of the language itself," he said, "and the general practice of the nation, constitute propriety in speaking."

Other grammarians, in Webster's view, had made one major mistake in their treatment of English: "They lay down certain rules, arbitrary perhaps or drawn from the principles of other languages, and then condemn all English phrases which do not coincide with those rules. They seem not to consider that grammar is formed on language, and not language on grammar." Here he was taking a swipe at rival grammar book authors, who modeled their grammar rules on those of Latin. He continued, "Instead of examining to find what the English language *is,* they endeavor to show what it *ought to be* according to their rules."

To eighteenth-century grammar book authors—and the people who bought their books—these were fighting words. They contradicted all the accepted ideas about what grammar was for and how to teach it. Webster had just fired the opening round in a battle that's still raging today. On one side are those who think that grammar should reflect what the English language is, on the other are those more concerned with showing what it ought to be.

The lecture eventually expanded into a broader examination of the English language. For twenty-five cents (worth about the price of a movie ticket in today's terms), eighteenth-century audiences expected a thorough exploration of the speaker's topic lasting at least two hours. Webster sketched a brief history of English, including its foreign influences, and touched on its convoluted spelling practices, another of his linguistic concerns.[5]

At the end of his lecture he returned to the question of American speech standards and called again for a new approach. Standards should be based on the obvious patterns of the language. Where no clear pattern existed, grammar rules should be based on "the opinions of the learned, and the practice of the nations." In other words, standards should come from what most people deemed acceptable speech. That did not necessarily coincide with the rules found in the currently popular British grammar books.

In spite of Webster's shortcomings as a lecturer, his subject found a ready audience. Each succeeding talk drew a larger attendance. His discussions ranged widely, from a sweeping review of the world's languages and how they evolved to an examination of controversial word pronunciations in different areas of the country. Whatever the issue, he kept returning to his argument that Americans should take charge of their own speech.

This belief led him to champion some usages that were frowned on by most grammarians of the time. He noted that while *It is me* was not considered strictly grammatical, it was far more prevalent than *It is I*, and therefore should be acceptable. He also thought *Who do you speak to* was preferable to *Whom do you speak to* because the latter was never heard in ordinary speech. In Webster's opinion, *whom* was "hardly English at all"—more of a corruption from Latin. Again and again, he emphasized that American speech standards should be based on America's linguistic realities, not the language of the British king and court or the irrelevant patterns of Latin grammar.

By the time Webster had finished presenting the complete series of talks on October 26, he was able to note with satisfaction in his diary, "The lectures have received so much applause that I am induced to revise and continue reading them in other towns." He later wrote to a friend that his ideas had been well received, including his criticisms of other grammarians. He explained, "My criticisms are *new* and no person here is capable of disproving my remarks." With characteristic self-confidence, he then restated his determination to change how Americans talked: "I have begun a reformation in the language and my plan is yet but in embryo."[6] He hoped that with more lecturing and writing, he could draw Americans away from British grammar books and toward a more natural form of speech.

Webster's lectures attracted an audience partly because questions of language use were on people's minds during and after the Revolution. In the heady aftermath of declaring independence, Americans were faced with the dilemma of how much they should separate themselves culturally from the mother country. Among the issues troubling them was whether they should continue to accept British speech standards as the model for their own language use.

In the two centuries or so between the first English settlements in North America and the Revolution, the American version of English had grown distinctly different from the British version. All languages evolve over time. From one generation to the next, small changes occur in people's pronunciations and how they structure sentences. Word meanings shift, obsolete words disappear, and new words take their place. Although these changes happen slowly, eventually they add up. Because American and British English speakers were separated by an ocean, the two forms of the language had evolved in two different directions.

Americans had invented dozens of words to describe their new environment—*backwoods, rapids, muskrat*—and adopted dozens more from the natives—*squash, possum, hickory.* New expressions arose and usages such as *It is me* became more common. Pronunciations had changed noticeably. Travelers from Great Britain often commented on the distinctive American accent, usually describing it as a drawl. They also remarked on the nasal quality of American speech.

Americans were proud of the cultural and political differences that separated them from the old country. Nonetheless, most Americans still looked to England for linguistic guidance. Suggestions for establishing American grammatical standards typically assumed that the starting point should be the best version of British English.

Most proposals took a top-down approach. One popular idea was to found an American Academy of Language that would determine principles of correct speech. Some were already imagining this possibility in the run-up to independence. Language was a serious enough issue to inspire commentary, even in the midst of planning for a war.

In January 1774, the *Royal American Magazine* printed a letter patriotically signed "An American." (Signing letters to the editor with a meaningful pseudonym was common at the time.) The writer argued that although British English had improved greatly over the past century, "its highest perfection, with every other branch of human knowledge, is perhaps reserved for this land of light and freedom." He then proposed the formation of an American Society of Language, with members who will "publish some observations upon the language and from year to year, correct, enrich and refine it."[7]

Founding father John Adams also favored language reform from above. In a 1780 letter, he urged the president of Congress to consider instituting an academy "for correcting, improving, and fixing the English language," which he believed "would strike all the world with admiration and Great Britain with envy." (By "fixing" the English language, Adams meant deciding on a standard that could be permanently "fixed" in place.) Adams thought that American speech should grow out of British traditions. He explains in his letter, "We have not made war against the English language any more than against the old English character."[8] Adams and other backers of an academy weren't interested in creating a new linguistic standard from scratch. They simply wanted to perfect the old one.

Webster's idea was more unusual. He envisioned starting from the bottom up. Two years before his Baltimore talks, in the introduction to his spelling book (*A Grammatical Institute, Part I*), he used an imaginative metaphor to state his position: "For America in her infancy to adopt the present maxims of the old world would be to stamp the wrinkle of decrepit age upon the bloom of youth."[9] As citizens of a new country, Americans had a unique opportunity to make their own rules. Webster wanted those rules to be based on current American speech.

In this he was in the minority. Most Americans relied on British grammar books—the very grammars that Webster had attacked in his first lecture—to teach them the best version of their native language. One of the most popular and earliest to be imported was *A New Guide to the English Tongue* by English schoolmaster Thomas Dilworth. Dilworth's Spelling Book, as it was popularly called, appeared in England in 1740. Benjamin Franklin first reprinted it in Philadelphia in 1747. It went through numerous editions and by 1785 a copy could be found in many homes and nearly all classrooms.[10] Webster used it as a child. In the small farming hamlet of West Hartford, where he grew up, it was the only book the district school owned, apart from the Psalter (Book of Psalms) and the New Testament.

An even more popular grammar book in 1785 was *A Short Introduction to English Grammar* by Anglican clergyman, later Bishop of Oxford, Robert Lowth. Bishop Lowth's book appeared on the scene later than Dilworth's—it was published in London in 1762 and in Philadelphia in 1775. It had a more lasting impact, however. Both Harvard and Yale used it as a textbook until the middle of the nineteenth century and later grammar writers borrowed from it freely.

Several of the most familiar rules of "proper" grammar originated or were popularized in Lowth's book. Lowth banned double negatives with the formula still universally accepted today—"Two negatives in English destroy one another, or are equivalent to an affirmative."[11] He argued that when two people or things were compared, the second should be treated as the subject of a missing verb—*You are wiser than I (am)*, not *You are wiser than me*. Lowth also objected to the use of *whose* for inanimate objects, preferring *of which*, even though it can result in awkward constructions like *This is the book the pages of which are badly stained*. (One rule that he doesn't mention is the "split" infinitive rule—the ban on inserting an adverb between *to* and the verb, as in *to quietly depart*. That issue wouldn't begin

13

appearing in grammar books until the middle of the nineteenth century.)

Most famously, Lowth ruled against stranding prepositions at the end of a question or relative clause, giving the example *Horace is an author whom I am much delighted with.* He admitted, "This is an idiom which our language is strongly inclined to," but felt that "the placing of the preposition before the relative is more graceful . . . and agrees much better with the solemn and elevated style." (Ending the first of these sentences with the preposition *to* instead of saying *to which our language is strongly inclined* might have been a mistake, but also could be a subtle way of demonstrating his point.)[12]

The preposition-stranding rule offers a good example of how one grammarian's style judgments can gradually harden into absolutes. Lowth meant his principle to apply mainly to "the solemn and elevated style." He admitted that the sentence-final preposition "prevails in common conversation, and suits very well with the familiar style." In other words, it was fine for everyday speech. This nuanced statement was lost in later grammar and usage guides. Over the years, the ban on sentence-final prepositions expanded until it covered every situation, including prepositions that form part of complex verbs like *sit down* and *stand up.* Lowth never proposed such an extreme restriction.

Not only sentence-final prepositions, but most of the structures Lowth rejected, had prevailed in "common conversation" for centuries. They had also appeared in the work of famous authors. Lowth often illustrated what he saw as incorrect usages by quoting examples from writers such as Pope, Swift, Shakespeare, and the authors of the King James Bible. His example of too many negatives comes from Milton's *Paradise Lost*—"*Nor* did they *not* perceive the evil plight / In which they were, or the fierce pains *not* feel."[13]

❧ The fact that great writers had made use of certain grammatical constructions did not persuade Lowth of their acceptability. On the contrary, he thought that it underlined the necessity of studying grammar as a separate subject. He writes, "Our best authors have committed gross mistakes, for want of a due knowledge of English grammar, or at least of a proper attention to the rules of it."[14] This point of view led to the teaching technique known as false syntax. Lowth describes it in his preface as teaching "what is right, by showing what is wrong." For nearly half a century after Lowth, grammar books would routinely include examples of false syntax, using the literary greats to show students what not to do.

A Short Introduction to English Grammar permanently changed the landscape of standard English. Lowth presented his strictures more as style advice than a set of rigid rules—distinguishing, for instance, between elevated and casual speech—but future grammar book authors would treat his pronouncements as articles of faith. In spite of recurrent attempts to dislodge them, starting with Webster's, Lowth's guidelines would remain part of the grammatical orthodoxy until modern times. Although these rules no longer appear in up-to-date style guides, they are still what people think of first when they hear the word "grammar."

Usage prescriptions were only a small part of any late-eighteenth-century grammar book, including Dilworth's and Lowth's. Many taught reading and spelling as well as sentence structure. Dilworth's book was one of these. It's divided into five sections, with the first two devoted to the alphabet and spelling and the final two to reading practice. Only the third section deals with grammar.

Even grammar itself was not primarily about usage. Its main

purpose, at least theoretically, was to describe current English in its most elegant form. At the beginning of *A Short Introduction to Grammar,* Lowth defines grammar as a set of "principles which are common to all languages" and explains that the purpose of English grammar (or the grammar of any particular language) is to apply those common principles "according to the established usage or custom" of the language.[15] Later grammar books would typically adopt a similar definition. In practice, grammar book authors didn't confine themselves to describing an accurate version of the best current English. They often followed their personal tastes or the pronouncements of earlier grammarians to rule out widespread, previously accepted usages.

Some of the books' content strikes modern readers as stilted and odd. For instance, *thou* and *thee* appear as second-person singular, as in *thou hast* and *thou wilt. Ye* as well as *you* is a possible second-person plural. Unfamiliar verb forms are listed, too—*speak/spake, chide/chid, thrive/throve, work/wrought.* The writing seems overelaborate, especially for books aimed at teaching children. Lowth's explanation of natural gender in English begins with this convoluted sentence: "The English language, with singular propriety, following nature alone, applies the distinction of masculine and feminine, only to the names of animals." Such vocabulary today would probably be considered too challenging even for older students.

Grammar books also talk about issues that are unknown to modern English speakers. For example, they include detailed rules for the uses of *shall* and *will.* To express simple future tense, *shall* was used with first person—*I shall arrive tomorrow*—and *will* went with second and third person—*they will arrive by noon.* However, their use could be reversed to give a different spin to the meaning. *Shall* used with second or third person—*you shall go*—implied insistence or a threat. That is, the speaker plans to make you go. *I will go,* on the other hand, suggests determination—

the speaker plans to go in spite of opposition. These uses were already becoming less common two hundred years ago. Today they are obsolete. Americans seldom use *shall* at all, and it's usually in the form of a question—*Shall we go?*

All these features, which make eighteenth-century grammar books sound arcane to modern readers, would have seemed unremarkable to grammar students of that day. They expected lesson books to be written in what Lowth calls the elevated style. That meant including *thee* and *thou,* which were no longer much used in speaking but were still fairly common in written language. It also meant an ornate style and a formal tone. And of course it meant exploring subtle usage details, as in the case of *shall* and *will.*

Grammar books were typically organized to present information in memorizable chunks, taking students from the smaller pieces of language—the alphabet in some cases—to larger chunks, such as sentences, poems, and short essays. Students eventually memorized and recited all the book's lessons, the idea being that when they had thoroughly absorbed all the material, they could apply it to their own speech with ease.

Grammar study usually encompassed orthography (spelling), prosody (pronunciation), and etymology (parts of speech), as well as syntax (sentence grammar). The parts of speech were the same ones found in modern grammar books—nouns, verbs, adjectives, adverbs, prepositions, conjunctions, articles. Authors defined each part of speech and then discussed how it worked. Definitions didn't change much from book to book. In fact, later grammar book authors frequently lifted definitions word for word from older volumes. Dilworth defines a noun, or "substantive," as "the name of any being or thing, perceivable either by the senses or the understanding." Lowth describes it in a more convoluted but essentially similar way as "the name of a thing; of whatever we conceive in any way to subsist, or of which we have any notion."[16] (The now-common formula "person, place, or thing" wasn't used until the early nineteenth century.)

After defining a part of speech, grammarians demonstrated its features. Here is where Latin comes into play. Latin was a high-status language in the eighteenth century, normally studied only by the educated upper classes. Considered excellent mental training, it formed a major part of the curriculum at private boys' schools and was a requirement for college admission. For these reasons, many grammar book writers adopted Latin as a template for English. Not only was it thought to be a superior organizing tool for English, using it as a model was meant to prepare students for the eventual study of Latin itself.

In fact Latin is not that helpful for studying English—the structures of the two languages are very different. In Latin, a word's exact form varies according to its relationship to other words in the sentence. Nouns, for example, feature various endings, depending on their "case," or what part they play in the sentence. Subjects are in nominative case, direct objects in objective case (also called accusative), possessives in genitive case, and objects of prepositions in a variety of cases, depending on the preposition. Students learned the language by memorizing lists of the different forms. This practice was called noun declension. The declension of *liber,* the Latin word for "book," is nominative *liber,* genitive *libri,* dative *libro,* accusative *librum,* vocative *liber,* ablative *libro.*

Dilworth and most other grammar book writers used the same system for English, even though English nouns don't change their form no matter what role they play in a sentence. Whether *a book* is the subject of the sentence or the object, it's still *a book.* That meant students spent their time "declining" pointless lists of identical nouns—nominative *a book,* genitive *of a book,* dative *to a book,* accusative *a book,* vocative *O book,* ablative *from a book.*

Verbs were typically organized according to mood and tense. Classifications differed, but were again based on Latin. Most authors included indicative mood (statements), imperative mood (commands), subjunctive mood (conditional or contrary to fact), and potential mood (combining with *may, can, might, ought, could,* and similar words). Tenses included past, present, and future, as well as occasional subcategories, such as pluperfect (*had loved*). As with nouns, students memorized mostly unchanging lists of verb forms—*I love, thou lovest, he loves, we love, ye love, they love*—an exercise known as verb conjugation.

When Webster attacked grammarians who "lay down certain rules . . . drawn from the principles of other languages," he was thinking of these lists. In the preface to *A Grammatical Institute of the English Language, Part II*—the grammar volume—he makes his view even clearer, calling Dilworth's book "a mere Latin grammar, very indifferently translated."[17]

Lowth's grammar is unusual in not providing lists of Latin-based noun declensions. Instead he notes that English has only two noun forms—the noun itself, which he labels nominative, and possessive, which uses *'s.* He adds an objective case for pronouns that follow a verb or preposition. Lowth does, however, provide the usual lists of verb moods and tenses for students to memorize.

Lowth also invented a form of mental exercise called "grammatical resolution," or sentence parsing. In sentence parsing, a sentence is broken down word by word and each word defined by its place in the sentence. For his parsing exercise, Lowth chose a passage from the Gospel of Luke that begins, "In the fifteenth year of the reign of Tiberius Caesar."

First Lowth sets out the passage. Then he analyzes each word— "*In* is a preposition; *the* the definite article; *fifteenth* an adjective; *year* a substantive, or noun in the objective case; *of* a preposition; *the reign* a noun, objective case; *of Tiberius Caesar,* both substantives, proper names"; and so on through the entire passage.[18] This laborious method of teaching sentence structure remained a feature of most grammar textbooks until the end of the nineteenth century. (Sentence diagramming, a way of representing the parts of the sentence visually, came into vogue around that time, as shown in chapter 6.)

Lowth's parsing exercise illustrates another feature of grammar books in early America. Reading and grammar exercises were nearly always religious or morally improving. Dilworth's first practice sentence, for words of one syllable, is "No man may put off the law of God." His practice verses bear such sobering titles as "Life is short and miserable" and "The duty of man." Books often included fables that taught a lesson—"He that will not help himself shall have help from nobody"—or prayers thought to be suitable for schoolchildren. Dilworth's suggested prayer for wisdom and knowledge begins, "O Almighty Lord and merciful Father, Maker of Heaven and Earth, who of thy free Liberality givest Wisdom abundantly to all who with Faith and full Assurance ask it of Thee: Beautify by the Light of thy Heavenly Grace the Towardness of my Wit."[19]

Before the widespread availability of grammar books, American children practiced their language skills by reading from the Psalter or the New Testament. Grammars carried on the tradition of giving students moral instruction along with their parsing practice. For early American students, virtue and grammar would have been tightly connected.

Noah Webster's ambition to create a grammar strictly for Americans was no doubt partly inspired by his family history and early life experiences. He came of age during the Revolution and was intensely involved in the political issues of the day. A proud New Englander, he traced his ancestry on his father's side to John Webster, who arrived in Massachusetts from Warwickshire sometime in the 1630s. In 1636 John Webster followed Puritan leader Thomas Hooker to Hartford to help found the Connecticut colony. Twenty years later, he was chosen to be Connecticut's governor.

Noah Webster's mother, Mercy Steele, also came of old New England stock. She descended from William Bradford, governor of the Plymouth Colony. A later ancestor, John Steele, arrived in Hartford about the same time as John Webster, although not as one of Hooker's followers. Like John Webster, Steele participated in the colony's public life, holding the post of town recorder.

Webster's father, also named Noah, continued the family commitment to public service. For many years he was a justice of the peace and a deacon of the Congregational church in his home village of West Hartford. Although the senior Noah Webster was uneducated, he appreciated books. In 1753 he joined other church members in founding West Hartford's first Book Society. This "subscription library" was an early version of a public library. Members subscribed by paying a certain sum. The Society then used the money to purchase books that subscribers could borrow. The elder Webster's respect for books and learning would later make him sympathetic to his son's desire to go to Yale, normally an impossible goal for an impoverished farmer's son.

Webster's sense of his family traditions bolstered his lifelong confidence in his own opinions and intellectual worth—or, as some called it, arrogance. While living in Philadelphia in 1787, he often contributed comments to the editorial pages of the city's newspapers. When one reader of the *Freeman's Journal* expressed astonishment at a lowly schoolteacher writing books and lecturing on language, Webster replied that this "mere schoolteacher" belonged to one of the "oldest and most respected families in America, and his ancestors governed provinces fifty years before Pennsylvania was settled."[20]

Webster was born in the parlor of the family's modest farm-house on October 16, 1758, the fourth of five children. He would be the only one to receive an education beyond Dilworth's speller and the Bible readings of West Hartford's tiny school. Unusually for colonial America, schooling was compulsory in Connecticut. However, schoolrooms were often poorly equipped. Many years later, Webster would remember the local school's reliance on Dilworth as its only textbook. No history or geography was taught and there were no reading or arithmetic books.[21] When Webster wrote the *Grammatical Institute, Part III*—the reader—he included essays on history and geography to make up for the lack of such books in most schoolrooms.

❧ Farm children in the eighteenth century attended school only when they weren't needed on the farm. They were expected to start working alongside their parents by the age of ten. Young Noah nonetheless found time for books. According to family tradition, words fascinated him as a child, especially their exact meanings and use. A family story described how he would often take a Latin grammar out to the fields with him and spend his rest times reading it under the apple trees.

By the time Webster was fourteen, he had read and studied enough to know that he wanted to attend college, which in eighteenth-century Connecticut meant Yale. His father was reluctant at first. The farm just barely provided the large family with a living—college fees would be a heavy expense. Noah's desire for learning eventually persuaded his father. The elder Webster became a committed supporter, mortgaging the farm to cover his son's expenses.

❧ Before Noah could begin his studies at Yale, he had to prepare. The local school couldn't teach him what he needed—mainly Latin, Greek, and rhetoric—so he began studying with Rev. Nathan Perkins, the pastor of West Hartford's Congregational church. (Clergymen were often the best-educated people in small towns. As such, they routinely "fitted" young men for college.) After two years of diligent study Webster was ready for Yale. He began classes in September 1774. The next few years were the beginning of his passionate lifelong engagement with ideas, including ideas about language.

New Haven, forty miles from Webster's home, was a town of about 3,500, spreading out from a busy harbor on Long Island Sound. Much of the town's community life took place around a central square known as the Green. Several important buildings, including the imposing brick statehouse, the schoolhouse, the large two-story post office, the dilapidated prison, and several churches clustered on or near the Green. At its northwest edge stood Yale College.

Conditions at the college were spartan. Webster and his fellow students had to chop their own firewood if they wanted heat in their rooms. The dining hall food was reputedly very poor. Midday dinners usually consisted of an "Indian pudding" made of cornmeal cooked in broth, followed by meat and two potatoes each, with cabbage, turnip, or dandelion greens. The young men drank cider, which they passed around in pewter cans that everybody drank from. Supper was brown bread and milk.[22]

As a freshman, Webster's first class would have started at 7:00 a.m., immediately after morning prayers. Only when this class ended would he be allowed time for breakfast. Then he would continue to attend classes throughout the day. Latin and Greek made up the bulk of the studies all four years. Freshmen also studied arithmetic. Sophomores tackled logic, geography, rhetoric, algebra, and geometry. Upperclassmen added natural philosophy, a combined study of biology, geology, astronomy, and physics. Everyone studied divinity on Saturdays. Juniors and seniors also practiced "disputation," or debate, twice a week. When Webster graduated, Yale president Ezra Stiles commented that the young man had been especially strong in that subject.[23]

While Webster was still a freshman, events in the outside world disrupted his life as a scholar. In April 1775 the first shots of the Revolutionary War were fired in Lexington and Concord. Patriotic Yale students took to holding military drills on the Green. On Saturdays they built breastworks around New Haven. When Gen. George Washington traveled through the town on his way to Cambridge in June 1775, the students were invited to march to the house where he was staying and demonstrate their drill.

Webster later recalled the episode in a speech, noting that Washington and his companions "expressed surprise and gratification at the precision with which the students performed the customary exercises." The Yale students accompanied the men part of the way out of town, providing marching music as they walked. Webster, a flute player, told his listeners proudly, "he who stands before you was one of the musicians."[24]

In the winter of 1777, the war touched Yale more directly. Classes had to be disbanded because the college couldn't acquire enough food for the students. Webster and his classmates were sent home. That autumn Webster marched with his father, his two brothers, and several other West Hartford men to join the American army fighting at Saratoga, New York.

As the small band passed along the east bank of the Hudson, they saw Kingston in flames on the other side of the river and the residents fleeing in panic. As they approached Albany, however, they were met by a courier shouting the news that British General Burgoyne had surrendered. By the time the West Hartford men reached the battle scene, their help was no longer needed. They returned home soon afterward.

Although this brief episode was Webster's only war experience, it made a lasting impression. In later years, he couldn't speak of hearing the courier's shouts without being moved to tears. This episode, along with his war-related activities at Yale, buttressed his patriotic pride in all things American—including American speech.

Webster was back at Yale by the spring of 1778 to finish his classes. In July he took his final exams and in September he received his diploma. Because of the war, there was no public ceremony.

About a year after Webster's graduation, his Yale tutor Rev. Joseph Buckminster wrote him a long letter, reflecting on the class of 1778 and offering his former pupil a few pieces of advice. Reverend Buckminster said, "The independent spirit which was peculiar to you as a class . . . exposed you and will still expose you to errors and mortifications. I was however pleased to see it because it assured me that you would not be wanting in attempts to do something for your honor." Reverend Buckminster was right in predicting that the revolutionary spirit would continue to inspire Webster and his classmates. He and several others would take an active part in shaping the new country.

Reverend Buckminster then commented on Webster's previous letter to him: "The resolutions that you form in your letter are good, to obtain a knowledge of your own country, of the genius, manners and policy of our fellow citizens is commendable." Webster was evidently already intrigued with America's cultural uniqueness, and perhaps already thinking about how to contribute to it.

Buckminster then gave Webster some carefully worded guidance relating to his future behavior: "You must endeavor not to be forward in applying for this knowledge to persons with whom you have but a slight acquaintance, nor be too frank in opening your heart to them. Such is the perverseness of human nature they will be disposed to ridicule you and perhaps set you down among those who have too high an opinion of their own importance."[25]

This was sound advice that Webster would choose not to take. He never hesitated to voice his ideas publicly or to ask influential men with whom he had "but a slight acquaintance" for help in promoting his projects. He corresponded with George Washington, Benjamin Franklin, James Madison, and others about issues that affected American life.

He also published forceful essays and books about those issues—not just language use, but politics, government, education, even a two-volume work on infectious diseases—and was impatient with differing views. As Buckminster foresaw, his former student was often attacked for vanity and self-importance. Webster didn't hesitate to respond to his critics—fierce intellectual skirmishes were a regular occurrence in his life.

The Revolutionary War affected Webster in practical, as well as philosophical, ways. The class of 1778 graduated at an unfortunate moment. After years of war, the American economy was in shambles and the value of the currency issued by the Continental Congress had collapsed. Job prospects for new graduates were dim. Webster had hoped to study law, but the depressed economy limited his chances of apprenticing himself to a lawyer. He couldn't expect any more help from his father, who was struggling to make the farm pay. He would have to strike out on his own. The path he decided on led to a lifelong commitment to the American language.

After an uncomfortable interlude back home on the farm, the twenty-year-old Webster resolved to try his hand at schoolmastering. In the days before specialized training and certification, teaching was simply a matter of finding a school in need of a teacher, or even simpler, advertising for pupils. Webster took a temporary position with a school in nearby Glastonbury, the first of several. The next five years were to be deeply frustrating for Webster. He moved frequently, taking short-term teaching positions in various Connecticut and New York towns and never earning quite enough to live on comfortably.

Webster finally found an opportunity to study law in 1780. He went to work in a lawyer's office, learning on the job and reading law books at night. In April 1781 he passed the bar exam. His new professional status, however, didn't pay the dividends that he had hoped. The economy still hadn't recovered from the war and there was little work for new lawyers. Eventually, he resigned himself to teaching once again, opening his own school in the small rural Connecticut town of Sharon.

The school prospectus shows that Webster had already formed strong views on grammar. It announces not only the usual training in "the common arts of reading, writing, and arithmetic," but a thorough grounding in English grammar. Webster criticizes the usual level of language teaching, saying, "The little regard that is paid to the literary improvement of females . . . and the general inattention to the grammatical purity and elegance of our native language, are faults in the education of youth that more gentlemen [schoolmasters] have taken pains to censure than correct."[26] He assures prospective clients that his school will do better.

Things went well at first. The school drew a number of students from affluent New York families who had fled to Connecticut to escape the fighting in their home state. Then Webster's personal life took a devastating turn. He fell in love with a young woman who already had another suitor—a major in the Continental Army. When the major unexpectedly returned to Sharon, she wavered between the two. In the end she decided in the major's favor. Distraught, Webster closed his school in October 1781 and left town less than a year after settling there.

Now nearly four years out of Yale and with a series of failed career attempts behind him, Webster wandered miserably around

Connecticut for the next few months, trying to find work. Finally, when he was nearly destitute, he settled over the border in Goshen, New York, and once again opened a school.

In his old age, Webster remembered the "extreme depression and gloomy forebodings" of this difficult time.[27] Gradually, however, he got caught up in his teaching. He began to think seriously about the shortcomings of the textbooks that were available, and especially about the limitations of using British imports. Fired with patriotic enthusiasm, he decided to write a new and improved series of textbooks specifically for Americans.

Webster's enthusiasm for language study rescued him from his misery. As the challenge of writing gripped him, his depression disappeared. He worked steadily through the spring and summer of 1782 on a speller that, in his view, would be "better adapted to assist the learner than that of Dilworth." Writing about the project to a friend, he said, "Popular prejudice is in favor of Dilworth . . . but he is not only out of date; but is really faulty and defective in every part of his work." At the end of the letter, Webster sounded the theme that would run through all his writing about language: "America must be as independent in *literature* as she is in *politics*—as famous for *arts* as for *arms*."[28]

Before Webster could publish his improved speller, however, he would have to overcome some obstacles. His friend and former classmate, the poet Joel Barlow, pointed these out in a letter. Barlow wrote, "You know our country is prejudiced in favor of old Dilworth, the nurse of us all, and it will be difficult to turn their attention from it." He reminded Webster that printers could be sure of selling Dilworth, so they would print large runs of the book and "afford it very cheap." If the unknown Webster printed such large runs, he was likely to be left with unsold books. Smaller runs, on the other hand, would be expensive to print. Webster would either have to charge more or earn fewer profits.[29]

Barlow was right in thinking that printers would not be eager to take on the risk of an unknown author. Webster was finally able to convince Hudson & Goodwin, publishers of the *Connecticut Courant* newspaper, to undertake the printing at Webster's expense. As he didn't have the money to pay the printers in advance, he had to commit himself to repaying the costs once the book was printed. If the book failed to sell, he would be bankrupt.

Webster's gamble paid off. *A Grammatical Institute of the English Language, Part I* appeared in October 1783, priced at fourteen pence a copy (about fifteen cents) or ten shillings a dozen (about $1.50). By the following May the first edition of 5,000 copies had sold out. Hudson & Goodwin printed a second edition, this time paying the costs themselves. The book appeared at a good time. The war was over, and with peace came a renewed interest in education. The demand for schoolbooks was on the rise. Webster's speller was easy to use and its American slant appealed to newly independent patriots.

One of Webster's innovations was a pronunciation key. He assigned a number to the various long and short vowel sounds—for instance, "1" represents the long vowel sounds of *a, e, i, o, u*. When pupils encountered *find* or *lace* marked with a "1" over the *i* or *a*, they immediately knew how to pronounce the word. Webster also brought the representation of words ending in *–tion* more in line with reality by treating the ending as a single syllable. Dilworth and others artificially divided it into *ti-on* for recitation purposes although that pronunciation had disappeared from ordinary speech.

Material designed to appeal to Americans was scattered through the book. Webster Americanized a number of place-names that were still commonly spelled using the original French orthography. *Ouisconsin*, for example, became the more English-looking *Wisconsin*. His reading lessons and lists featured topics that would interest citizens of the new country, such as American money values, facts about the states, and how to pronounce American place-names.

Hudson & Goodwin had sold 12,000 copies by the end of 1785. By 1790 they were printing about 20,000 copies annually for sale in Connecticut, now with the simplified title *The American Spelling Book*. Webster had licensed printers in other cities to produce and sell thousands more copies in their regions. By 1807 an estimated 200,000 copies were selling each year. Webster's speller was on its way to becoming one of the largest-selling books in American history. Eventually it would become a fixture in American classrooms. Familiarly known as the "Blue-backed Speller" because of its blue cloth cover, this first volume of the *Grammatical Institute* sold an estimated 15 million copies by 1837, an astonishing number considering that the country's population in the 1830s was under 13 million.[30]

After *Part I* of the *Institute* was published, Webster began writing the remaining two volumes. *Part II*, the grammar book, appeared in March 1784 and *Part III*, the reader, in February 1785. Hudson & Goodwin undertook to publish both. Unfortunately, neither of these volumes would sell nearly as well as the speller. *Part II* was the least popular of the three volumes. Americans preferred Lowth and other conventional grammar books, Latin and all.

A Grammatical Institute, Part II was actually not as unconventional as Webster sometimes claimed. Because he wanted teachers to adopt it for the classroom, he followed a traditional format for the most part, borrowing elements from both Dilworth and Lowth. As his linguistic attitudes grew more radical, he would revise future editions of the grammar to reflect his changing ideas.

Although Webster's preface attacks Dilworth as being too dependent on Latin and "invariably wrong" when describing features that are specific to English, he nonetheless organizes his book along the same lines as Dilworth's grammar section. Like Dilworth, he uses a question-and-response format. Similar in style to a Sunday school catechism, the question-and-response method was believed to be the easiest way for students to memorize and recite the material. Questions started with the general— *What is grammar?*—and moved to the particular—*Where is the adjective to be placed?*

Webster's answer to *What is grammar?*—"the art of speaking and writing our thoughts with propriety"—is almost identical to Dilworth's—"the art of writing and speaking properly and syntactically."[31] In later editions, Webster would revise his definition to bring it more in line with his evolving views, saying that "the use of English grammar" was "to teach the true principles and idioms of the English language." The more Webster thought and read about English, the more committed he became to idiomatic American English.

Webster was not yet disillusioned with Lowth when he wrote *Part II* of the *Institute*. He praises Lowth in the book's preface, saying Lowth is "well acquainted with the origin and genius of the language," although he thinks Lowth's "style and method are not suited to the capacities of youth." He agrees with Lowth on various points that he will later attack. For instance, he advises using nominative case after *be* (*It is I*) rather than the more natural *It is me*. He also takes the same position as Lowth regarding stranded prepositions, writing that *Whom did you give it to?*, or even worse, *Who did you give it to?*, is "generally inelegant" and "in the grave and sublime styles is certainly inadmissible."[32]

Later, *Who did you give it to?* would be one of the constructions he strongly supported. In the 1800 edition of the *Institute*, he says, "It is the invariable practice to use *who*" rather than *whom* in such sentences, "except among people who are fettered by grammatical rules." He continues, "In spite of rules, *Who is she married to?* is more agreeable than *Whom is she married to?*" In this same edition he changes his position on pronouns after *be*, coming down in favor of *It is me* and other objective-case pronouns (*It is him* or *her*) because they "have such a prevalence in English."[33]

Webster was moving gradually toward a defense of common American usages. He explains his new attitude in the preface to the 1800 edition, saying, "It is the business of grammar to inform the student, not how a language might have been originally constructed, but how it is constructed. . . . Anomalous phrases creep into a language in its infancy and become established idioms. . . . This is my reason for admitting some phrases as good English which the most respectable writers on this subject have condemned as ungrammatical." His arguments would take on a more aggressive tone in later writings.

Webster adopts Lowth's idea of illustrating incorrect grammar with false syntax, but invents many of his own examples. These straightforward sentences are much simpler to follow than Lowth's literary illustrations. When writing about double negatives, he replaces Lowth's Milton quotation with the example *I do not know nothing about it,* a statement that would be familiar to students from their everyday speech.

Webster also provides a parsing exercise, but one distinctly different from Lowth's Bible passage. Instead he takes an excerpt from Henry Home's 1774 *Sketches of the History of Man.* Because the book was only ten years old, the language would have sounded more modern than that of the Gospels. Still, it must have been daunting for young schoolchildren. The first sentence of the exercise reads, "A woman who has merit, improved by a virtuous and refined education, retains in her decline an influence over men more flattering than even that of beauty." Webster suggests in a footnote that children use a pocket dictionary to help them understand the vocabulary.[34]

The American flavor of the *Institute* comes through in some of Webster's examples. He lists *Mississippi* and *Philadelphia* as examples of proper nouns and demonstrates the use of articles before names with the phrase, "a traitor is called an Arnold." In 1784, with the Revolutionary War just over, he knew his readers would immediately catch his reference to Benedict Arnold and approve of the sentiment expressed.

In his Baltimore lectures, given hardly more than a year after he wrote *Part II,* Webster would distance himself much more sharply from Lowth and other contemporary grammarians. Writing to his friend Timothy Pickering, Webster says that he "most pointedly" opposed Lowth in his talks and received no argument from the audience. He admits to Pickering, however, that although lecture audiences accepted his criticisms of popular grammar books in theory, they continued to buy them in preference to his own volume. He notes ruefully, "I convince the judgment, tho' I may not reform the practice."[35] Webster's *Part II* was the first American grammar to achieve widespread classroom adoption, but it never reached the popularity of the British imports.

Webster's travel plans gained a new focus with the success of his Baltimore lecture series on the English language. Although he had already been on the road for six months, he decided to take the lectures to other cities. He still wanted to sell books, but now that wasn't his only goal. He also wanted to convince Americans to abandon Latin-based grammars and embrace the natural structure of English. He wrote enthusiastically to his friend, "I shall make one *General* effort to deliver literature and my countrymen from the errors that fashion and ignorance are palming upon Englishmen."

Webster's decision meant another round of travel, no light undertaking in the late eighteenth century. Travel in colonial America was slow, uncomfortable, and often hazardous. Most roads were poorly maintained. So-called "corduroy" roads, made out of unfinished logs laid in rows, were treacherous for horses and wagons. In the South, where most people lived on remote plantations rather than in towns, roads were scarce. Unless travelers were headed for a courthouse, church, or other public gathering place, they had to forge their own path across fields and through forests.

Webster traveled on horseback most of the time, carrying his personal belongings in two heavy saddlebags and sending his books down the coast by sloop. Occasionally, he traveled by sloop himself or took the stagecoach. Both methods were uncertain. A sailing trip from Norfolk to Charleston, which should have taken only a few days, stretched out to nearly three weeks as squalls were followed by lack of wind. On one ill-fated stagecoach trip from Baltimore to Alexandria, the vehicle overturned on a corduroy road, leaving Webster to "curse all stage wagons" and return to town, where he hired a horse.

Webster would spend the next seven months speaking in cities all along the Eastern Seaboard, including Philadelphia, Dover, Trenton, and Albany. At the end of May 1786, thirteen months after setting out, he finally returned to his home in Hartford. He didn't stay long, however. By mid-June he was lecturing again, first in Hartford and New Haven, then farther afield—Boston, Providence, Salem, Newport.

Besides lecturing on grammar, Webster kept up a steady stream of essays on topics that interested him. He wrote an essay on manners and one on government. He wrote frequently to the newspapers, putting forth his opinions about language and politics and often drawing heated responses. News of Webster's contentious ways traveled to his father in West Hartford, who wrote advising him to "have courage but temper the same with prudence."[36]

On a return trip to Philadelphia he was offered a teaching post at the Episcopal Academy, where he stayed for several months. The chance to teach was a lucky opportunity for Webster to earn some extra money. Financial gain had not been the only reason for Webster's lecture tour, but he had hoped to earn more than he did. Webster's typical audiences, at around thirty or forty, had been disappointingly small, although he occasionally drew a crowd as large as three hundred. Sales of *A Grammatical Institute, Part II* also continued to lag well behind sales of the speller.

In June 1787 the twenty-eight-year-old Webster gained another reason for wanting a steady income. He became engaged to a young Bostonian woman named Rebecca Greenleaf and needed money to marry on. Webster stayed in Philadelphia just long enough to shepherd a revised edition of his spelling book through the press and to write an essay explaining the principles of the new federal Constitution, signed "a citizen of America." Then he moved to New York City to found a monthly journal titled *The American Magazine.* He hoped journalism would prove more profitable than grammar.

Webster's journal published an ambitious mix of political, scientific, and literary writing, including poems by Webster's friend Joel Barlow and others. The title page displayed the magazine's forward-looking motto, "Science the guide, and truth the eternal goal." He also found time to start a Philological Society, dedicated to the study of American English. (*Philology* was the usual eighteenth-century term for language study, from the Greek for "love of language.") Webster occasionally read essays before the Society and was able to persuade them to recommend his speller, although they balked at approving the more unorthodox grammar.

Unfortunately, *The American Magazine* never caught on with the general public. Webster lost money on it and was forced to suspend publication after less than a year. At the end of 1788, Webster left New York. He continued his usual round of business travel for several more months, while Rebecca waited at her family home in Boston. Eventually he settled once again in Hartford for another try at the law. Gradually he started to build a practice.

On the strength of a generous $1,000 gift from his future brother-in-law James Greenleaf, a prosperous merchant, Webster felt financially stable enough to marry Rebecca. They wed on October 26, 1789, shortly after his thirty-first birthday. He wrote in his diary, "I am united to an amiable woman, and if I am not happy, shall be much disappointed." Although Webster would continue to face obstacles in his career, from now on his family life would be a source of comfort and consolation.

A few months before Webster married, he brought out his lecture series in the form of a book titled *Dissertations on the English Language,* which he had printed in Boston. Webster's challenge to Latin-based grammars is more forcefully stated here than in the *Institute.* In the book's preface, he writes dismissively, "Our modern grammars have done much more hurt than good. The authors have labored to prove, what is obviously absurd, viz. that our language is not made right; and in pursuance of this idea, have tried to make it over again, and persuade the English to speak by Latin rules, or by arbitrary rules of their own." He goes on to attack Lowth by name, saying, "Very few of the alterations recommended by Lowth and his followers can be vindicated on any better principle than some Latin rule or his own private opinion."[37]

Between the first edition of *A Grammatical Institute* and the publication of *Dissertations,* Webster's anti-Latin bias received strong reinforcement from a 1786 book by an English radical politician and language scholar named John Horne Tooke. Horne Tooke's book, ponderously titled *Winged Words, or The Diversions of Purley,* is a forcefully argued attempt to prove that all English words derive from a small set of Anglo-Saxon (Old English) nouns and verbs. Later linguistic discoveries would show that Horne Tooke's analysis of English was mostly wrong, but when his work first appeared, it captured the imagination of Webster and many others. Horne Tooke was well known in America for his vocal defense of the American Revolution, which might have further influenced Webster in his favor.

Webster uses Horne Tooke's theories to buttress his arguments against basing English grammar on Latin. For instance, he argues that typical verb classifications, such as those in Bishop Lowth's grammar book, are inaccurate because they are influenced by Latin. Lowth (and most grammarians) assumed a future tense for English. Webster points out that, while Latin verbs are marked for future tense with a special ending, English verbs have no such form. They simply combine present-tense verbs with *shall* or *will* for a "future" meaning. After providing several examples of this sort, he concludes, "It is astonishing to see how long and how stupidly English grammarians have followed the Latin grammars."[38]

Dissertations argues for the same constructions that Webster had been promoting to his lecture audiences, but now he fleshes out his arguments with etymological evidence. He writes, "*Who did you speak to? Who did he marry?* are challenged as bad English, but *whom did you speak to* was never used in speaking . . . *who* in the Gothic or Teutonic has always answered to the Latin nominative *qui,* the dative *cui,* . . . and the ablative *quo* . . . So that *who did he speak to? who did you go with?* were probably as good English in ancient times as *cui dixit?*" It's more than probable, in Webster's opinion, that "*who* was once wholly used in asking questions, even in the objective case . . . until some Latin student began to suspect it [of being] bad English because not agreeable to the Latin rules."[39]

Webster was not always consistent in his views. In spite of his belief that the most common usage should determine what was standard, he did have pet peeves. He complained, for instance, that speakers didn't understand how to use *shall* properly and were increasingly replacing it with *will*. He also thought upper-class New England pronunciations sounded more educated than those of other regions. He urged Americans in other parts of the country to abandon their own local dialects and adopt New England speech in the interests of a uniform national language.

Webster wrote in his preface that he hoped *Dissertations* would be useful to "all classes of readers," but the book was too esoteric to have wide appeal. Besides the original material of his lectures, Webster included essays on topics that had recently caught his interest. These included a proposal for spelling reform and a section demonstrating Horne Tooke's method of deriving prepositions, conjunctions, and other parts of speech from ancient Saxon verbs. Such abstruse topics made the book heavy going for readers who were simply hoping to improve their grammar skills. Although *Dissertations* added to Webster's stature as an expert on language, it was not successful as a practical grammar guide.

Webster lost $400 on the publication of *Dissertations,* a hefty sum at that time. Many workingmen earned less than half that in a year. In 1791 he wrote wryly to Timothy Pickering, "My dissertations, which cost me a large sum of money, lie on hand and must, I believe, be sold for wrapping paper."[40] Earlier, Webster's brother-in-law Nathaniel Appleton had tried to reassure him by writing "The work has, undoubtedly, merit, and the next generation will acknowledge it."[41] But Webster was far more than one generation ahead of his time. Several decades would pass before a group of grammarians made another attempt to inject more natural usage standards into American grammar books, and nearly a century would pass before linguists began challenging the very notion of prescriptive grammars.

Dissertations on the English Language would be Webster's last linguistic publication for the next seventeen years. Meanwhile, his writings in support of the Constitution and a strong federal government led to a new opportunity. In 1793 a group of Federalists, including Alexander Hamilton and John Jay, approached Webster about starting a Federalist journal in New York City. They wanted to counteract anti-Federalist newspapers such as the Philadelphia *Aurora,* which was publishing vitriolic attacks on President Washington. To get the project started, each man in the group gave Webster a no-interest loan of $150 on the condition of being repaid in five years.

The new project would give Webster a powerful platform for his political views. It would also give his income a much-needed boost, allowing him to pay off his debts. In October Webster moved his family, which now included two small daughters, from Hartford to New York. On December 9 he published the first issue of his journal, *The American Minerva.* Beneath the title was the motto "Patroness of Peace, Commerce and the Liberal Arts." The *Minerva* would prove to be a success. Webster now committed himself to public affairs. For the first few years, until he could afford an assistant, he worked long, arduous hours producing all the paper's editorial content himself. This heavy schedule left little time for other writing.

Although the speller remained popular, Webster's grammar books soon sank into obscurity. His famous dictionary was decades in the future. In the meantime, a rival grammarian was about to publish the book that would sweep all others off the market.

2.

Grammar for Different
Classes of Learners

While Noah Webster was in New York laboring in the Federalist cause, an expatriate named Lindley Murray who lived several thousand miles away in old York, England, was beginning work on his own version of an English grammar book. In many ways Murray was the antithesis of Webster. He didn't write the book to express his own theories of language use—his views were entirely orthodox. Nor was he especially interested in making money. Growing up in a family of prosperous Quaker merchants, he had always been well off and had earned enough income as a lawyer and businessman to retire at the age of thirty-nine. Unlike Webster's *Institute* or *Dissertations,* Murray's grammar book was not written with the American public in mind. Yet during most of the nineteenth century, Americans would invoke the name *Murray* as a synonym for proper grammar. Today, although his name is virtually unknown, his ideas about usage live on in America's favorite style guides.

Lindley Murray was a Pennsylvanian by birth, but when he began writing *English Grammar, Adapted to the Different Classes of Learners* in 1794, he and his wife, Hannah, were living on the outskirts of York. They had moved there nearly a decade earlier, hoping a cool climate would benefit Murray's health. The forty-nine-year-old Murray had recently become an invalid, unable to walk more than a few yards without exhaustion. At first the

Murrays hoped to return to New York after two or three years. Unfortunately, instead of improving, Murray's health grew worse. He developed increasingly debilitating muscle weakness, which would have made travel a serious challenge, so they stayed in York. (No one knows exactly what was wrong with Murray. One suggestion is that he had post-polio syndrome, brought on by a childhood polio attack. Other possibilities are that he suffered from some form of multiple sclerosis or myasthenia gravis, a chronic autoimmune disease that causes muscle weakness.)[1]

Murray and his wife lived quietly in the small village of Hold-gate (now called Holgate). Because he was unable to move around, Murray's days were circumscribed. He spent his time mainly in his sitting room, a large, comfortable space where a fire burned year-round. The room featured two bow windows, one overlooking the garden, the other the road to York. Those views were as close as Murray got to the outdoors most of the time. Once a day, if he could, he walked slowly out to a closed carriage, using a plank to level out the space between the front steps and the vehicle. The coachman then drove him around for an hour or so to enjoy the fresh air.

Visitors often remarked that Murray, a tall, slender man with pleasant features, looked remarkably well considering his condition. He kept his health stable by following a regular schedule of light meals and plenty of sleep. He also followed a work schedule as well as he could. His wife wheeled him into his sitting room in the morning using a wheeled armchair. He then moved onto the sofa. Here, using a portable writing desk, he spent most of the day reading, writing, and conducting business.

In spite of Murray's infirmity, he was active in his community. One reason why he and Hannah had chosen to settle near York was the area's vibrant Quaker community, the second largest in England. Murray notes in his memoirs that the two had hoped to settle among "religious and exemplary persons."[2] Shortly after their arrival they applied to join the York Monthly Meeting (the local congregation) and were not only accepted as members, but were quickly appointed as Elders. That meant they had responsibility for the spiritual education of fellow members, both adults and children. Murray's limited trips away from home often took him to the Quaker meetinghouse.

Murray's first book grew out of both his circumstances and his religious beliefs. In 1787 he compiled a collection of "testimonies"—thoughts on illness, affliction, and death—titled *The Power of Religion on the Mind*. As he explains in his memoirs, he was inspired to write the book after reflecting on the "lively pleasure and satisfaction" that he received from "perusing the sentiments of eminent and virtuous persons on the subject of religion and futurity when they approached the close of life." He later wrote to a friend that he wanted to promote "piety and virtue . . . without the design of advancing . . . any one religious profession."[3]

The book features an eclectic group of people from far-flung countries and various times—Confucius to John Donne, Caesar Borgia to Isaac Newton. *The Power of Religion* was instantly popular, foreshadowing the tremendous success of his grammar writings. His way of handling its publication and distribution, as well as the resulting profits, was also typical of his later books.

Murray was not initially interested in selling the book at all. Instead, he had 500 copies printed and distributed anonymously to prominent citizens of York. The response was so enthusiastic that he then decided to have a London publisher print a larger edition. Several more editions quickly followed. With the sixth edition, Murray revised and enlarged the book and finally put his name on the title page. He then assigned the copyright to a bookseller, feeling that if it "circulated more diffusively" his purpose in writing it—to share ideas that he had found inspiring—would be "still more effectually answered."

Within the next few decades, the book went through eighteen editions.[4] Murray did not accept any of the profits.

Although Murray was tied to his sitting room sofa, he was not isolated. An even-tempered, kindly man, he welcomed visits whenever he felt well enough to talk. Those who spent time with him often commented on his gentle manner. Before his illness he enjoyed a lively social life. As an invalid he still welcomed neighbors to his sitting room to share their news and talk over events in the larger world. When his condition worsened and he was no longer able to go out, many church-related activities such as mentoring necessarily took place in his sitting room as well.

Murray's grammar book grew out of one such activity. In 1794, while Murray was recovering from a bout of acute illness, he received a letter from three young women who taught at the Trinity Lane School, a recently founded Quaker girls' school. Murray sometimes acted as an advisor to the school's directors. When the teachers were first hired, school administrators deemed them insufficiently qualified to teach grammar, so Murray tutored them at his house. Now the young women were asking for something more substantial. They wanted a complete English grammar, "with examples and rules annexed, proper for this and similar Institutions." In their joint letter, they write that they are "well assured" of his "incomparable abilities" and "humbly solicit" his acceptance of this important task.[5]

Murray hesitated over the request, feeling that he wasn't competent to write an original work on grammar. Eventually, he agreed, after receiving permission from the Quaker authorities in London, and with the understanding that the book was destined only for Trinity Lane and its sister school in Clonmel, Ireland.

Murray didn't have any of the usual motivations for writing a grammar book. Unlike most authors, he had never been a schoolteacher and didn't need a volume for the classroom. He didn't have strong views on usage, as Noah Webster did. At the start, he wasn't even writing with a general audience in mind. He was simply doing his best to help out his young friends. Yet his amateur effort was destined for a success that Webster and other grammar book authors could only envy.

Because Murray was writing for a limited readership of Quaker schoolgirls, he didn't worry about providing original content. He concentrated on organizing and explaining his material in an accessible way. In the introduction to *English Grammar,* he begins cautiously by observing, "When the number and variety of English grammars already published, and the ability with which some of them are written, are considered, little can be expected from a new compilation." He hopes to make his contribution by "a careful selection of the most useful matter, and some degree of improvement in the mode of adapting it to the understanding and the gradual progress of learners."[6]

This humble disclaimer didn't impress Murray's later critics—mainly rival grammarians. They would claim that his heavy reliance on previous writers, especially Lowth, crossed the line from compilation into plagiarism. He was far from alone, however, in basing his grammar rules on those already published. Standards for borrowing from previous authors were looser in Murray's day and borrowing from Lowth was especially common. Murray always insisted that his aim of clarifying traditional material was legitimate.

Although much of Murray's material came from other books, he did introduce innovations. These set his book apart and helped turn it into a runaway bestseller. Murray was the first to print the most important rules and definitions—"the most proper to be committed to memory"—in large type as a way of making lessons easier to absorb. Detailed explanations and investigation of specific points appeared in smaller type. Beginning students learning the basics simply focused on the large-type passages, which were arranged so they made sense even when readers skipped over the intervening small type.

The greater clarity of Murray's book is immediately obvious when it's compared with competing grammar books. *English Grammar* is much less discursive than works by Lowth, Webster, and other writers. Rather than introducing a part of speech or other item of grammar and then exploring the fine points, Murray lists and defines all the parts of speech together, then briefly discusses each one in turn before moving on to issues of sentence grammar. In the days when learning grammar meant memorizing it, this straightforward arrangement must have made the beginner's task much less onerous. Many later grammar book authors, including some who criticized Murray's excessive borrowings, adopted this sensible way of organizing material.

Murray's reliance on Lowth is most evident in his definitions and grammatical rules. He describes nouns in nearly the same elaborate language as Lowth. Lowth's *Short Introduction to English Grammar* defines a noun as "the name of a thing; of whatever we conceive in any way to subsist, or of which we have any notion." Murray defines it as "the name of any thing conceived to subsist, or of which we have any notion." His definition of a verb is, word for word, the same as Lowth's—"A verb is a word which signifies to be, to do, or to suffer [be the subject of]."[7] Murray also follows Lowth in avoiding Latinate noun declension. For nouns, he lists only nominative—the default—and possessive—the only case with a special ending. He classifies pronouns as nominative, possessive, or objective.

Unlike Lowth, he explains in small print the difference between the structures of English and Latin and why it's best to avoid adopting Latin noun categories. He writes, "The English language, to express different relations and connections of one thing to another, uses for the most part prepositions. The Greek and Latin . . . vary the termination . . . of the substantive [noun] to answer the same purpose"—that is, Greek and Latin use varying word endings to show whether nouns are subjects, objects, or something else. Murray provides an example of Latin noun declension so students can see the difference.

Murray then goes on to suggest that if the term *case* means "the variation of a noun or pronoun by termination" it should not also be used for "the relations signified by the . . . addition of prepositions."[8] In Murray's view, labeling preposition-noun combinations such as *to a book* and *of a book* with case names like *dative* and *genitive* doesn't make sense. It's better to treat the noun separately from the preposition that precedes it. Elucidations like these are no doubt another reason why learners vastly preferred Murray's grammar.

After outlining the parts of speech, Murray moves on to syntax, "the agreement and right disposition of words in a sentence." Here he recapitulates all the conventional grammatical restrictions. Like Lowth and others, he calls for nominative case after *to be*—*It is I*—and bans the use of *who* and *whose* with non-humans. The familiar double negative rule—two negatives are equivalent to an affirmative—is stated in exactly the same words as those of Lowth and other grammar books. Murray also adopts Lowth's rule on prepositions left stranded at the end of a sentence in virtually the same words, except that he corrects Lowth's grammar. Instead of Lowth's "This is an idiom which our language is strongly inclined to" he writes, "This is an idiom to which our language is strongly inclined."[9]

Some of the issues Murray addresses have a familiar ring. He writes about the use of *they* with a singular antecedent, giving as one example, *Can anyone, on their entrance into the world, be fully secure that they shall not be deceived?* Since *anyone* is singular, Murray says, the correct pronouns are *his* and *he*. To-day's grammar purists largely agree with Murray, but might be surprised that the usage was common enough to be mentioned in an eighteenth-century grammar book. Typically, critics today assume that speakers use *they* with singular nouns in order to avoid using *he* alone or the awkward *he or she*. In fact, this usage came naturally to English speakers long before sexist pronouns were a concern.

Murray also discusses another nonstandard usage that still causes widespread annoyance—using the wrong pronoun case in conjoined phrases. His examples include *My sister and her were on good terms* (should be *my sister and she*); *He entreated us, my comrade and I, to live harmoniously* (should be *my comrade and me*); *His wealth and him bid adieu to each other* (should be *his wealth and he*). Present-day sticklers for correctness usually assume that nonstandard pronouns, especially nominative case after verbs and prepositions, as in *between you and I*—sometimes called "hypercorrection"—are a contemporary issue. Evidently, however, incorrect nominatives were just as trouble-some two centuries ago.

Even more than other grammar book authors, Murray took advantage of his practice exercises and example sentences to mix moral training with grammar lessons. In his memoirs, he explains that he was especially concerned with "the propriety and purity of all the examples and illustrations."[10] This attitude makes sense, as he was writing specifically with the adolescent girls of Trinity Lane School in mind. Murray's example sentences are often taken from the Bible, but he also includes short, mor-ally improving aphorisms. For instance, his parsing exercises feature such sentences as "Peace and joy are virtue's crown" and "The man is happy who lives wisely."

At the end of *English Grammar,* Murray offers another innovation in the form of an appendix titled "Perspicuity," where he lists a number of rules for improving clarity in writing. Today this section would be called a style guide. Much of Murray's advice sounds familiar. That's because it still appears in one form or another in many twenty-first-century writing manuals.

Murray begins by explaining that perspicuity requires "purity, propriety, and precision." Under the heading "purity," he counsels students to avoid using words that are obsolete—*erewhile*; newly coined—*incumberment*; or not English—*politesse*. Under "propriety," he lists rules such as "Avoid low expressions," "Avoid injudicious use of technical terms," and "Keep clear of double meaning or ambiguity." Two examples of low expressions are *topsy-turvy* and *hurly-burly*.

Murray spends the most time on "precision," which he describes as expressing an idea fully, but without unnecessary words. Offenses against precision include overlong sentences and incorrect synonyms. Murray offers plainspoken writing advice, such as, "In order to write or speak clearly and intelligibly, two things are especially requisite; one, that we have clear and distinct ideas of our subject; and the other that our words be approved signs of these ideas."[11]

The final paragraphs in the precision section list rules for composing effective sentences—for example, weaker assertions should come before stronger ones, and sentences should be pruned of redundant words. With his fifth rule, Murray brings the issue of sentence-final prepositions once more into play.

Here Murray asserts that writers should avoid concluding sentences with "an adverb, a preposition, or any inconsiderable word." As an illustration, he gives a typical example of preposition stranding: "Avarice is a crime which men are often guilty of." He suggests that "Avarice is a crime of which men are often guilty" is stronger. Then he goes a step further. In Murray's opinion, prepositions should never end a sentence, even when they are part of verb-preposition combinations like *clear up*.[12] A strong verb is a better choice.

Although Murray takes the no-prepositions rule to a new level, he sets it in the larger context of pleasing style—prepositions at the end of sentences are not so much ungrammatical as awkward. They are not the only part of speech that he feels should be avoided. He also rules out adverbs and pronouns at the end of a sentence. His reasoning is that the reader can't help pausing for a few seconds on the last word of a sentence, so it's better to end with a word—like a noun or verb—that conveys an idea. Early grammarians such as Lowth and Murray often framed their rules in terms of pleasing style. Later grammar books would tend to repeat their rules without the mitigating explanations, turning them from style suggestions into inviolable laws of grammar.

Murray wraps up his grammar book by drawing a direct parallel between good grammar and more substantial virtues. "Embarrassed, obscure, and feeble sentences," he admonishes readers, "are generally, if not always, the result of embarrassed, obscure, and feeble thought." In contrast, he says, "those who are learning to compose and arrange their sentences with accuracy and order are learning at the same time *to think with accuracy and order*; a consideration which alone will recompense the student for any care and attention that may be suitably employed on these occasions."[13]

English Grammar, Adapted to the Different Classes of Learners quickly gained an audience far broader than Quaker schoolgirls. Although Murray had originally stipulated that the book was only for use in two schools, he apparently overcame his qualms about having it widely distributed. By 1797 *English Grammar* was being printed and sold in London as well as Yorkshire.

Once it hit the larger market, its success was immediate and phenomenal.

That same year Murray published a book of exercises designed to give students extra practice. It offered exercises in spelling, punctuation, and parsing, as well as syntax. He also provided an answer key, as he says in his memoirs, "for the convenience of teachers and for the use of young persons who had left school and who might be desirous, at their leisure, to improve themselves in grammatical studies." He explains that he hopes to encourage the student by giving him "the pleasure of feeling his own powers and progress" in language learning. He also wants to "imbue his mind with sentiments of the highest importance" by "weaving principles of piety and virtue with the study of language."[14]

An abridged version of the grammar for younger students and anyone just beginning grammar study also appeared in 1797. Written mostly in short declarative sentences, with a tight organization and few footnotes, it's a comparatively easy read. Eventually Murray added a reader, then an introduction and a sequel to the reader, and finally a spelling book. The schools and the public snapped up each volume as soon as it appeared.

In a 1799 letter to a friend, Murray writes, "In four years there have been printed of the Abridgment, the Grammar, the Exercises, and Key, forty-six thousand copies; [and] eight thousand of 'The English Reader.' " He tells his friend that "an eminent" London bookseller offered him £1,050 for the copyrights of the grammar, exercises, and reader, which he has accepted. He sold the abridgment earlier for £100. Concerned that his correspondent will think he's benefiting financially from these sales, he hastens to reassure him: "I have appropriated the whole . . . for the benefit of others, without applying any of it to my private use."[15]

Until 1800, each edition of the grammar, exercises, and abridgment consisted of about 5,000 copies. Subsequent printings were about 15,000 copies each. By 1832, fifty-two editions had been printed in England, amounting to well over half a million volumes. Over the next few decades at least 3 million copies of Murray's various language study books were printed and sold in England.[16]

Murray was now deeply committed to his grammar writing. Just as Webster had pulled himself out of depression by writing the *Grammatical Institute*, Murray discovered that the mental engagement involved in writing language books cheered his spirits and improved his health. Eager to see his works distributed as widely as possible, he soon sold all the copyrights to Quaker booksellers in Yorkshire and London who had the capacity to produce large print runs and who would also advertise. Although Murray did not have radical ideas about grammar, in his own way he was just as passionate as Webster about the importance of the subject. He felt he was doing good by helping as many people as possible gain grammatical skills.

Even after he sold the copyrights, Murray continued to be closely involved in the books' production. He spent much of his time meticulously revising each new edition, as well as adding new material. By the 1824 edition *English Grammar* had grown from an original 222 pages to 310. He paid careful attention to comments and criticisms and tried to respond to them by correcting and rewording the relevant parts of the next edition. He explained to a friend, "By the change of a word, a slight variation in the form of a phrase, an additional sentence, or a short note, I have, as I think, frequently removed an objection or difficulty."[17] Murray always remained humble about his work and open to suggestions even after his books became bestsellers. Such humility was a rare trait in the contentious world of grammar book writing.

Murray's modesty didn't prevent him from taking a business-like interest in sales. Nor did the fact that he wasn't keeping what he earned on the books. He was highly skilled at marketing and put a great deal of time into it. From his sitting room sofa, he sent many letters to booksellers inquiring about the number of copies of a given edition they still had on hand, when they expected to print a new edition, and whether they had any useful suggestions for improving the work before then. When he received positive reviews, he sent them to be inserted as "characters," or advertisements, in later editions. He made sure that announcements of his other books were also included at the back of each book.

One way to distribute his grammar books more widely was to introduce them to the country of his birth. He asked his brother John, a New York businessman, to take charge of American printing and sales. The first American edition of *English Grammar* was published in New York in 1800. Shortly afterward, publishers in Philadelphia and Boston also produced printings. As in England, both the textbook and the related volumes that followed were immediate hits. In 1800 alone, ten American editions appeared.

By 1808 the grammar had been through twenty-five American editions and the abridgment through forty. This amounted to around three-quarters of a million books in circulation, in a country with only a little over 7 million people. From 1800 until 1840, when sales gradually began to decline, Americans would purchase as many as 12 million copies of Murray's various grammar and reading books. He was even more popular in the United States than in England.

No doubt part of the reason for his booming sales was the lack of international copyright laws. American printers didn't pay royalties to British authors, so printing Murray's books was financially attractive. It was also easy to crank out pirated editions, and dozens appeared on the market.

Another reason for the book's remarkable success is surely

Murray's genius for promotion. He collected positive English reviews and sent them to his brother John to use in American advertising, along with copious instructions about where they should appear. After quoting from one review of his speller, he tells his brother, "This character [advertisement], besides being circulated in the papers and periodical works, should be printed at the end or front of the American editions." He also asked his brother to keep him informed of any positive American reviews so he could use them in England.[18]

Murray made sure that readers were aware of the various improvements that came with each edition. For example, in the 1797 edition of the exercise book, he explains in a notice at the front of the book that he "has felt it incumbent upon him to give the *seventh* edition every improvement in his power, without enhancing the price of the book." Among the changes are "expunging some obscure and uninteresting sentences, inserting a number of examples adapted to the latest improvements in the grammar; and adding to the Syntax many useful exercises."[19]

Murray was also expert at networking. He frequently shipped copies of his latest editions to people who might be in a position to spread the word about them. For instance, he sent a box of books to the well-known geographer and Congregationalist minister Jedidiah Morse, explaining in the accompanying letter, "The books which accompany this note lately received new editions, in which the author hopes there will be found some improvements." He goes on to say that he has enclosed duplicates, in case Dr. Morse "should incline to promote American impressions [that is, American printings of the book], he may do it the better from having the latest editions."[20]

Murray also sent books to New York state politician Samuel Latham Mitchill. In 1804, shortly after Mitchill was elected to the U.S. Senate, Murray sent him a copy of the latest edition of *English Grammar* with a note asking for Mitchill's opinion. He expressed gratification that the book had been well received in his native country, and especially that Yale and other universities had adopted it. "It would be very pleasing," he told Mitchill, "to know that in the college of New York they were also received."[21]

Aside from Murray's energetic promotional activities, the grammar itself must have had some special appeal to sell so well. Americans no doubt recognized that it was much more practical than other grammar books on the market. Although later editions were longer and more detailed than the original volume, Murray kept essentially the same clearly organized structure. Following Lowth, Murray didn't obfuscate with too much Latin. Students were not faced with long lists of verb conjugations and noun declensions to be memorized. Murray also provided material targeted to specific groups. For young children and other beginners, the abridgment was available. For those who wanted extra practice, there was the exercise book.

The overall message of *English Grammar* was also clear and straightforward, in contrast to *A Grammatical Institute, Part II.* Murray did not explore alternative theories of usage or argue that *It is me* and *Who did she speak to?* should be accepted as standard speech because everyone said those things. His stated purpose was to teach his readers to speak and write with elegance and precision. Americans eager to improve their language skills could rest assured that if they mastered Murray's grammar they would sound like educated people. That, rather than a deep understanding of the American idiom, was their goal.

The American embrace of Murray is ironic in some respects. While it's true that he was an American and always spoke of the United States as his home, he spent the second half of his life in England. During the Revolutionary War, Murray's father was a prominent Loyalist and most likely Murray himself was sympathetic to the British. Neither Murray's Tory leanings nor his long residence in Yorkshire kept Americans from buying his books.

Murray's American roots were not very deep. When he was born on March 27, 1745, his father, Robert, had not been in the country long. Robert had immigrated to Pennsylvania as a boy, coming from Ireland in 1732 with his brother John and their father. They settled in Swatara (then known as Swetara), about eighteen miles northeast of Harrisburg. Shortly after the family's arrival, the elder Murray bought a large parcel of land along Swatara Creek and set up a successful flour mill. Robert took it over while still a young man.

Murray's mother, Mary Lindley, was also the daughter of recent immigrants. They, too, came from Ireland, but unlike the Presbyterian Murrays, they were Quakers, part of the wave of Quaker immigrants who arrived in Pennsylvania during the early eighteenth century. Mary Lindley's father, Thomas, settled in Philadelphia. He flourished, first as a blacksmith, then as the owner of an iron forge. Around 1733 he bought a large parcel of land outside Swatara, where he quickly became a prominent citizen. He served as a justice of the peace and later became a member of the Pennsylvania Assembly.

In 1744 Robert Murray and Mary Lindley married after Murray converted to Quakerism. Lindley was born a year later. He was the first of twelve children, although only five would survive to adulthood. Robert Murray had ambitions beyond the flour mill. He made several profitable trading trips to the West Indies when Lindley was still a baby. Then in 1753, after moving to North Carolina for a brief time, he settled with his family in Manhattan. Here he established a successful shipping business. By the 1760s he was one of New York's wealthiest merchants, well connected among the Quaker families of the city, and the owner of an impressive mansion overlooking the East River. (The mansion stood at what is now Park Avenue and 36th Street, a neighborhood still known as Murray Hill.)

Young Lindley's education was distinctly different from that of Noah Webster and others who attended village schools before the Revolution. Around the age of eleven, he spent a year at the prestigious Academy of Philadelphia, founded by Benjamin Franklin. In his memoirs, Murray recalls being "agreeably exercised in the business of parsing sentences." He also remembers enjoying a book titled *The Travels of Cyrus*, which tells the story of a young Persian prince's travels through the ancient world.[22] Such books would rarely have come the way of public schoolchildren.

Later Murray attended a good New York school, where he claimed to have made "the usual progress of young learners," in spite of occasionally skipping school. Eventually he grew to love reading and scholarship, and when his father took him from school as a teenager to work in the family countinghouse, young Lindley resisted. He was not interested in being a merchant. After one unusually explosive clash with his father, he packed his bags, took the money he had saved, and ran away from home. His intention was to enroll in a well-known Quaker academy in Burlington, New Jersey, and study French.

Murray arrived at the school and signed up as a boarder, apparently covering the expenses himself. His parents discovered his whereabouts almost immediately, but allowed him to remain at the school for a time. Eventually he was coaxed back home and he and his father reconciled. After Murray's return, Robert Murray agreed to allow him a private tutor. Murray writes in his memoir, "I pursued this new career with great alacrity of mind. I sat up late, and rose early, in the prosecution of my studies."[23] He also joined a young men's debating society that met weekly.

Murray was more than ever convinced that he wanted to pursue a scholarly career. He decided that he would like to study law and, after some initial reluctance, his father agreed. Lindley became a pupil of Robert Murray's lawyer, Benjamin Kissam. In 1767, at the age of twenty-two, he was admitted to the New York bar.

Recently married to Hannah Dobson, Murray settled down to practice law. About a year later his career was briefly interrupted when his father traveled to England on business and the rest of the family, including Murray and his wife, accompanied him. Murray returned to New York in 1771 and resumed his law practice. He had a wide circle of business connections and did very well until the upheavals of the Revolution shut down the courts.

At about the same time Murray suffered an episode of severe illness. When he recovered, the Murrays decided to move to Islip, a quiet hamlet on the south shore of Long Island. In this idyllic spot Murray hoped to regain his health. Another motivation was to escape New York until, in Murray's words, "the political storm should blow over, and the horizon become again clear and settled."[24]

The extent of Murray's loyalty to England is unclear. His evident wish to avoid involvement in the Revolution may have stemmed from Tory sympathies, but it might also have been inspired by a Quaker opposition to war. Murray's mother and other family members were known to support the American cause. His father, however, was a committed Loyalist. Robert Murray openly traded with the British before and during the war, and almost certainly was part of a supply chain providing the British army with flour. After the king's army captured and occupied New York, its officers were welcomed into the elder Murray's Manhattan home.

Whatever the son's views, after four years in Islip spent mostly fishing and sailing, he was ready to return to New York. Murray had begun to feel as though he needed to earn money again. He joined his father in the import-export business and was extremely successful. By the end of the war, he had amassed a large enough fortune to retire.

Murray and his wife then purchased what he describes in his memoirs as "a country seat" on the banks of the Hudson, about three miles outside the city. They planned to settle down to a bucolic life, surrounded by extensive gardens and their own cattle pastures. No thoughts were in Murray's mind of a writing career. Before they could settle into their new home, however, Murray's always-fragile health broke down completely. Besides fever and chills, he experienced muscle weakness so severe he could barely walk. After a time he improved, but he never fully recovered. From then on, Murray's health would dictate the shape of his life.

The Murrays tried different remedies. They traveled to the Pennsylvania countryside, where they spent several weeks getting to know the Moravian community. When temperatures rose into the 90s, they traveled into the mountains for relief. They visited medicinal springs, where Murray sampled the waters. Nothing improved his health. Gradually he noticed that hot summer weather had an especially damaging effect. When Murray and his wife began to think of relocating to a cooler climate, Murray's doctor suggested Yorkshire.

At the end of 1784 the Murrays sailed for England, believing that they would return to New York after a few years. In fact, they would remain in Yorkshire for the rest of their lives—more than forty years. The gentleman farmer's existence that Murray had planned for himself would never materialize. Instead he was a little more than a decade away from writing the books that would make him famous and define grammar study until the middle of the nineteenth century.[25]

Sometime in 1803 Lindley Murray mailed a copy of his gram-mar book to Noah Webster, enclosing a friendly letter. It opens, "I take the liberty of requesting that the Author of 'Dissertations on the English Language' will do me the favour to accept a copy of the new edition of my grammar as a small testimony of my respect for his talents and character." After further compliment-ing Webster on his "ingenious and sensible writings," Murray asks that Webster look over the grammar and convey any sug-gestions he may have for improvement.[26]

This letter was the only direct communication that Murray and Webster would have. Webster's answer would not appear for sev-eral years and when it did, it would take a form far different from the letter that Murray expected. Instead Webster responded by writing a new grammar book of his own. He was more firmly convinced than ever of the ideas that he had formed while writ-ing his grammar lectures in 1785, and also more disapproving of conventional grammar books. Any "suggestions for improve-ment" that Webster had for Murray were incorporated into his book as attacks. Webster later claimed that he had sent Murray a copy of his new book, along with what he termed a polite let-ter, but Murray apparently never received it.

❧ The past decade had been a busy one for Webster, although little of it had been spent in language writing. His energies were mainly channeled into the political writing that appeared in his Federalist newspaper, *The American Minerva*. Webster and his family returned to New Haven in 1798 after five years in New York, but Webster continued to edit and publish the *Minerva* un-til 1801. Then a rival Federalist journal, the *Evening Post*, began siphoning off Webster's readers. He decided to sell the paper and get out of the journalism business. Afterward he continued writ-ing vigorously on a variety of topics. He published *A Brief His-*

tory of Epidemic and Pestilential Diseases in 1799, after an outbreak of yellow fever piqued his interest in the subject. In 1805 he brought out the two-volume *Elements of Useful Knowledge*, a survey of American history and geography.

At the same time he returned to his first love, American English. In 1806 Webster published *A Compendious Dictionary of the English Language*. This dictionary was his first attempt at recording American words. Although much less comprehensive than his monumental 1828 dictionary would be, the *Compendious Dictionary* was a substantial piece of work. It featured five thousand new words not recorded in previous dictionaries, and cemented Webster's reputation as a language scholar.

As usual with Webster's publications, not everyone was happy with the book. Some critics were scandalized by Webster's audacity in attempting to compete with the great British lexicographer Samuel Johnson, whose 1755 *Dictionary of the English Language* was considered the gold standard. Others were troubled by the inclusion of "low" words (*bamboozle*) and Americanisms (*presidential, deputize*), as well as a number of simplified spellings (*aker* for *acre, tung* for *tongue, wimen* for *women*). Most commentators, however, considered the book a major accomplishment.

In the first few pages of the dictionary's preface, Webster talks about his latest views on grammar, a preview of the grammar book that he would publish the following year. Writing to his friend Joel Barlow in 1807, he describes his new grammar project: "My grammar had its run but it has been superseded by Murray's. Both are wrong. I have lately published one on Horne Tooke's plan, which President Smith of Princeton pronounces the best analysis of the language ever published."[27] Webster's new version of English grammar gave him a chance to correct what he saw as his own earlier mistakes, while pointing out those of Murray and other grammarians. His goal, as before, was to rescue Americans from linguistic ignorance and make them aware of how their language really worked.

◊ *A Philosophical and Practical Grammar of the English Language* represents the culmination of Webster's thinking about English over twenty years. When he wrote the book, he was still in thrall to British linguistic philosopher John Horne Tooke's theory that all English words—including prepositions, conjunctions, adjectives, and adverbs—originated as Anglo-Saxon nouns and verbs. Part of his purpose was to reanalyze English grammar according to this idea. Webster's preface asks rhetorically, "Have we not Grammars enough already?" He answers with a firm no, "for if the theory . . . unfolded in Horne Tooke's 'Diversions of Purley,' is well founded, we have not hitherto had *any* correct Grammar."[28] As Webster has seen nothing in new grammar books except "fresh editions of the same errors," he intends to construct a grammar based on true principles of the language.

Webster was not writing for scholars only. He planned to market *A Philosophical and Practical Grammar* as a textbook. He organized it in typical grammar book style, beginning with the alphabet and including the usual sections on parts of speech ("Etymology"), sentence structure ("Syntax"), and pronunciation ("Prosody"). Webster also included many examples of false syntax and the usual type of parsing exercise. Over this basic foundation, however, he built a highly idiosyncratic grammatical edifice.

Webster's radical remodeling begins with the basic building blocks. He explains in the preface that, in order to more accurately describe "the true state" of English, he has had to change the names of most parts of speech. While he is aware that the names have been customary since classical times, "in the sciences prescription cannot legalize error."[29]

Webster divides words into two classes—primary and secondary. In the primary category are verbs and nouns—the words on which the rest of the language depends. He keeps the term *verb* because he can't think of another one that is more descriptive, but he relabels nouns as *names*. The secondary category covers the remaining parts of speech. All except prepositions are re-named. These include substitutes (pronouns), attributes (adjec-tives), modifiers (adverbs), and connectives (conjunctions).

Webster then discusses each part of speech, often exploring its origins and usage in lengthy footnotes. His attacks on other grammarians typically appear in these notes. His usual method is to cite an example sentence or statement from another gram-mar book and then argue that it's wrong. Although Webster rails against other grammarians generally, he singles out Murray for special abuse. His hostility probably stemmed at least partly from frustration over his declining book sales. *English Grammar, Adapted to Different Classes of Learners* was inexorably pushing *Grammatical Institute, Part II* out of schoolrooms and homes.

The attacks on Murray begin in the preface. Webster mentions in a footnote that English grammar books have not shown much improvement since the days of Charles II. He admits that Lowth has "supplied some valuable criticisms," but then says dismis-sively, "Murray, not having mounted to the original sources of information, and professing only to select and arrange the rules and criticisms of preceding writers, has furnished little or noth-ing new."[30]

Webster again compares Murray unfavorably with Lowth in his discussion of *a* and *an*. This extended footnote gives a taste of the book's overall tone. Webster starts by explaining that gram-marians have normally labeled these two words indefinite arti-cles, in contrast to the definite *the*, arguing that they don't identify one specific person or thing. Webster disagrees. He believes that because *a* and *an* do limit a noun to a single item or individual they constitute "the most definite word imaginable."

Webster then argues his point in more detail. He quotes

Lowth's definition of *a*—"A is used in a vague sense to point out one single thing of the kind, in other respects indeterminate"— and follows it with Murray's definition—"A is styled the indefinite article; it is used in a vague sense to point out one single thing of the kind, in other respects indeterminate." He comments tartly, "So great scholars write, and so their disciples copy!"

He notes that Lowth's book is titled *A Short Introduction to English Grammar* and wonders whether Lowth would agree that the *A* in this instance refers to something indeterminate. He believes that Lowth would consider his book a very specific thing. To cap his argument he continues sarcastically, "Suppose *a* man to have received *a* severe wound, *a* fracture of the leg, or of the skull; however indeterminate the man may be, his grammars will hardly convince him that *a* broken head or leg is a very indeterminate thing."[31]

Like many of the book's other extended explorations of the true nature of a word, this one does not have any practical application. Webster has committed himself to a perverse interpretation of *a* and *an*, but he isn't suggesting that they should be used differently. He just thinks that they should be labeled differently.

Anti-Murray footnotes are scattered throughout the book. Webster quotes Murray's rule that the phrase *as follows* should always be singular—*The rules are as follows*, not *The rules are as follow*. Then he huffs, "On this passage, which is an error from beginning to end, I will just remark that had it been written in the days of Johnson and Lowth, the errors it contains must have been pardoned. . . . But to frame such an explanation . . . after the publication of the 'Diversions of Purley' admits of no apology." Webster also disagrees with Murray about the proper form for joint possessives. Webster believes that when several people possess a thing, each possessor gets an *'s—It was my father's, mother's, and uncle's opinion.* He then notes, "The contrary rule in Murray is egregiously wrong, as exemplified in this phrase: 'This

was my father, mother, and uncle's advice.' This is not English."
Never mind that in both cases the weight of consensus was—
and still is—on Murray's side.[32]

A Philosophical and Practical Grammar was hopelessly un-
suited to classroom use. Besides the unfamiliar terminology and
long digressions on word origins, Webster continued to push his
unorthodox ideas about usage. As he did in *Dissertations on the
English Language* several years earlier, he supports using *who* in
Who did she speak to?, saying, "This idiom is not merely colloquial; it is found in the writings of our best authors." He still believes that *It is me* is grammatical and accepts the use of *whose*
with nonhumans.

Webster also advocates some unusual plurals. He writes,
"*Women* is one of the grossest errors in our language. The true
original plural is *wimmen.*" He encourages English-style plurals
with common Latin words—*focuses, mediums, funguses* instead
of the more usual (at that time) *foci, media, fungi.* He insists that
when *you* refers to only one person, the following verb should
be *was.* Referring to the trend toward replacing *thee* and *thou*
with *you,* he argues, "If a word, once exclusively plural, becomes
by universal use the sign of individuality, it must take its place
in the singular number." Webster backs up his argument with
examples from print sources, including contemporary court
transcripts—"Was you there when the gun was fired?"[33]

In Webster's opinion, it's only a matter of time before this usage becomes completely acceptable. He says, "The compilers of
grammar condemn the use of *was* with *you*—but in vain. The
practice is universal, except among men who learn the language
by books."[34] Webster was wrong about *you was.* It was fairly
common in his day, but became increasingly unacceptable as
time went on. Standard grammar books continued to reject it,
along with Webster's other pet usages.

If Webster had hoped to wean large numbers of Americans

away from Murray's grammar, he was disappointed. *A Philosoph-ical and Practical Grammar* sold poorly, although a second edi-tion appeared in 1822. The reactions of an 1808 reviewer express what many readers probably felt about the book. The reviewer rejects Webster's novel terms on the ground that they are im-practical. If grammar rules are arbitrary anyway, he asks, what is the use of confusing people by changing the terminology? "The parts of speech" he argues, "seem like the tools of a mechanick; and if Mr. Webster would have us call a *gimlet* a *perforator,* we see not how it will better perform its original office."[35]

He is also repelled by the "veneration" in which Webster holds "the language of the vulgar." He quotes Webster's passages on double negatives and *it is me* without comment, assuming that their faulty reasoning is obvious. He also rejects *focuses, radi-uses,* and similar plurals. He admits that "had we a new language to form," the inclusion of *you was* would make sense. Since *you were* is already established, however, it seems best to keep it. He concludes with a ringing affirmation of current grammatical standards. "We . . . believe that our language will be the same three hundred years hence, . . . in spite of the exertions of Mr. Webster. . . . We scorn the notion of an American tongue, or of gaining our idiom from the mouths of the illiterate."[36] Many people reading the review would have nodded their heads in agreement.

In 1828, two years after Murray's death, Webster brought out his *American Dictionary of the English Language,* with a com-pact version of his 1807 grammar included at the front. Here Murray's shortcomings get another airing. Webster introduces the grammar section by telling readers, "In the year 1803, I re-ceived a letter from Lindley Murray, with a copy of his Gram-mar." He quotes Murray's letter in full. He then explains how his changing view of the structure of English led him to write *A*

Philosophical and Practical Grammar, partly as a response to Murray.

Webster further explains that he sent Murray a copy of the book when it was first published, but later learned from Murray's friends that he never received it. Webster is convinced that Murray nonetheless read the book. In the very next edition of Murray's own grammar, which appeared in 1808, Murray admits that he "examined the most respectable publications on the subject of grammar that had recently appeared," and accordingly had been able to "extend and improve" his own work. In tones of controlled outrage, Webster fumes, "On carefully comparing this work with my own Grammar, I found most of his *improvements* were selected from my book."

Webster goes on to claim that Murray borrowed from at least thirty passages of Webster's book, "so incorporated into his work that no person except myself would detect the plagiarisms without a particular view to this object." Webster does not identify any of the plagiarisms. He concludes by saying that because Murray has only given Webster credit for one extended quotation—Webster's system for classifying verbs—American students are unaware that they are "learning *my* principles in Murray's Grammar."[37]

Since Webster doesn't cite any specific instances, it's difficult to say whether Murray borrowed from *A Philosophical and Practical Grammar.* He may well have. His remarks in the new edition's introduction indicate that he was comfortable incorporating other people's material. He says, "In a work which professes itself to be a compilation, and which, from the nature and design of it must consist chiefly of materials selected from the writings of others, it is scarcely necessary to apologize for the use which the Compiler has made of his predecessors' labours; or for omitting to insert their names." Most of the grammar books coming off the presses during this era have a sameness of language, especially in their definitions and their syntax rules. All books including Webster's, for instance, continue to quote Lowth's rule against double negatives—two negatives in English destroy one another—almost verbatim.

In any case, Webster's attacks on Murray in *A Philosophical and Practical Grammar* appear not to have had much impact on the 1808 edition of Murray's grammar. The rules that Webster specifically criticized remain unchanged. Murray continues to define *a* and *an* as indefinite articles. He still thinks joint possessives should take only a single *'s*. He does enlarge his discussion of *as follows,* saying that grammarians disagree about whether it should always be singular and outlining competing points of view. In the end, however, he recommends that it be treated as singular. He tells readers that those in doubt may paraphrase.

The majority of Murray's users would never have become aware of Webster's accusations. They wouldn't have abandoned Murray's grammar books even if they had. At least another decade would pass before Murray's books began to disappear from classrooms, and they would not be replaced by Webster. Instead, the new grammar books would be very much like Murray's. Americans remained unconvinced by Webster's arguments in favor of basing grammatical standards on their own homegrown speech.

Murray's success opened the floodgates for grammar book writers. By 1800, several Americans a year were turning out their own versions of Murray-like grammars, with around three hundred titles published in the first half of the nineteenth century.[38] All of these authors were hoping to capture a slice of the vast grammar book market that Murray's spectacular sales had revealed.

Most would fail. Even so, writing a grammar book was considered a promising way for teachers and literary men to earn some extra income.

Two of the most successful of Murray's competitors were Goold Brown and Samuel Kirkham. Brown, a New York schoolmaster, published *The Institutes of English Grammar* in 1823. Brown's preface suggests that he was fully aware of Murray as the major obstacle to his own book's sales. He savages Murray in language that makes Webster seem measured by comparison. (Brown also indirectly attacks Webster with remarks on "some [who] have . . . wasted their energies on eccentric flights, vainly supposing that the learning of ages would give place to their whimsical theories." He saves his most brutal criticisms, however, for Murray, his chief competitor.)

Brown uses much of his preface to denigrate Murray. He sneeringly points out that Murray opened his grammar book with remarks to the effect that "little is to be expected" of a new grammar compilation, considering how many volumes were already in print. "From the very first sentence of his book," Brown says, "it appears that he entertained but a low and most erroneous idea" of the duties of a grammarian. In Brown's view, "Murray was an intelligent and very worthy man, . . ." but "in original thought and critical skill" he fell far below most of the authors he relied on for his materials. He comments austerely, "It is certain and evident that he entered upon his task with a very insufficient preparation."[39] Brown points out that Murray never actually taught children, unlike Brown himself, who had many years' experience in the classroom.

Furthermore, Brown says, Murray seemed to think that writing a grammar book consists solely of compiling the most useful materials and arranging them conveniently for students. "As if," he exclaims, "to be master of his own art—to think and write well himself, were no part of a grammarian's business!" Brown has decided to write his own book because "to expect the perfection of grammar from him who cannot treat the subject in a style at once original and pure, is absurd."[40] Brown intends to provide more than a mere compilation.

Like most grammar book authors, Brown tries to strike a balance in his preface between assuring readers that his grammar rules are authoritative and claiming originality for his scholarship. "The nature of the subject," he concedes, "almost entirely precludes invention." On the other hand, "many false and faulty definitions and rules [have] been copied and copied from one grammar to another, as if authority had canonized their errors." Brown believes he has avoided this problem through diligent research. He has "carefully perused" over fifty grammar books, and glanced over many others that, in his opinion, were not worth reading.[41]

Brown also believes that his practice exercises are an improvement over what has come before. He says, "Murray evidently intended that his book of exercises should be constantly used with his grammar; but he made the examples in the former so dull and prolix, that few learners, if any, have ever gone through the series agreeably to his direction." Brown then dissects several of Murray's parsing examples to show where Murray has gone wrong.[42]

Although Brown has mentioned earlier in the preface that he didn't think it necessary to "encumber his pages with a useless parade of names and references, or to distinguish very minutely what is copied and what is original," he holds Murray to a higher standard and winds up his assault with charges of plagiarism. He complains that *English Grammar* is not only riddled with errors, but the best parts of it are really other people's work. "There is no part of the volume more accurate," Brown claims, "than that which he literally copied from Lowth." Not that later grammarians have done any better, in his view. He comments, "It is curious to observe how frequently a grammatical blunder committed by Murray . . . has escaped the notice of . . . many others who have found it easier to copy him than to write for themselves."[43]

In spite of Brown's harsh criticisms of *English Grammar, The Institutes* shows more than a hint of Murray's influence. Like Murray, Brown presents his main rules and definitions in large type and his comments in smaller type. An appendix titled "Of Style" divides the basic features of style into the same three categories that are found in Murray's "Perspicuity" chapter—purity, propriety, and precision—and defines them in almost the same words.

Like Murray and others, Brown pays tribute to the notion that general use should determine what constitutes good grammar, but adopts the same rules that were laid down in the earliest eighteenth-century grammar texts. He calls for nominative case after the verb *be* and after comparatives, as in *He is taller than I*. He declares that *To whom did he speak?* is "in general more graceful" than *Whom did he speak to?* He also rejects double negatives, stating flatly that they are "vulgar." As an illustration, he presents the same line from Milton—"Nor did they not perceive their evil plight"—that Lowth quoted several decades earlier.

Brown's book does show some original features. Most of his definitions and rules are freshly worded. His description of nouns—the name of any person, place, or thing that can be known or mentioned—is an early version of what would later become the standard formula. His definition of verbs also sounds more modern than earlier ones—a word that signifies to be, to act, or to be acted upon.

Brown takes an innovative approach with parsing exercises. He doesn't wait until students have memorized most of the book's material, but begins presenting exercises immediately. The first set comes right after he defines the parts of speech.

More exercises appear after each new section and Brown explains each time what he wants from the students: "It is required of the pupil—to distinguish and define the different parts of speech, and the classes and modifications of the articles and nouns."[44]

His parsing exercises differ in another way, too. Most of his contemporaries' books presented the text to be parsed, then provided the "resolution," which demonstrated the actual parsing. Brown gives learners texts to parse on their own, without the corresponding answers. That way they have to work out the resolution themselves rather than merely memorizing it. He provides a separate answer key for the convenience of teachers and "private learners."

Brown's exercises mainly consist of simple, original sentences rather than quotations (although, surprisingly, he occasionally quotes a sentence from Murray's book). He supplements the parsing examples with basic questions about the material, such as "What are tenses in grammar?" He also makes heavy use of false syntax exercises.

The Institutes reflects changes that have occurred in the English language and how it's analyzed. Brown's book is one of the first to list participles as a separate part of speech. Like most other grammar books by this time, he drops the question-and-response method of teaching in favor of straightforward presentation of the material. He avoids excess Latin-style noun cases, keeping only nominative, objective, and possessive. He also notes the fact that *you* is now commonly used for second-person singular as well as plural, although he still includes *thou* when demonstrating verb forms.

Brown's *Institutes* went through at least fifty editions, replacing *English Grammar* in the schools of his native New York and challenging it in other places. The differences between Brown's approach and Murray's, or maybe the fact that *The Institutes* was a newer book, clearly won over some schoolteachers. Nonetheless, Brown never succeeded in eclipsing Murray as he had hoped.

Samuel Kirkham, whose 1825 *English Grammar in Familiar Lectures* was also widely popular, took the opposite approach from Brown. He made no attempt to escape from Murray. On the contrary, he admits frankly in his preface that he is aware of the public's preference for "the doctrines contained in Mr. Murray's grammar." He therefore plans to "select his principles chiefly from that work." Kirkham then devotes a paragraph to pointing out to Murray and any other competitors the well-known fact that "similar investigations and pursuits often elicit corresponding ideas in different minds." If they notice similarities between his book and theirs, they shouldn't be too quick to accuse him of plagiarism.[45]

Like other aspiring grammar book authors, Kirkham struggled to set his book apart in a crowded field. He touches all the usual grammatical bases, but does include some distinctive features. He addresses students directly throughout the book, telling them exactly what he wants them to do. After his section on progressives, for instance, he says, "Now please to turn back, and read over this and the preceding lecture *three* times, and endeavour not only to understand but also to *remember* what you read." When he first introduces parsing he says, "To analyze or *parse* a word means to enumerate and describe all its various properties . . . If you persevere you will . . . find it of great utility."[46]

A long footnote on philosophical grammar near the beginning of the book shows that Kirkham has been reading Webster, although he doesn't mention him by name. Kirkham explains that while he thinks it's absurd to try to teach English grammar based on a system like Horne Tooke's, he knows that "a strong predilection for philosophical grammars exists in the minds of some teachers." He therefore plans to intersperse "Philosophical Notes" throughout the text. These are Webster-style explorations of word origins for anyone who wants to study the language in more depth.

𝒪 Kirkham also includes a unique list of provincialisms organized by region, along with the standard alternative. For example, he lists the New England expression *He lives to home* and corrects it to *He lives at home.* He corrects the southernism *Tote the wood to the river* to *Carry the wood to the river.* He says *I seen him,* often heard in Pennsylvania, should be *I saw him.* Aside from Webster's writings, this fascinating list is one of the few glimpses of regional variation to be found in an early nineteenth-century grammar book.

Although Brown and Kirkham took different routes, they shared the same goal—to knock Murray from his publishing throne. Murray's *English Grammar* was the acknowledged benchmark in the world of grammar books. For the next few decades, all hopeful grammar book authors would market their products by claiming to have improved somehow on Murray, whether through better teaching methods, original exercises, or a more readable format.

The innovations and improvements they claimed were matters of style, not substance. The core of all grammar books—the rules themselves—remained the same. Bishop Lowth's restrictions on sentence-final prepositions, double negatives, and pronoun case, first expounded in 1762, lived on in his successors' books, their wording virtually unchanged. With millions of Murray's books circulating in every part of the country, these rules became familiar maxims to people of every social class. They achieved the status of established truths.

Murray still dominated the grammar book market when he decided to give up writing. Toward the end of his memoirs, completed in 1809, he announces that he will no longer write grammar books. A year earlier he produced a two-volume "octavo" version of his *English Grammar,* much revised and enlarged.[47] The first edition sold out within months. "I had the satisfaction to perceive," he says, "that all my literary productions were approved . . . But I was fully persuaded that an author ought to terminate his labours before the tide of favour begins to turn; and before he incurs the charge of being so infected with the morbid humour for writing, as not to have the discretion to know when to stop."[48]

Part of Murray's reason for retiring from grammar book writing was his worsening health. By the end of 1809 he was so weak he could no longer go out for his daily carriage rides or even sit in the garden. Often his vocal muscles were so weak he couldn't speak above a whisper. He spent the next seventeen years, until the end of his life, confined to his house. Besides his chronic muscle weakness, he faced recurring bouts of severe illness, probably brought on by his lack of movement. Only by keeping to his strict schedule and careful diet was he able to continue some semblance of normal life.

In his memoirs, Murray expresses the hope that there will "still remain for me other sources of employment and some degree of usefulness, better adapted to . . . my growing infirmities of body."[49] From the confines of his sitting room, Murray remained engaged with the larger world. He was a member of the Anti-Slavery Society and supported William Wilberforce, Yorkshire's member of Parliament, who led the fight to abolish England's slave trade. He involved himself in local charitable causes, ranging from a school for poor children to the animal welfare league. He also wrote two brief essays on religious subjects. Like all his writing, these were well received.

Whenever he felt well enough, he continued to tinker with his books. Whether or not Murray fully absorbed the ferocious comments of Webster, Brown, and other critics is unclear. He certainly took seriously any errors or gaps that came to his attention. He diligently reworded and polished until problems were corrected to his satisfaction, bestowing what a friend termed "parental care" on all his publications.

Murray's grammar books had made him a celebrity. He was awarded honorary memberships in New York's Historical Society and Literary and Philosophical Society. Scholarly and literary people asked to meet him and afterward wrote about their visits. One such person was a Yale professor of chemistry named Benjamin Silliman. He arrived on a November day in 1805 when Murray was fortunately able to talk. Professor Silliman reports, "Our conversation related principally to literature, morals, and religion, and the state of these important subjects in the United States and England." After his visit, he rode back to York "with impressions of the most agreeable kind."[50]

By the time of Murray's death in 1826, just short of his eighty-first birthday, his name had become one to conjure with. Reviewers who wanted to suggest that a book's style could use some improvement would say that the author seemed unfamiliar with Murray. In contrast, those who wrote well were said to have obviously studied their Murray. "Murray" was shorthand for good grammar.

Murray's grammar was used to fill out descriptions of fictional characters. Dickens includes the book in a miscellany of items strewn around schoolmaster Wackford Squeers's study in *Nicholas Nickleby*. In *Uncle Tom's Cabin,* Harriet Beecher Stowe describes Haley the slave trader by saying, "His conversation was in free and easy defiance of Murray's grammar."

Memoirs and biographies also frequently mention the grammar. Yorkshire clergyman Andrew Reed, recalling his sister from around 1812, says, "She then went through Murray's Grammar, . . . not merely committing its rules to memory, but understanding and applying them." African Methodist-Episcopal bishop Daniel Payne, recalling his efforts at self-education during the same period in South Carolina, tells his readers, "I began with 'Murray's Primary Grammar,' and committed the entire book to memory." Then, feeling that he didn't really understand the book, he went through it a second time.[51]

Murray's grammar was enough of an institution to figure in comic sketches. In an 1845 book of elocution exercises, a character named Mrs. Grumpy tells a schoolmaster whose school she's thinking of patronizing, "I've *heerd* a great deal about your school, and I've determined to send you one of my *gals,* if you can only satisfy me on one *pint.* They tell me you have some new-fangled notions on the subject of grammar; and I never will have *nothing* to do with *no* one that does not know Murray's Grammar."[52] The schoolmaster assures her that all his pupils receive a thorough grounding in Murray.

Gradually, newer books would replace Murray's. New teaching methods evolved and updated texts gained favor. Until at least the middle of the nineteenth century, however, people concerned with improving their minds and their circumstances would define being educated as having a good understanding of Murray's *English Grammar.*

3.

The Value of Grammar

Three years after Lindley Murray's death, when his books were still enjoying peak sales, America entered a new cultural and political age—the age of Andrew Jackson. Jackson was the first "people's president." The six presidents before him had all come from families that were as close to being aristocrats as was possible in the United States. Washington, Jefferson, Madison, and Monroe were wealthy plantation owners; the Adamses were patrician New Englanders. Jackson's election broke with this tradition. The son of working-class Irish immigrants, he had grown up in the rugged Carolina backcountry and begun his adult career in the wilds of frontier Tennessee.

Like the election itself, Jackson's inauguration on March 4, 1829, was distinctly different from what had come before. Previous presidential inaugurations had been formal, indoor affairs with invited guests. Jackson's took place under the Capitol's East Portico, and anyone who could find a spot on the lawn was welcome to attend. In the days before the event, thousands of exultant Jacksonians streamed into Washington, D.C. One observer who was not a Jackson supporter remarked unhappily that it seemed as if half the country had rushed at once into the capital— "like the inundation of the northern barbarians into Rome."[1]

On the morning of the inauguration itself—luckily, a sunny day—the multitudes swamped the Capitol grounds. Supreme

Court justice Joseph Story estimated that the number of spectators reached at least ten thousand. They thronged together so tightly that it was difficult for the president-elect, who was on foot, to push his way through to the Capitol. Someone had tried to contain the crowd by stretching a ship's cable across the East Portico steps, but this barrier almost snapped as those in front reached out to touch their hero. When Jackson finally appeared under the portico, a cheer went up that, as one attendee described it, "seemed to shake the very ground."

❦ Most of that tumultuous crowd had never heard of Lindley Murray, or else had forgotten all they once knew. The majority of Jackson supporters were laborers or small farmers who had only a few years' basic schooling at most. Some were recent immigrants. They hailed largely from the rural areas of the South and the western frontier. A large percentage were men who, because of their low economic status, had only recently gained the right to vote.

When the United States was first formed, only men who owned a certain minimum amount of property were allowed to vote (mainly white men, but also free black men in some states). Elections were the business of a select few. This situation changed when frontier states like Tennessee, Kentucky, Ohio, and Illinois began joining the union. The hardy individualists who settled these areas felt that they were just as entitled to a voice in the government as wealthier citizens. They demanded and received their voting rights. Most of the original thirteen states soon loosened their voting laws as well.

Andrew Jackson was the ideal candidate for these new voters. A self-made man, he had risen from a humble backcountry childhood to become one of the largest landowners in Tennessee. He was the famous hero of the War of 1812 who led the victory over the British during the Battle of New Orleans. He had also put down the 1814 uprising of the Creeks. His troops nicknamed him

Old Hickory as a tribute to his toughness. Like his followers, he believed in individual rights and a limited federal government. He was like them in another way, too. He received most of his education from a "common school"—a public school that taught only basic levels of reading, spelling, and arithmetic.

This fact alone distinguished Jackson sharply from earlier presidents, although he was not completely deprived of higher education. As a child, he studied for three years at a private Presbyterian academy that offered Latin and Greek, as well as English grammar and other advanced classes. Later he attended a private school briefly to brush up on his Latin before studying for the bar exam. These experiences made him better educated than many Americans. They didn't compare, though, with his predecessors' privileged educations, which included exclusive private schools, tutors, and in some cases colleges such as Harvard and Princeton.

The election of 1828 was remarkable for the no-holds-barred campaigning on both sides. Andrew Jackson and his opponent, incumbent president John Quincy Adams, had already squared off during the 1824 election, when Jackson won the most votes out of four presidential candidates, but not an outright majority. The lack of a clear winner sent the decision to the House of Representatives, which voted Adams into office. Now supporters of both men were prepared for a brutal return match.

Adams supporters seized on Jackson's limited formal schooling and shaky spelling skills as a major campaign issue. The pro-Adams *National Journal* went on the attack by publishing a note that they claimed to have received in Jackson's own handwriting. Filled with lurid vocabulary and laughably bad spelling, it seemed to prove that Jackson was as ignorant as his enemies claimed he was: "When the midnight assasins plunges his dagger to the heart & riffles your goods, the turpitude of this scene looses all its horrors when compared with the act of the secrete assasins poinard levelled against femal character by the hired minions of power."[2] (The note probably alludes to the vicious insults leveled at Jackson's wife, Rachel, during the campaign, which newspaper readers of the time would have realized.)

Other Adamsite papers followed up by claiming to have seen letters by Jackson in which "many of the plainest words of the language" were misspelled, such as *solem* for *solemn* and *goverment* for *government,* and "good English" was "shockingly violated." These were "proof positive," declared one editor, "that the man who aspires to the chief magistracy is incapable of writing a commonly decent letter." To Adams supporters, this lack of literacy was evidence of Jackson's "absolute incapacity" to hold the office of president. Adams considered Jackson "a barbarian who could not write a sentence of grammar and hardly could spell his own name." Adams, in contrast, had once been a professor of rhetoric and oratory at Harvard.[3]

Naturally Jackson's supporters jumped to his defense. The fervently Jacksonian *United States Telegraph* published a forceful editorial against the *Journal*'s "pitiful and contemptible slander." The paper revealed that the supposed "note" was actually a printed pamphlet, almost certainly written by someone other than Jackson. Another pro-Jackson writer enlarged on this idea with the suggestion that the pamphlet was a hoax meant to trick the Adams people into making fools of themselves. Yet others declared that they were in possession of letters from Jackson that not only displayed "perspicuity and precision," but were "almost fastidiously correct" in their spelling.[4] They also argued that other office holders spelled just as badly. To demonstrate this point, one supporter went to the Library of Congress and unearthed facsimile letters from famous politicians such as former vice president Elbridge Gerry.

Portrayals of Jackson as a nearly illiterate bumpkin were obviously exaggerated. His successful legal career would have required substantial reading and writing. He had risen to the rank of major general during the War of 1812, and had served as the military governor of Florida, and as both a representative and a senator from Tennessee. He could not have filled these positions successfully if he had not had able to handle the written word reasonably well.

On the other hand, Jackson made no pretense of being scholarly. He didn't read for pleasure and was apparently unfamiliar with the classics in spite of having studied Latin. As president, he admitted to one of his aides that anyone going through his private papers would find examples of "false grammar and bad spelling."[5] Although he could be a powerful and eloquent speaker, his style tended toward the folksy rather than the elevated.

Washington Globe editor Francis P. Blair, a member of Jackson's informal "Kitchen Cabinet," remarked, "He was not . . . what is commonly termed an orator. But he was a fluent, forceful, and convincing speaker. . . . When perfectly calm or not roused by anything that appealed to his feelings . . . he spoke slowly, carefully, and in well-selected phrase. But when excited or angry, he would pour forth a torrent of rugged sentences more remarkable for their intent to beat down opposition than for their strict attention to the rules of rhetoric—or even syntax."[6]

Jackson's grammatical and compositional skills, or lack of them, were beside the point. His ability to sway his audience and "beat down opposition" was what counted. The adoring crowds that had clamored to touch the new president weren't interested in Jackson's spelling capabilities or grammar. They had voted for him because he was a man of action from an ordinary background like themselves. They preferred him over an elitist rhetoric professor. As Duff Green, editor of the *United States Telegraph*, put it: "To argue against the presumption of General Jackson's fitness for the Presidency because he cannot spell is absurd. We care not if *he spell Congress with a K*. He may . . . understand the rights and duties of that body, or of the people, or himself, as well as if he spelled it correctly."[7]

⟨After the inauguration, Jackson's supporters followed him as he rode on horseback to the White House to host a reception. Here the crowd turned into a mob. They swarmed into the building in a suffocating mass, shoving to get at the tubs of orange punch and other lavish refreshments. Eager to get a glimpse of Jackson, they climbed onto delicate damask-covered chairs in their muddy boots. A horrified Justice Story later described the event in a letter to his wife: "The president was visited by immense crowds of all sorts of people, from the highest and most polished, down to the most vulgar and gross in the nation. I never saw such a mixture. The reign of King Mob seemed triumphant. I was glad to escape from the scene as soon as possible."[8]

President Jackson also escaped eventually by climbing out a side window. He spent the remainder of the evening at a nearby hotel while the partiers continued their celebration. The public rooms of the White House were soon a welter of broken glass, stained carpets, and smashed furniture. Only when waiters carried the tubs of punch out onto the White House lawn did the crowd begin to disperse.

Although Justice Story and other traditionalists were horrified that a man like Andrew Jackson could be elected, many Americans admired the rough pioneer virtues that he embodied. They respected his war record and saw him as a champion of average Americans, especially fellow frontier residents. That these virtues came along with a lack of sophistication and verbal polish didn't worry them.

This attitude was the countervailing force against the widespread notion that the first step on the road to success was a good education. Jackson's fellow Tennesseean David Crockett expressed the feelings of many Jacksonians in the preface to his autobiography. Addressing potential critics of his book's homespun writing style, he tells them, "I can only say . . . that while critics were learning grammar, and learning to spell, I and 'Doctor Jackson, L.L.D.' were fighting in the wars. . . . Big men have more important matters to attend to than crossing their t's and dotting their i's."⁹

David Crockett himself is the archetypal simple backwoodsman who rose to prominence without the aid of formal schooling. Although poor and barely educated, he was elected to Congress three times. Once there his forthright personality and colorful brand of western "tall talk" captured the imagination of the American public, especially easterners who viewed the Tennessee frontier as exotic territory. He was known as "the gentleman from the cane," a reference to the stands of canebrake that still covered some western wilderness areas.

Crockett lore proliferated. Popular writers dubbed him "Davy Crockett" and spun his persona into an outsize American character. His motto—"Be always sure you're right, then go ahead"—became famous. By the time the real Crockett died gloriously at the Alamo at the age of forty-nine, he was a national icon.

Crockett's life inspired a genre—exaggerated tales of the intrepid men who settled west of the Appalachians. Among the Crockett-inspired writings were fake biographies, a play, and several issues of *Davy Crockett's Almanack*. The *Almanack* provided instructions on frontier skills—how to hunt wild hogs, the basics of rifle care—and sensationally titled anecdotes told in "Davy's" voice (although not really written by Crockett). Typically they relate remarkable deeds in boisterous, backwoodsy language. One volume includes the stories "A Tongariferous Fight with an Alligator" and "A Corn Cracker's Account of his Encounter with an Eelskin [Yankee peddler]."

In 1830, shortly after Crockett's first congressional term, James

K. Paulding wrote a play called *The Lion of the West,* modeling his hero, the Kentuckian Nimrod Wildfire, on the mythical version of Davy Crockett. *The Lion of the West* was hugely popular. The play introduced eastern audiences—and later Londoners—to the western tall-talk tradition of extravagant boasts and fanciful word inventions. In a letter to his aunt and uncle that announces his pending visit, Nimrod writes, "And let all the fellers in New York know—I'm half horse, half alligator, a touch of the airth-quake, with a sprinkling of the steamboat!" Later he boasts to a new acquaintance, "Of all the fellers on this side the Alleghany mountains [sic], I can jump higher—squat lower—dive deeper—stay longer under and come out drier! . . . I've got the prettiest sister, fastest horse, and ugliest dog in the deestrict."[10]

A cobbled-together variant of Nimrod's speeches appeared in a fictional biography titled *Sketches and Eccentricities of Col. David Crockett of West Tennessee* and has sometimes been attributed to Crockett himself. According to this story, a drunken stranger staggers up to Crockett in a tavern and cries, "Hurrah for Adams." When Crockett indicates that he's a Jackson man, the stranger asks, "Who are you?" The great man replies, "I'm that same Davy Crockett, fresh from the backwoods, half-horse, half-alligator, a little touched with the snapping turtle; can wade the Mississippi, leap the Ohio, ride upon a streak of lightning, and slip without a scratch down a honey locust."[11]

Nimrod Wildfire and his like were partial to overblown words and expressions. They were responsible for such verbal concoctions as *rumbunctious* (hot tempered), *lickspittle* (a bootlicker), *exflunctify* (wear out), and *conbobberation* (commotion), and phrases like *kick the bucket, see how the cat jumps,* and *knee high to a frog.* Although it's likely that some were created especially for a particular story, others were genuine westernisms. David Crockett helped popularize several regional expressions including *bark up the wrong tree* and *go the whole hog.*

Lindley Murray and other grammarians would no doubt have classified these fantastic figures of speech as low expressions, but American audiences loved them. Many entered the permanent vocabulary. Grammarians would also have frowned on nonstandard forms like *knowed* for *knew* that typified "stage western" speech. To millions of readers and playgoers, these linguistic quirks were a big part of what made tall tales so entertaining.

David Crockett's real life was less spectacular than his legend, but still remarkable. He was born in 1786 in rural Tennessee. The family was extremely poor and David (as he always called himself) had to scramble for a living from a very early age. He remarks in his autobiography that his father had neither the means nor the opportunity to give his children any "learning." Like other poor children of the time, they were put to work as soon as possible. He recounts how his father hired him out when he was twelve to accompany an old Dutchman who was driving his cattle from Tennessee to Virginia. After traveling four hundred miles with his employer, young David made his way back home on his own. Although it was winter, much of his return trip was on foot.

❧ Not until after this adventure was he finally sent to the local school. His school days didn't last long. Within the first week he got into a fight with an older boy, waylaid him after classes, and beat him up. Fearful that the teacher would punish him for fighting, he then stayed away from the schoolhouse. When his father discovered his truancy and threatened to beat him if he didn't return to school, David ran away from home.

He spent the next two years on the road, picking up casual work wherever he could. He only returned to his family after deciding that enough time had passed to soften his father's wrath. Crockett concludes his story, "But it will be a source of astonishment to many who reflect that I am now a member of the American Congress . . . that at so advanced an age, the age of fifteen, I did not know the first letter in the book."[12] He later attended school briefly to learn basic reading and arithmetic skills, but his formal education totaled less than a year.

Crockett began his political career in 1821 with a run for the state legislature. In his autobiography, he explains his inexperience with electioneering by saying, "I knowed no more about [it] than I did about Latin, and law, and such things as that. . . . I had never read even a newspaper in my life, or anything else, on the subject [of politics]."[13] He realized early in the campaign that formal speeches were not his strength. Instead he charmed the voters at campaign rallies by telling humorous anecdotes. In contrast to the other candidates, who bored the crowd with lengthy speeches, he shared amusing stories and occasionally shared a "horn" of liquor with them.

Crockett served two terms in the state legislature. Then in 1827 he won election to the House of Representatives. He describes his method of canvassing, wearing a buckskin hunting shirt with two large pockets. In one pocket he carried a good twist of tobacco, in the other a bottle of whiskey. As he chatted with voters, he would offer them a slug from the bottle. They had to remove their "chaw" of tobacco to take it, so he would offer them a fresh one off his twist. This down-home approach, along with his tales from the canebrake, won him the majority of the votes, with no necessity for polished oratory or elegant grammar.

Near the end of his time in Congress, Crockett decided to counteract the outlandish tales circulating about him—as well as further his political career and explain his break with Jackson—by writing the true story of his life. His book appeared in 1834 with the title *A Narrative of the Life of David Crockett of the State of Tennessee.* The first few printings quickly sold out. The *Narrative* is written in the folk vernacular of rural Tennessee and includes plenty of country words and phrases—*varmint, frolic, I reckon, a mighty ticklish business, root hog or die.* Nonstandard grammar also turns up from time to time—*I know'd what I come for*—and occasional misspellings—*Christmass*. For the most part, the spelling and grammar is conventional.

Crockett addresses this issue in his preface with seeming frankness. "I would not be such a fool," he tells readers, "or knave either, as to deny that I have had it hastily run over by a friend or so, and that some little alterations have been made in the spelling and grammar." Nonetheless, he insists, every "sentence and sentiment" is his own. Furthermore, he tells readers, he has instructed his editors to leave many of the original spellings and grammatical structures in place because they sound better to him than artificial correctness. He sums up his views by saying, "I despise this way of spelling contrary to nature. And as for grammar, it's pretty much a thing of nothing at last, after all the fuss that's made about it."[14]

This casual dismissal of grammar by an admired national figure might suggest that the importance of grammar was on the wane in the 1820s. American voters—a larger number of people than ever before—had elected Andrew Jackson to the White House, in spite of his admittedly wobbly command of grammar and spelling. They had made a folk hero out of David Crockett, a man with even less schooling and an apparent contempt for the language arts. Americans seemed to have arrived at a moment when they could appreciate more natural American speech.

The Jacksonian era was potentially ripe for an embrace of common usages like Noah Webster's *you was* and *It's me*. Americans might even have been inspired to adopt his simplified spellings or to abandon spelling standards entirely. Their enjoyment of Crockett's evocative regionalisms and respect for Andrew Jackson's plain talk might easily have led them to a new acceptance of everyday American speech patterns. These men's success seemed to argue that language training was an unnecessary frill. Qualities such as common sense and an independent spirit were more crucial.

Yet the rejection of standardized grammar rules never happened. Instead the art of speaking and writing with propriety—the textbook definition of grammar—remained a powerful ideal goal. As a *North American Review* writer put it in an 1826 essay on the state of education, "Popular custom requires this study to be pursued. . . . There is a mystery hanging about it, to the eyes of most parents . . . but there is a vague and indefinable impression on their minds that grammar is something very important, and indeed, essential."[15]

Grammar books had been selling extremely well since the first years of the nineteenth century. Half a dozen or more new textbooks were released in a typical year. After 1800, increasing numbers of public schools included the study of English grammar in their curriculum. From being an advanced subject before the Revolution—off limits to all but boys being privately educated—grammar took its place among the educational basics. In 1819 Princeton became the first college to demand a knowledge of grammar as an entrance requirement. Other colleges followed suit.

Part of the reason for grammar's increasing popularity is that Americans saw it as more practical than the study of Latin and Greek grammar, yet it carried some of the same mystique. While the classics were essential only to those training for top-flight careers, learning how to express yourself eloquently in your own native tongue was valuable to almost everyone. As with Latin and Greek, the study of English grammar was seen as excellent mental training. Besides giving students a fundamental grounding in elegant speech habits, it was meant to discipline their minds and prepare them for more advanced subjects like rhetoric and philosophy.

This reverent attitude was reflected in the way grammar books presented their topic. Authors often described the purpose of grammar studies in moral, aesthetic, or even spiritual terms. The most popular grammar books of the day adopted this tone. In the address to young learners that introduces Samuel Kirkham's 1825 *English Grammar in Familiar Lectures,* Kirkham tells his pupils, "This is not only a pleasing study, but one of real and substantial utility; a study that directly tends to adorn and dignify human nature." Kirkham sees grammar as the foundation for all further study. It "opens the door to every department of learning," and at the same time, "cannot fail of being serviceable" even to those "destined to pass through the humblest walks of life." It is valuable in "every situation, under all circumstances, on all occasions."[16]

Goold Brown, in his 1823 *Institutes of English Grammar,* places the virtues of grammar even higher. He tells readers, "The grammatical use of language is in sweet alliance with the moral." It "forms the mind to habits of correct thinking." He considers parsing the most important of all the school exercises because it trains students to unite grammatical correctness with fluency, a skill they can carry with them into ordinary life.[17]

Americans had a patriotic rationale for acquiring a good education. People at every social level were aware of themselves as embarking on a novel and potentially dangerous political experiment. A government that represented all the people, one that allowed men from lowly backgrounds to rise as far as the presidency, wouldn't work unless citizens were prepared to make informed and rational choices. For that, they needed to be educated. Female education also started to matter more. Women couldn't vote or run for office, but they were responsible for raising sons who could. As the century progressed, a complete education increasingly encompassed grammar, composition, and rhetoric in addition to reading and penmanship.

Grammar books were the self-help manuals of their time. Ambitious adults who had missed their chance at formal lessons studied on their own, hoping to raise themselves to a higher economic and social level. Grammar books, spellers, and readers were easy places to start. They were readily available even outside the cities. Print shops and general stores sold them and traveling peddlers carried them into remote areas. The multitude of editions ensured that there were always plenty of secondhand copies around. Grammar book writers expected many of their books' users to be adults. The subtitle of Lindley Murray's grammar book is *"Adapted to the Different Classes of Learners,"* and Kirkham and Brown both mention "private learners" on their title pages. For this reason, many authors provided answer keys.

Men such as David Crockett seem to be exceptions to these trends. Crockett was not as impervious to grammar, however, as he first appears. The "friend or so" that he mentions in his introduction was Thomas Chilton, a congressional representative from Kentucky. Crockett admits that Chilton "ran over" his book looking for grammar and spelling errors. In reality, the congressman did much more. He essentially acted as a ghostwriter. Not only did he collaborate closely on Crockett's autobiography—perhaps writing it to Crockett's dictation—he routinely helped him with letters, circulars, speeches, and other official utterances.

Crockett's unedited letters are filled with misspellings and grammar mistakes. In a letter describing his intention to tell his own life story, he writes, "I am ingaged in prepareing a worke that may be of little prophit to me but I consider that justice demands of me to make a statement of facts. . . . no doubt but you have saw a book purporting to be the life and adventers of my self that book was written without my knowledge . . . and in fact the person that took the first liberty to write the book have published a second addition."[18]

Crockett's natural writing style is a far cry from the carefully placed regionalisms and occasional slight misspellings of his autobiography. Crockett's audience was delighted with the book's colorful frontier idiom, but they would not have wanted to read page after page of real spelling and grammar mistakes.

Crockett was canny enough to realize this. The *Narrative* gives readers a taste of the Tennessee backwoods, but a smoother version than the raw natural product. The book's language aims for a version of Crockett's authentic speech that educated people would find acceptable. Even folk heroes had to meet certain linguistic standards—at least if they wanted to be taken seriously as writers and political figures.

One strand of American culture celebrated uniquely American dialects, but a more dominant strand embraced grammar standards as an important part of being educated and socially mobile. Andrew Jackson and David Crockett were popular figures. Nonetheless, Jackson's linguistic weaknesses were subject to scathing criticism, and Crockett felt the need to tidy up his natural speech before publication. In spite of superficial appearances, early nineteenth-century Americans valued proper grammar.

The significance of grammar training is also obvious from the fact that not everyone had equal access to it. Until the Revolution, females were one deprived group. During most of the eighteenth century, education for girls was spotty at best. They were not always allowed to attend school. When they did, they were taught separately from boys and limited to brief classes at the beginning or end of the day. Most girls, even those from the upper classes, learned only basic reading and writing.

Outside the upper classes, a majority of women remained illiterate. Others learned to read, but not to write. Women didn't need to write as much as men did—they didn't write business letters or keep records. Reading was a more practical skill. It allowed women to read the Bible, or read aloud to their children. (Many lower-class men were also illiterate, but the numbers were not nearly as large as for women. Families of every class often included a literate husband and an illiterate, or a semi-literate, wife.)[19]

Grammar studies were out of reach for all except those rare privileged girls who received a masculine private education. One such was Aaron Burr's daughter, Theodosia. Burr's commitment to equal education for girls meant that his daughter learned Latin and Greek, as well as English grammar and composition, at an early age, but his idea of what constituted a suitable female education was very much in the minority. While Burr was away from home in the 1790s as a senator from New York, he wrote almost daily letters to Theodosia. He advised her on what to study next and critiqued the spelling, grammar, and style of her letters to him. His letter of January 8, 1794, instructs his eleven-year-old daughter, "Learn the difference between *then* and *than*. You will soonest perceive it by translating them into Latin."[20]

By the turn of the nineteenth century, young women's prospects for learning grammar had improved. Nearly two hundred female-only institutions sprang up between 1790 and 1830.[21] These new schools usually offered a greater range of subjects than they would have earlier. Traditionally, daughters of the upper classes who attended private academies had been taught literacy and simple arithmetic, but spent much of their day learning genteel accomplishments such as music, dancing, drawing, and needlework. The new schools added more serious subjects, including classical and modern languages, rhetoric, and English grammar.

The belief that girls should learn grammar was still a novelty in 1782, the year that Noah Webster started his school in Sharon, Connecticut. Webster mentioned the issue specifically in the newspaper advertisement announcing the school's opening. The ad deplores "the little regard that is paid to the literary improvement of females, even among people of rank and fortune," and promises that Webster's school will give full attention to the education of young ladies as well as gentlemen.[22]

At around the same time as Webster was starting his school, Caleb Bingham, a teacher in a Boston girls' school, brought out *The Young Lady's Accidence*. (*Accidence* is a term for a beginning-level grammar book.) Bingham's book was "designed principally for the use of young learners, more especially those of the fair sex, though proper for either."[23] The author was evidently thinking of his own pupils, but he must have recognized a growing niche market as well when he specified that his grammar book was mainly for girls.

Bingham doesn't say what makes the book particularly suitable for females. The content is virtually the same as that of any other late-eighteenth-century grammar book. It is unusually short at sixty pages and includes only a few footnotes, and Bingham may have assumed that these features would make it easier for "young learners, especially those of the fair sex" to grasp. In any case, the book met with the public's approval. In the first few decades after its publication, Webster's speller was the only language textbook that sold better.

Increasing numbers of girls from the lower classes were also studying English grammar after 1800. The decades following the war saw a push for state-supported schooling for children of both sexes. The main purpose of common schools was to train boys and girls who couldn't afford a private education to become useful citizens. Advanced subjects such as the natural sciences were seldom offered because they didn't have a practical application. According to proponents of widespread general education, English grammar did. They believed that encouraging students to learn and use a uniform version of English helped turn them into patriotic citizens. The same democratic principles that called for basic education for girls also supported grammar study.

Those in favor of female education frequently emphasized the point that well-educated girls made better Americans. Girls weren't being offered improved educations for their own benefit, but to turn them into more rational companions and more qualified mothers. Revolutionary leader and influential physician Benjamin Rush was a prominent supporter of this notion. He spelled out the practical aspects of educating young women in his 1787 address to visitors at the Young Ladies' Academy of Philadelphia. His speech outlined the sort of education that he believed was most suitable for girls.

Rush began by declaring that girls' education should be tailored to the "situation, employments, and duties" that fell to most American women. Americans' tendency to make early marriages shortened the time available for schooling, so Rush thought lessons should focus on the areas that provided obvious advantages. The duties of most wives would include acting as "stewards and guardians" of their husbands' property; ensuring a good education for their children, even if they didn't do all the teaching themselves; and most important of all, instructing their sons "in the principles of liberty and government."[24] Female education, Rush believed, should prepare young women for these tasks.

Rush then outlined the subjects that he thought were most essential for girls. First on his list was English grammar. He explained, "She should not only read, but speak and spell [the English language] correctly. And, to enable her to do this, she should be taught the English grammar, and be frequently examined in applying its rules in common conversation."[25] Other areas of study that Rush suggested included penmanship, bookkeeping, vocal music, dancing, and the kind of general interest reading that would qualify a young woman to be "an agreeable companion for a sensible man." Grammar study came first though. By teaching girls to comprehend good writing and to be articulate themselves, it underpinned most of the other subjects.

❡ While women's chances to learn grammar improved greatly during the early nineteenth century, those for African Americans remained elusive. In the 1820s, around 233,000 free blacks lived in the United States, mostly in cities. Like whites, they had better educational opportunities after the Revolution. Charitable groups such as the Quakers operated a number of "African free schools," meant to provide freed slaves with a basic education. African Americans also set up their own tuition-charging schools in cities like Boston and New York. They were normally excluded from public schools, although in a few cities local school committees provided minimal funding for separate schools.[26]

A basic education did not mean the same thing for black children as for white children. Specifically, it did not include grammar studies. As with other public schools, the main point of African free schools was to turn students into useful citizens. Those organizing the free schools argued that because most free blacks were restricted to menial employment—cleaning houses, waiting tables, polishing boots—higher subjects such as grammar and rhetoric were a waste of time. In many places the committees expressly forbade teachers to offer English grammar to African American students.

One African American who clearly understood the power of grammar was David Walker. Best known for his rousing seventy-six-page antislavery pamphlet *An Appeal to Coloured Citizens of the World,* Walker was born free in Wilmington, North Carolina, in 1796. His mother was one of the few free black women living in Wilmington and his father was a slave. Little is known of his early life or education. Sometime between 1810 and 1820, Walker moved to Charleston, South Carolina. His commitment to abolition almost certainly started there, when he joined an

African Methodist-Episcopal church whose members were active against slavery. By the early 1820s he embarked on travels that took him, in his words, "through a considerable portion of these United States." He probably spent time in several southern states before settling in Boston in 1825. At some point along the way, he educated himself, a process that included memorizing Murray's *Grammar.*

Walker started a used clothing business in Boston and married a local woman. He immersed himself in the community. In a short time he had gained a name as an antislavery activist and a community leader. He joined Boston's African Mason's Lodge. He also became a member of the African Methodist-Episcopal church headed by the outspoken abolitionist Rev. Samuel Snowden. In 1829, at the age of thirty-three, he published his *Appeal.*

Walker's *An Appeal to Coloured Citizens of the World* is both an outraged indictment of black oppression by whites and a call to fellow African Americans to fight for their rightful place as citizens. It lays out in fiercely eloquent language what Walker sees as the chief causes of black wretchedness. Among the more obvious evils stemming from slavery and the lack of civil rights, he names ignorance as a major source of misery. He exhorts his readers, "You have to prove to the Americans and the world that we are MEN, and not *brutes,* as we have been represented. . . . Remember to let the aim of your labours among your brethren . . . be the dissemination of education."[27]

To Walker, the most devastating evidence of ignorance is the lack of grammatical knowledge. "It is lamentable," he writes, "that many of our children go to school, from four until they are eight or ten, and sometimes fifteen years of age, and leave school knowing but a little more about the grammar of their language than a horse does about handling a musket." He cautions against imagining that being able to read or "to scribble tolerably well" is the same as being educated. He tells the story of an elderly man who boasts that his adult son has a good education, saying, "He can write as well as any white man." Walker then questions him: "Did your son learn . . . the width and depth of English Grammar?" When the man replies in the negative, Walker tells him, "Your son . . . has hardly any learning at all."[28]

He ends his discussion of education by relating "the very heart-rending fact" that he has examined schoolboys and young men in various parts of the country "in the most simple parts of Murray's English Grammar, and not more than one in thirty was able to give a correct answer." He has found that barely five in one hundred are able to correct false grammar. Part of the problem is the difficulty of acquiring grammatical learning. A young man of Walker's acquaintance who has been attending a Boston school under a white schoolmaster tells him, "My master would never allow me to study grammar." The local school committee, says the young man, "would not allow any but the white children to study grammar."[29]

David Walker would certainly have rejected any suggestion that he should adopt a more natural speech style. He recognized that a command of standard grammar was a powerful social advantage. So did the white school committees that tried to restrict its teaching.

African American leaders had particular cause to be concerned about education in the early nineteenth century. At that time, most whites who rejected slavery, or who believed that it would eventually end, also favored resettlement of free blacks outside the United States. A number of political leaders, including Thomas Jefferson, James Madison, and Andrew Jackson, supported colonization. In 1816 the American Colonization Society (ACS) was founded to further the cause. ACS members argued that freed slaves would lead happier lives in Africa because racism and their own limitations would keep them from fitting into

American society. As evidence they pointed to African Americans' supposed intellectual shortcomings and lack of education. Walker wrote his *Appeal* partly in response to these arguments.[30]

Another response was the New York–based *Freedom's Journal*, the first African American newspaper. *Freedom's Journal* began publication in 1827, two years before Walker wrote the *Appeal*, and he became the paper's Boston agent. In the first issue, the editors explain why they intend to make education one of their main topics. Those hostile to the black community, they write, "enlarge upon the least trifle which tends to the discredit of any person of colour." In the editors' view, most of the negative behaviors that people attribute to African Americans stem from a lack of early education. Therefore, they assure readers, "Useful knowledge of every kind . . . shall find a ready admission into our columns."[31]

Articles on education feature frequently among the weekly paper's four or six pages of domestic and foreign news, marriage announcements, poetry, meeting notices, and offers to buy used clothing. Besides discussions on education, nearly every issue carries at least one notice of a school about to open. The first several issues advertise that B. F. Hughes plans to open a school for children of both sexes in the basement of New York's St. Philip's church. Subjects offered will include reading, writing, arithmetic, geography, history, and English grammar. The cost is $2 to $4 per quarter.

Later issues carry ads for other schools. While some are for children, others are evening schools for adults. All mention English grammar as one subject on offer. One teacher, a Mr. Gold, offers nothing but grammar. His advertisement runs under the title "English Grammar" and promises to teach grammar "upon a new and improved plan by which a pupil of ordinary capacity may obtain a correct knowledge of the principles of the English language."[32] Grammar was central enough to education to call for a class of its own.

After *Freedom's Journal* stopped publication in 1829, one of its editors, Samuel Cornish, started *The Rights of All*. This paper, which lasted only one year, published Walker's *Appeal* over several issues. Walker circulated his essay in other ways as well. Sailors, both black and white, brought stacks of copies to their ports of call all along the Atlantic Coast. There they handed the pamphlets to local ministers or circulated them among the free black and slave populations. Those who were literate read them aloud to crowds of people who were not.

Three editions of the pamphlet came out within the year. Wherever it was distributed, this strongly worded call to action frightened slave owners and other whites, while blacks, in the words of one newspaper article, rejoiced in its principles "as if it were a star in the east, guiding them to freedom and emancipation."[33] Walker's emphasis on the need for self-education must surely have been one of the items that frightened whites. Shortly after the pamphlet's appearance, state governments took steps to make black educational opportunities even narrower. Formerly, slaves had sometimes been taught to read and write, but by the 1830s it was against the law to do so in the southern states. In the North, African Americans continued to be limited to separate, poorly funded public schools. Few of those schools taught higher subjects like rhetoric and grammar.

David Walker did not live long enough to see the full impact of his pamphlet. He died of tuberculosis in September 1830 during an epidemic that swept through Boston. His infant daughter had succumbed to the disease a week earlier. His son, Edward, was born after Walker died.

Edward (also called Edwin) must have believed in the possibilities of self-education as strongly as his father did. He attended

Boston public schools as a child and later became a successful leatherworker. Then he advanced further through his own reading. During his activities as an abolitionist in the 1850s, he acquired Sir William Blackstone's classic legal treatise *Commentaries on the Law of England*. The book inspired him to study law. He passed the Massachusetts bar exam in 1861, becoming one of the first African Americans to be admitted to the bar in that state. In 1866 he became one of the first two African Americans elected to the Massachusetts legislature.

Thirty-two years after Andrew Jackson took office, another man from a humble background was elected president. Like Jackson, Abraham Lincoln grew up on the western frontier. Lincoln's family, like Jackson's, was poor and undistinguished. Lincoln's school days were even briefer than Jackson's, amounting by his own estimate to less than a year. Like Old Hickory, Honest Abe projected a rustic image. This led his political enemies to smear him as an ignorant bumpkin who lacked grammar skills. In fact, Abraham Lincoln is the prime example of an American who rose from modest beginnings to the highest rung of the social ladder with the help of grammar books.

Lincoln was born on February 12, 1809, on a small farm in Hardin County, Kentucky. The area was sparsely settled and living conditions were harsh. Lincoln's father, Thomas, was a carpenter and farmer who gradually acquired substantial land, but later lost it through disputed land titles. Thomas Lincoln was apparently literate, but not educated. Neighbors remembered him as a steady, dependable man, but unlettered, and Lincoln once commented that his father "suffered greatly for want of an education." His mother, the former Nancy Hanks, was "passionately fond of reading" and taught her son to read the Bible. Like so many women of the time, however, she could not write.[34]

Schooling options were extremely limited on the Kentucky frontier, especially for children of the poor. Lincoln's earliest education took place in what was known as an A.B.C. school—a school that taught the alphabet, but not much more. Most teachers in these schools were only minimally qualified for the job. They offered basic reading and penmanship, and possibly simple arithmetic.

Young Abraham attended an A.B.C. school near his house for a short time when he was seven years old. Many years later, one of Lincoln's childhood neighbors recalled the teacher in unflattering terms. In the neighbor's memory, this young man could "perhaps teach spelling, reading and indifferent writing and perhaps could cipher to the rule of three (a way of calculating proportions), but had no other qualifications of a teacher except large size and bodily strength to thrash any boy or youth that came to his school."[35] In a small, poorly heated room where students of all ages spent long hours sitting uncomfortably together on backless benches, such a talent probably came in handy.

After Thomas Lincoln lost his title claims, he decided to move his family to southern Indiana. He staked out a parcel of remote forestland in what is now Spencer County, and the family came to live there at the end of 1816, just as Indiana became a state. The Lincolns' new home was even less settled than Kentucky. Bear and other wild animals still filled the forests. Dense stands of trees and underbrush had to be backbreakingly cleared before any planting could take place. Abraham became skilled with an axe while still a child, leading to his later nickname, "Rail Splitter." During the presidential campaign of 1860, both sides referred to him this way. To his supporters, the name was an indication of his strength and grit, but to his detractors, it was a reminder of his lowly background.

Lincoln's next bout of schooling took place in the winter of 1820 when he was eleven years old. A little over a year earlier, his mother had died. His father had recently remarried a widow named Sarah Bush who had three small children. Lincoln, his older sister, Sarah, and his three stepsiblings were all sent to a fee-charging school about a mile from their farm. It was a common type of frontier school known as a "blab" school. Because books and writing implements were scarce, classes at blab schools were mostly oral. Teachers recited the lesson to the students, who would repeat it back in unison until they had it memorized. Individual students would then recite what they'd learned. Sometimes the children would also take turns reading aloud from whatever schoolbooks were available. All ages and both sexes went to these one-room schools.

As an adult, Lincoln was contemptuous of the "schools, so called" that he attended as a child, saying, "No qualification was ever required of a teacher beyond *'readin, writin, and cipherin'*." Expectations for education were so low that if anyone in the neighborhood was rumored to understand Latin, "he was looked upon as a wizard."[36] Lincoln attended his first blab school for only one winter term. When the weather warmed up, he was needed around the farm. He later attended similar schools sporadically, ending his formal education when he was about fifteen. Skimpy as the subject offerings were at these schools, they gave the young man the foundation he needed to keep learning on his own.

Lincoln started his self-education in the same way as so many other people of the time—with spellers, readers, and grammar books. His familiarity with spellers started in childhood when he and his sister studied Dilworth's spelling book. In the early nineteenth century, Dilworth was still ubiquitous, even on the Kentucky frontier. It was probably one of the few books found at the A.B.C. school. Lincoln later obtained Webster's speller and several readers, including Murray's. He once commented that Murray's reader was "the best schoolbook ever placed in the hands of a child."[37] Another favorite reader was a collection of literary excerpts titled *The Kentucky Preceptor*. He committed several of the *Kentucky Preceptor*'s selections to memory.

After the move to Indiana, Lincoln graduated to books other than texts. His stepmother owned several books, including *Aesop's Fables,* the popular Christian allegory *Pilgrim's Progress, Robinson Crusoe,* and William Scott's *Lessons in Elocution.* Morally improving books such as these were the most commonly owned volumes, after textbooks and the Bible. Lincoln read and reread them. He also got hold of an etymological dictionary from one of his mother's relatives.

Scott's elocution book, a collection of excerpts from well-known authors, is designed to turn students into polished readers, writers, and speakers. It includes prose, poetry, speeches, sermons, and passages from famous plays such as *Hamlet.* For completeness, the author provides an introduction to English grammar in an appendix. Here are the familiar rules, beginning with definitions of the parts of speech. The appendix ends with a discussion of common grammar errors—*between you and I, who did you give it to, this is them, more wiser.* These notes were probably Lincoln's first introduction to standard grammar rules.

Scott encourages his readers to learn chunks of the text by heart and practice reciting them while standing. Lincoln may have done this, as he was a strong memorizer. His stepmother recalled that whenever he lit on a passage in a book that appealed to him, he scribbled it down—on boards if no paper was at hand—and repeated it until he learned it. No doubt his capacity for memorization helped him when he began to study grammar, and more complicated subjects like the law.

When Lincoln exhausted his stepmother's small supply of books, he borrowed whatever he could get from neighbors. The Lincoln family was always in dire need of money, so Lincoln's father often hired out his adolescent son to do rough jobs like clearing brush and mending fences. While working at the neighbors' homesteads, Lincoln took advantage of their libraries. He told an acquaintance that as a young man he had borrowed and read every book he could hear of for fifty miles around. He read biographies of Franklin and Washington. He also enjoyed the poetry of Robert Burns and Shakespeare's plays, and memorized long passages of both.

The Lincoln family moved yet again to central Illinois in 1830, when Lincoln was twenty-one. By late 1832, he was living on his own in New Salem, a village along the Sangamon River. He was earning an uncertain living as the co-owner of a New Salem general store, but his ambitions reached much further. He took a lively interest in local politics and had already run unsuccessfully for the state legislature. He was also contemplating the possibility of studying for a law degree. He decided that he needed to know more about grammar.

Lincoln's interest in serious grammar study came at a time in his life when he was struggling financially and had not yet settled on his ultimate life's work. Like many other adult learners, he realized that a knowledge of standard grammar would give him an advantage, no matter which direction he chose to take. Sharper writing and speaking skills were always valuable.

He learned that a farmer in the area owned a copy of Kirkham's *English Grammar in Familiar Lectures.* By the 1830s Kirkham was seriously challenging the dominance of Murray's *English Grammar* and Lincoln apparently decided that it was worth walking several miles to borrow the farmer's copy. He then set about mastering the book in the traditional way. He systematically committed large portions of it to memory. He also asked for help from his friends, including the local schoolmaster. With the book as a guide, they would ask the young man questions—"What is a noun?" He would respond with the memorized phrase—"A noun is the name of any person, place, or thing."

The store was seldom busy, so Lincoln had plenty of time to spare for his studies. He completed his study of the book in only a few weeks, helped by Lynn M. Greene, a fellow New Salem resident who was attending Illinois College. Before entering college, Greene may have had to pass a grammar exam. He definitely would have worked his way through several grammar books, so he would have been able to tutor Lincoln in the fine points. Lincoln also borrowed a copy of Murray from another friend and spent time working through that volume as well. Lincoln was proud of his proficiency in standard grammar. When writing a sketch of his life for his campaign biographer, he noted that he had "studied English grammar, imperfectly of course, but so as to speak and write as well as he now does."[38] Lincoln later went on to educate himself in the law and passed his bar exam in 1836.

Lincoln's opponents brutally criticized his grammatical skills during the 1860 presidential contest. The nomination of Lincoln as the Republican candidate for the presidency caught many people by surprise. Having only served one term in Congress before losing reelection, he was not as well known or experienced as the other three contenders. However, he had impressed Republicans with his performance in a series of debates against Democrat Stephen Douglas during the 1858 Illinois senate race. He had also delivered a masterful speech at Manhattan's Cooper Union several months before the nominating convention. In the Cooper Union speech he argued against expanding slavery into the territories.

Democrats, angered by Lincoln's antislavery stance, reacted to his nomination with furious disgust. Democratic newspapers attacked him in the most personal and insulting terms. His modest family background, his ungainly appearance, his youthful work as a rail splitter—all were fodder for hostile editors. One major source of criticism was his supposed ignorance of proper grammar.

After the nomination was announced, the *New York Herald* expressed its outrage that the Republican Party, in "a remarkable instance of small intellect growing smaller," had selected a "third-rate western lawyer." The newspaper fulminates, "They pass over Seward, Chase, and Banks, who are statesmen and able men, and they take up a fourth-rate lecturer who cannot speak good grammar." The editor then reveals the main cause of his complaint—Lincoln's recent public speeches. He reminds readers that Lincoln has been in New York during the past few months, delivering "his hackneyed, illiterate compositions at two hundred dollars apiece.... when in return for the most unmitigated trash, interlaced with coarse and clumsy jokes, he filled his empty pockets with dollars coined out of Republican fanaticism."[39]

Other newspapers jumped on the same bandwagon. The Albany *Atlas and Argus* declares, "He . . . is not known except as a slang-whanging stump speaker." The *Philadelphia Evening Journal* compares his style unfavorably with that of his main rival for the nomination, Sen. William Seward: "His coarse language, his illiterate style, and his vulgar and vituperative personalities in debate contrast very strongly with the elegant and classical oratory of the eminent Senator from New York."[40]

The newspapers' criticisms of Lincoln's grammar were probably not meant to be taken literally. As the *New York Herald* editor's remarks indicate, Lincoln was a popular and respected public speaker, which suggests some skill in putting sentences together. "Bad grammar" was really a code phrase. Saying that Lincoln didn't know how to use language correctly was an indirect way of saying that he was from the lower classes and therefore unworthy to be president. Ignorance of standard grammar implied a whole range of other social deficits. The newspapers' readers would have gotten the message. In contrast Senator Seward, the son of a prosperous businessman and a graduate of

Union College in Schenectady, New York, was credited with superior linguistic abilities.

Many people in Lincoln's contemporary audiences thought his unadorned prose style was too simple and unpolished. Mid-nineteenth-century listeners expected heavily ornamented speeches full of extended metaphors and classical allusions. Lincoln's approach was more straightforward. Like Andrew Jackson, David Crockett, and other frontier politicians, he often made use of the colloquial style. In his daily life, he used regionalisms like *reckon* and *howdy*. He also had a habit of telling humorous backwoods tales that struck some of his associates as undignified. Yet Lincoln's speeches have come down to us as among the most moving and memorable ever heard in this country. Contrary to what his enemies claimed, his speeches were carefully constructed. Lincoln was adept at the familiar style, but made effective use of the elevated style when the occasion called for it.[41]

Lincoln's well-known speeches show, among other things, that he had a sophisticated understanding of standard grammar. For example, the speech that he gave at Cooper Union on February 27, 1860, demonstrates correct use of several common grammar rules. He uses nominative case after the verb *to be* ("It was not we, but you, who discarded the old policy of the fathers"); uses the present subjunctive *unless you be* rather than *unless you are* ("Your purpose, then, plainly stated, is that you will destroy the Government, unless you be allowed to construe and enforce the Constitution as you please"); and correctly keeps the preposition *among* with its object *whom* ("I give [the Democrats] . . . all other living men . . . among whom to search").

The Gettysburg Address, delivered on November 19, 1863, includes the specialized use of *shall* with third person to promise or express determination ("We here highly resolve . . . that government of the people, for the people, by the people shall not perish from the earth"). As early as the 1780s, Noah Webster had complained that few people knew the proper uses of *will* and *shall.* By the early nineteenth century, these specialized uses would have been even less common outside of grammar books. Yet Lincoln obviously understood them.

None of the formal grammar rules that Lincoln applies in his speeches would have been acquired naturally while growing up on the Indiana frontier. He could only have learned them by studying Kirkham, Murray, and other grammarians. Grammar books promised to set their users on the path to scholarly and social achievement. In this case at least, those promises were fulfilled.

4.

Rational Grammar

In spite of Lindley Murray's overwhelming popularity during the 1820s, linguistic reform was far from dead. While Noah Webster was laboring on his landmark dictionary, other grammarians took up the banner of natural American speech. Like him, they called for a more realistic approach to grammar, often using the same arguments as Webster—that grammar should be based on how people really speak and that common usages should be acceptable. They rejected Latin-based rules, just as he did.

The "rational" grammarians were like Webster in another way, too. They had fallen under the compelling influence of John Horne Tooke. Their fascination with his theory of word origins would prove to be a fatal diversion. Sensible grammar reforms were lost in the welter of long-winded arguments that prepositions, adjectives, and other parts of speech had originated as nouns or verbs. As a result, their books suffered the same failure as Webster's *Philosophical and Practical Grammar*. Reviewers, teachers, and the few members of the general public who were aware of these alternative grammar books preferred to cling to their trusty copies of Murray or Kirkham.

The most prominent of the reforming grammarians was a Bostonian educator and textbook writer named William Bentley Fowle. At around the same time that Andrew Jackson was preparing for his first inauguration, Fowle was writing to argue for an English grammar uncluttered by artificially imposed rules. "It is to be regretted," he writes in his 1827 book *The True English Grammar,* "that a grammar of our language was not formed at a period when our ancestors were free from any servile deference to Latin."

Fowle notes that Lowth modeled his grammar on Latin partly as a way to familiarize students with Latin terminology before they went on to study that language. For most students, however, learning Latin grammatical categories is a waste of time. "Not more than one child in a thousand studies Latin after having studied English grammar," argues Fowle. Since Latin is reserved for the privileged few, "is it not wiser to have a grammar which we can call our own?" In the true Jacksonian spirit, he calls on Americans to adopt the vernacular of "the common people." Although their nonstandard usages often "bring upon them the sneer of grammarians," these speakers are adhering to a more natural form of the language.[1]

Fowle's early experiences with grammar influenced his later attitudes. He was born in 1795, the third son of highly educated, though poor, parents. His father, Henry, had originally planned to pursue a literary career, but money troubles and a fast-growing family forced him into the trade of pump and block making. He nonetheless managed to keep up his interest in books and scholarship and owned a large, carefully chosen library. He sent his son to school at the unusually early age of three.

Young William first attended a "dame school"—a school for small children run by a woman rather than a schoolmaster. There he started his mental training by memorizing the Westminster Assembly's "Shorter Catechism." He learned it so thoroughly that he could repeat the whole thing "backwards as well as forwards," much to the delight of his teacher. She often called on him to perform this feat in front of school visitors. Fowle recalled, however, that he didn't understand much of the meaning in either direction.[2] This experience contributed to his later belief that memorization was a poor way to learn.

William's talent for rote learning stood him in good stead when he began studying grammar a few years later. By the age of six he had memorized Caleb Bingham's popular grammar book for young children, *The Young Ladies' Accidence.* Next he tackled an abridged version of Lindley Murray's grammar and soon had that committed to memory as well. At the age of ten he won a medal for grammar knowledge.

In spite of these achievements, Fowle hated grammar. He describes his early grammar classes in *The Teacher's Institute,* an advice book for young teachers that he wrote after twenty years as a schoolmaster. He recalls that pupils sat on twelve long benches, with six or eight boys to a bench. Each bench represented a different "form," or level of scholarly achievement. The boys took turns reciting grammar lessons at the rate of one bench a day, progressing from the more advanced pupils on the front benches to the less skilled at the back. A grammar lesson typically consisted of a boy spelling a few words and then reciting at least six lines memorized from the grammar book.

Those who performed especially well were moved to the front benches. That meant that their turn to recite a grammar lesson came around again more quickly than if they'd stayed in place. When a boy could recite every word of the grammar book three times in a row, he received the dubious reward of promotion to the first bench, where he was introduced to the mysteries of parsing. This system understandably squelched any potential enthusiasm for mastering the subject of grammar. "Such was the horror in which this exercise was held," recalls Fowle, "that boys, whose turn it would be to say grammar the next day, would miss words in spelling, so as to drop down to a lower form, and put off the evil day."[3] Many who had the opportunity to advance to the first form intentionally gave wrong answers to avoid the move.

In Fowle's view, teaching grammar by forcing students to memorize and recite it is not only mind-numbingly tedious, it's ineffective. To the boys who struggled with memorization, grammar lessons were a recurring nightmare. To those—like Fowle himself—who excelled at it, the lessons were less painful but still ultimately meaningless. The schoolmaster never discussed the context for the rules or explained how to apply them. Students simply parroted the lessons without comprehension.

Fowle discovered the uselessness of knowing grammar books by heart when he entered the prestigious Boston Latin School at the age of thirteen. One of his teachers tested his grammar skills by demanding the past participle of *love*. Fowle was humiliated to realize that he couldn't remember it. He concludes, "It is not to be wondered at, therefore, that I hated grammar, had no faith in the utility of teaching it as it was then taught, and determined to reform the method if I ever had a good opportunity."[4] That opportunity would eventually come, but Fowle would discover that grammar teachers—as well as their former pupils— were remarkably resistant to change.

After two years at the Boston Latin School, William was ready to enter Harvard. Unfortunately, his father was once again mired in financial difficulties, so instead of going to college, William signed on as a bookseller's apprentice. His master was none other than Caleb Bingham, author of *The Young Ladies' Accidence*— now retired from teaching and in the business of publishing and selling textbooks. Fowle's unhappiness with the way grammar was taught did not extend to his new mentor. He greatly respected Bingham. He later wrote of him as "a good scholar; a very successful and much beloved teacher; a gentleman in the best sense of the word."[5]

Fowle's apprenticeship dramatically influenced his ideas about education, including grammar education. Because the bookstore dealt only in textbooks, business was sporadic. Fowle had plenty of time to read and found that he enjoyed this informal way of gaining an education. He also began developing his own ideas about teaching. Bingham was a prominent school reformer, and the bookstore was a gathering place for like-minded teachers. Fowle often joined in their lively conversations.

The store was so congenial that when an acquaintance, theologian William Ellery Channing, offered to pay Fowle's way through Harvard, he declined. He later wrote that he was grateful that poverty had prevented him from attending college, "which would have furnished me with a diploma to wrap up and bury my intellect."[6] Instead he continued learning on his own. He formed the "Belles-Lettres Society," a group of a dozen or so shop clerks that met once a week to read each other original essays. The group stayed together for two years, and several members later became professional men or teachers.

When Bingham died in 1817, his family hired the twenty-two-year-old Fowle to run the business. Fowle spent five more years at the bookstore. Then he got the chance to put some of his educational theories into practice. Boston's Primary School Committee discovered two hundred young people who had somehow slipped through the school system's cracks. They were now too old to attend primary school, but not qualified to attend classes with pupils their own age. The Committee decided to educate them in a special school.

The sum allocated to furnish a schoolroom and hire a teacher was a barely adequate $1,000 (equal to about $21,000 today), so to save money, the school was organized on the "monitorial" system.[7] The monitorial system was a recently invented way to keep students with varying skill levels occupied while employing only one teacher. The teacher focused on instructing the oldest, most advanced students. These students—the monitors—would then listen to the younger children reciting their lessons. That way, the whole class could be active at once. Normally students sat silently much of the time, waiting for their turn to recite. Fowle, who was a member of the Primary School Committee, volunteered to do the teaching until a permanent instructor could be found.

Fowle's first experience teaching grammar, described in *The Teacher's Institute,* reinforced his disgust with mainstream grammar books. When quizzing the monitors on the parts of speech, he discovered to his chagrin that they could not correctly identify the parts of even the simplest sentences. Asked to parse the sentence *David smote Goliath,* one young woman guessed that *smote* was a preposition. Her reasoning—prepositions, according to Murray, "serve to connect words with one another and to show the relation between them." In this case, the student explained, *smote* connected David with Goliath. When asked what she thought the relation between them was, she ventured that it was not a very friendly one.

This incident, so reminiscent of Fowle's own embarrassing experience at the Latin School, made him realize that grammatical ignorance was common even among those who had studied the fabled Murray. He comments drily that his student's performance shook his faith in "the perfection" of that book.[8] No doubt it also strengthened his resolve to one day provide an alternative.

Fowle's temporary teaching assignment grew into a career. He approached it with the zeal of a born didact, introducing several innovations previously unheard of in Boston. These included using blackboards to write out grammar and spelling exercises and do arithmetic; teaching geography by drawing maps; and using instruments like air pumps to teach science. Instead of the usual instructional method of mindless repetition, he tried the novel approach of engaging the students according to their interests and capacities. Fowle also allowed girls to attend the school year-round, instead of the usual arrangement of teaching them only during the summer when the boys were busy elsewhere. Even more radically, he abolished corporal punishment.[9]

Fowle's reforms paid off. The special school was so successful that the School Committee eventually rewarded him with a regular teaching appointment and a schoolmaster's salary. In 1823 Fowle took over the headship of the Female Monitorial School—an early version of teacher training for young women. He remained there for seventeen years, until worsening health forced him to abandon teaching and return to bookselling.

Fowle's innovations gave him a taste of the hostile reception that radical reformers can expect. Conventional public schoolteachers saw Fowle's success as a threat. Not only would the monitorial system cut down on the need for their services, but they might be forced to introduce some of the same changes into their own classrooms. In an effort to close the special school after its first year, a teachers' group organized a campaign of letters to the newspapers, arguing that the new system was a way of cutting corners. They told parents it had nothing to recommend it but cheapness.

Although a placid, tolerant man in private life, Fowle reacted ferociously to attacks on his work. He jumped into the fray with a series of newspaper essays defending his methods and, incidentally, accusing other Boston schools of inefficiency. Under pressure, the City Council announced that the experimental school would be shut down. Later—after furious protests from the School Committee and perhaps after reading Fowle's essays—they changed their minds. The school was allowed to go forward with Fowle at its head. The furor over Fowle's school reforms was a preview of the violent reaction that his alternative grammar book would trigger several years later. It convinced him, as he would later write, that "there are no greater enemies to improvements in education than schoolmasters."[10]

While running a school and contesting with the City Council, Fowle still found time to write textbooks. Within a few years he produced a French-American dictionary, an arithmetic book, a geography book, a reading and spelling guide, and an introduction to linear drawing. He wrote over forty textbooks altogether during his career.[11] In 1827, he finally produced the grammar book that he'd been planning since his own school days. *The True English Grammar* was intended to make grammar study meaningful by explaining the true structure and history of the language. The detailed subtitle—*An Attempt to form a Grammar of the English Language, not modelled upon those of the Latin and Greek and other Foreign Languages*—makes Fowle's purpose clear.

Fowle's years of training teachers should have translated into a highly functional grammar textbook. Unluckily for the success of his project, he was diverted by John Horne Tooke. By the time Fowle began writing, Horne Tooke's two-volume work on the origins of English, *Winged Words, or the Diversions of Purley*, was more than two decades old. The second volume had appeared in 1805 and Horne Tooke himself had been dead since 1812. His influence was still strong, however, in the United States.

The Diversions of Purley (as it's usually called) strikes a bizarre note with modern readers. The "Purley" in the title refers to the country house of Horne Tooke's patron, where the book is set. Horne Tooke and his fellow guests at Purley—all scholarly men— "divert" themselves with a series of conversations about the origins of English words. These are really closer to monologues. They usually open with one of Horne Tooke's companions questioning some aspect of his theory that all parts of speech are ultimately traceable to ancient nouns or verbs. Horne Tooke then launches into a detailed defense of his ideas, pummeling his listeners with an overwhelming battery of facts and arguments in support of his claims. By the time he's finished, they are more than ready to admit that he's right.

Horne Tooke's arguments would not be so readily accepted today. His approach to word histories was slapdash at best. Modern etymologists uncover a word's history and development by carefully tracking its appearances in historical documents over time. Horne Tooke favored a more intuitive approach. Often he connected words based on little more than a spelling resemblance, twisting meanings in far-fetched ways to make the words in question fit in with his theory. As a result, many of his word histories are wrong, as later discoveries in etymology would show.

In one typical scenario, a member of the party questions how a preposition like *from* can really be a disguised noun or verb. It seems to him that *from* encompasses several complex meanings—indicating a source in *These figs come from Turkey,* a point in space in *That lamp hangs from the ceiling,* and a starting point in *That lamp is falling from the ceiling.* Surely all these meanings can't have come from a single term.

Horne Tooke replies that *from* has "as clear, as precise, and at all times as uniform and unequivocal a meaning as any word in the language. *From* means merely *beginning* and nothing else. It is simply the Anglo-Saxon and Gothic Noun Frum, . . . *Beginning, Origin, source, fountain, author.*" He then demonstrates that the word *beginning* can substitute for *from* in all these instances without changing the meaning—"Figs came BEGINNING Turkey . . . Turkey the *Place* of BEGINNING to come."[12]

(According to the *Oxford English Dictionary, from* derives from the Old English adjective *fram,* with the general meaning of "forward." Later the meaning shifted to "onward" or "away." By the ninth century, it was being used as a preposition. Gothic *frum,* meaning "to forward, promote, or supply," is indirectly related to *fram,* but its modern English descendant is the verb *furnish.*)

Challenged with sentences using *from* in different ways (*The alarm rang from morning till night*), Horne Tooke shows how each one really means *beginning* ("The alarm rang BEGINNING morning, i.e., Morning being the *time* of its BEGINNING to ring").[13] He bolsters his arguments with extended footnotes that feature such wide-ranging evidence as quotations from Chaucer, lines from early English poetry, the opinions of earlier linguistic philosophers, and related words in Dutch and German. He also uses the footnotes to take jabs at mainstream grammarians like Lowth and Murray.

It seems astonishing today that educated nineteenth-century readers could have taken this mixture of bombast and quasi-scholarship seriously. One explanation is that the scientific tone, no matter how spurious, strongly appealed to Americans of the Jacksonian era. They were enthusiastic about all types of scientific progress. Several institutions for the promotion of science were founded around this time. Philadelphia's Academy of Natural Sciences dates from 1812 and the Franklin Institute from 1824. New York's Lyceum of Natural History, later the New York Academy of Sciences, opened in 1817. In 1835, during Jackson's second term, the United States received the bequest under James Smithson's will that led to the Smithsonian Institution. The lyceum movement—named after the garden where Aristotle taught philosophy—also took hold during the 1820s, with lyceums springing up around the country. Americans eager to hear about the latest scientific discoveries and inventions could attend lectures sponsored by their local lyceum.

During these years, scholars were keenly interested in scientifically organizing and classifying the natural world, a trend that spilled over into grammar study. Grammarians began treating their subject more like a science. Lindley Murray and other eighteenth-century grammarians defined grammar as the art of speaking properly, but grammar writers in the 1820s talked about the science of language. Fowle was part of this new approach. He believed that by applying Horne Tooke's theories to the parts of speech, he was giving the structure of English a more rational and scientific basis.

As linguists a decade or two later started to construct a more genuinely scientific history of English, *The Diversions of Purley* would gradually fall out of favor. Horne Tooke's early detractors accused him of having a poor command of Anglo-Saxon English and other ancient languages. This criticism would appear even more obvious to the next generation of readers. By the time a new edition of *Diversions* appeared in 1840, the world had changed so much that a *Blackwood's* reviewer would scornfully describe the book as "one of the most consummate compounds of ignorance and presumption that ever practiced with success upon human credulity."[14] In the 1820s, however, the field of etymology was still in its infancy. Horne Tooke's incisive writing style made his word histories sound convincing and few were equipped to challenge them.

Fowle organized *The True English Grammar* like a typical textbook, but the conventional format is misleading. Although the book opens with a standard definition of grammar ("rules for writing or speaking the English language") and a conventional description of nouns, it quickly plunges into Horne Tooke territory. Fowle spends most of the book presenting detailed arguments for reclassifying almost every part of speech. Horne Tooke's influence is especially apparent in a long section titled "Contractions, Anomalies, Etc.," which is simply a shortened version of *The Diversions of Purley*. Here Fowle presents a list of several dozen words normally identified as prepositions or conjunctions, from *as* ("means the same as *it* or *that*") to *unless* ("the Anglo-Saxon verb *dismiss*"), and claims that they are really verbs or nouns.

Throughout the book Fowle notes his disagreements with other

grammarians in asides such as "in consequence of a mispercep-
tion . . . Mr. Murray has constructed his Passive voice" or "what
is called the imperative mood by Dr. Lowth and his followers."
He also criticizes Murray more directly in an appendix titled
"Strictures on Murray's Grammar." Fowle admits that anyone
correcting the great man faces an uphill climb. "In the United
States," he writes, "Murray's Grammar, under one form or another, is universally used; and so satisfied is the publick mind of
its perfection that any attempt to check its progress will be viewed
as a desperate adventure."[15] Even so, he feels that Murray's word
classifications should be revised.

In Fowle's view, the only reason why Murray and his followers have sorted English words into articles, prepositions, pronouns, and the like is to bring them into line with Latin word
categories. They've adopted case distinctions like nominative and
accusative for the same reason. He doesn't see any value in organizing English this way. Concluding that "we are surely as
competent to improve our grammar as to simplify and improve
our machinery," Fowle proposes that Americans abandon all
Latin-based linguistic complications in favor of his more logical
system.[16]

Fowle considered his book a practical guide to English, but he
provided almost no usage guidance. Typically, grammar book
writers of the time included a "Syntax" section where they pronounced on issues such as the importance of making pronouns
agree with their antecedents. Fowle omits this discussion. Nor
does he mention the nonstandard usages that Webster argued
for so insistently, such as *Who did she speak to?* and *It is me.* Although he praises the common man's linguistic instincts, he stops
short of actively encouraging nonstandard speech.

The book does offer some sensible suggestions for making
grammar easier to learn. Fowle labels nouns according to their
use in the sentence—"agent" or "object"—rather than with the

case names "nominative" and "accusative." He also provides easily intelligible definitions for the few parts of speech that he accepts, saying that nouns are "names of things" and verbs are "words which express what nouns do." He instructs teachers to explain the material so their students understand it rather than merely forcing them to memorize it. This approach, a clear improvement over the usual practice, was highly unorthodox at the time. Unhappily, these useful hints are nearly hidden among dense discussions about word origins.

Like Webster, Fowle had a sharp grasp of the realities of nineteenth-century American English. He saw the weaknesses of contemporary grammar teaching and his ideas for reform were enlightened and sensible. If they had been incorporated into a conventional grammar book, they might have taken root. Fowle spoiled his book's chance of classroom adoption—and his chance to influence the way Americans thought about English—by turning a grammar text into a treatise on etymology. As with Webster's *Philosophical and Practical Grammar,* his reasonable suggestions were swamped in a sea of linguistic proselytizing. Arguments for dropping Latin case names or accepting *It is me* lose much of their punch when they're accompanied by extended arguments that *from* is really a noun.

Other alternative grammar books appeared during the 1820s. Their authors all share the same general point of view as Fowle. They all criticize mainstream grammar books for purveying Latin-based nonsense. They also emphasize that standard English should be defined by the normal way that most people talk. They all make reasonable arguments for teaching grammar in a new way—one that starts from an appreciation of how English is really constructed and how Americans actually use it. Unfortunately, none of the authors can resist embellishing their main topic with speculative theories about word origins. Predictably, these eccentric books made no more headway with teachers or the general public than Fowle's had.

One book that received some attention was William Cardell's *Elements of English Grammar, Deduced from Science and Practice, Adapted to the Capacity of Learners*. Published in 1826, *Elements of English Grammar* focuses on the supposedly scientific aspects of Horne Tooke's theories. Cardell taught French and English in New York and also wrote boys' adventure stories. Several years earlier, he had been active in trying unsuccessfully to found an American Academy of Language. As he wrote in a letter to the elderly Thomas Jefferson, the academy hoped to "form and maintain . . . an English standard of writing and speaking, correct, fixed, and uniform, throughout our extensive territory."[17] (The former president approved of the idea, but declined to participate.)

Cardell wrote *Elements of English Grammar* in the hope of providing a more rational description of the language. He deplored the sloppiness of standard grammar texts. He asks, "Who, in teaching arithmetic, would say 'nine times nine makes a hundred;' and then offer as a reason for this misstatement that a hundred is a round number and easier to remember than the real product."[18] In his opinion, the broad generalizations that most grammar books make about parts of speech and word relationships are no less misleading.

Cardell attributes the misinformation that infects other grammar textbooks to their authors' lack of scientific training. He says, "Those who . . . devoted their lives to this study were in too great a degree mere linguists, and not persons of accurate scientific pursuits." He also argues that to get at the essence of English, grammarians need to return to the roots of language—"the strong, crude models of early expression." They must ignore artificially imposed rules and classifications and try to discover what English was like in its more primitive state.[19]

Cardell's book is more conventional than Fowle's. His definitions of the parts of speech are simple and straightforward (nouns are names of things, verbs signify actions), and his brief section on syntax consists of an uncontroversial list of the usual rules. Cardell also includes parsing exercises. Hints of Horne Tooke begin to surface as Cardell reviews each part of speech. For instance, in a footnote to his definition of nouns he tells students (incorrectly), "The word *thing* is derived from the old Saxon *thingian,* to think."[20] Eventually, he bogs down in the same etymological swamp that trapped Fowle.

Another writer who tried to inject scientific rigor into grammar study was John Lewis. Lewis, a Kentuckian, tutored young men preparing for college. He also wrote poetry and a popular novel of the western frontier titled *Young Kate.* Lewis added interest to his grammar book by presenting it as a series of conversations between a schoolboy named George and George's papa. He may have been inspired by the conversations in *The Diversions of Purley,* but livening up scholarly topics with invented dialogue was not that unusual in the nineteenth century.

Lewis's 1825 *Analytical Outlines of the English Language* opens with George expressing an interest in learning something about grammar. Papa tells him that the best way to start is to "become, in some measure, acquainted with that which is in your own head."[21]

Rather than recommending a grammar book for George to memorize, Papa encourages his son to formulate a grammar of English by thinking about what he already intuitively knows. Eventually George realizes that, contrary to what he has previously heard—"that we must learn [grammar] in order to write and speak correctly"—grammar arises out of speech itself. His father confirms that grammar is nothing but "the collected methods used in speaking and writing." The rules of grammar should conform to speech, says Papa, not regulate it.[22] That is, grammatical standards must be compatible with the speech patterns that people have already internalized.

Lewis's description of grammar is surprisingly modern—not that different from how linguists talk about it now—but Lewis soon abandons this intriguing direction. Instead, he concentrates on examining the parts of speech. At this point, he goes down the same tortuous path as Fowle, Cardell, and the other reforming grammarians.

"By tracing conjunctions, prepositions, articles, &c. to the original word," explains Papa as he introduces the subject to George, "Mr. John Horne Tooke has clearly proved that they are *nouns* or *verbs*." After further talk, he and his son improve on Horne Tooke's theory. They decide that even verbs were originally derived from nouns. "The noun is the material of which all the words of all languages have been formed," Papa summarizes. "The different parts of speech . . . we must therefore consider as subdivisions of one class."[23] By this time, Lewis and his two protagonists have strayed rather far from the practical aspects of grammar.

The comment of one reviewer—"We fear Mr. Lewis is rather too fervent a worshipper of John Horne Tooke"—could have applied to any of the authors of alternative grammar books. Not all the reviews were negative. Cardell in particular came in for praise. "His work will stand," predicts a reviewer for the *New York Literary Gazette,* "for it is based on good sense and sound philosophy." Even Lewis's reviewer concedes that the book is "a work of some novelty, and evidently proceeds from a thinking, rather than an imitative mind."[24]

Unfortunately, the authors' preoccupation with reclassifying the parts of speech overshadowed their more reasonable ideas and allowed most reviewers to dismiss them as cranks. A common complaint is that their books are impractical. "For all schemes of amendment," declares one of Fowle's reviewers, "there should be but one test. *They must be sound, and they must be practicable.*" In his opinion, Fowle's book falls far short. More harshly, a Cardell reviewer, while admitting that there is "room for improvement" in current methods of teaching grammar, says, "it is not for . . . wild theorists to make it."[25]

As for Lewis's dialogues, they are "couched in phrase too elaborate for the pupil," says his reviewer. Besides, they "raise an expectation of entertainment too high to be gratified" by a detailed analysis of grammar.[26] By modern standards at least, they are unquestionably heavy going, even for an adult. It's hard to believe that the schoolchildren Lewis was writing for would have felt anything but bewilderment.

Most reviewers treated the authors' claims about parts of speech as obvious absurdities. One of Fowle's reviewers declares that he sees no advantage in changing their names if the current ones still work. The main purpose of grammar, he says, is "general utility and not philosophical or abstract propriety." The same reviewer also attacks Horne Tooke, saying, "Besides being imperfectly acquainted with the Northern dialects, he was . . . essentially unqualified to pursue his researches in *etymology. . . .* Bear in mind that many of his derivations are fanciful."[27]

The reviewer for *North American Review* begins his critique of Fowle's book by announcing sarcastically, "The object of this manual is to rescue parents and teachers . . . from the whole tribe of grammars, which, since the days of Lowth and Murray, have so fearfully accumulated upon them." He then presents Fowle's main arguments in their silliest possible form. He ends the review by congratulating Fowle on "the great work of restoring our language to its primitive simplicity."[28]

After these blistering criticisms, Fowle felt compelled to write a second volume defending his work. In the introduction to volume two of *The True English Grammar,* published in 1829, he explains how his teaching experiences led him to compile "such an English grammar as the best authorities and the structure of our language authorized." This book has brought upon him "so much ridicule that its principles must be defended or abandoned."[29] The rest of this short volume is an impassioned defense of his ideas.

He continues to be infuriated by most grammar books' "servile deference to Latin." This misplaced reverence, he says, has led to the bizarre practice of using quotations from great authors as examples of incorrect speech. "There was a time before grammars were invented to clip the wings of fancy and shackle the feet of genius," Fowle cries, "when it was considered more important to express a thought clearly and forcibly than, as now, prettily and grammatically." Shakespeare couldn't have written with such brilliance if he had been forced to follow the rules in Murray.[30]

Fowle is stung by one reviewer's assumption that he copied his ideas from Webster. Although he admires Webster, he is unfamiliar with the contents of *A Philosophical and Practical Grammar.* "I endeavored to find it," he says, "but it was not for sale in the city." Sneers at Horne Tooke also touch him on the raw. "It has been fashionable for pert reviewers and grammarians to revile the great man to whom we are indebted, at least for showing the right path," he says, before mounting a sweeping defense of the man he admires. He reminds readers that Horne Tooke had been an outspoken advocate of the American revolutionary cause. Therefore, Americans have an additional reason to be grateful to him.[31]

Finally, Fowle denies charges that his book poses problems for children trying to learn grammar. "I defy the most captious to produce a single sentence in my book which authorizes any departure from good usage," he challenges.[32] He seems unaware that his lack of usage guidance, orthodox or otherwise, is one of the biggest problems with his book. Both teachers and learners preferred a grammar text that laid out concise rules in familiar terms. That meant continuing to patronize Lindley Murray and other grammarians who stayed with the tried-and-true formulas.

Nothing illustrates the power of established linguistic traditions in the United States better than the fate of Noah Webster's famous dictionary. When Fowle, Cardell, and Lewis were publishing their theories of grammar in the 1820s, Webster's voice was uncharacteristically missing from the debate. He had not abandoned his grammatical principles or his devotion to American English. He was simply engrossed in a new phase of his life's work.

Almost as soon as his 1806 *Compendious Dictionary of the English Language* was published, Webster began exploring the possibility of producing a much more comprehensive volume. His goal was to provide a complete picture of American English—more accurate, consistent, and scholarly than anything that had come before. He would spend most of the next two decades devoted to this staggeringly ambitious project.

Webster received little encouragement for his new enterprise. His friend Oliver Wolcott, responding to a letter in which Webster outlined his ideas, says frankly that he is doubtful about the dictionary's feasibility. Getting a publisher won't be easy. Wolcott has mentioned it to a number of publishers and booksellers, and they are leery of such an unprecedented project. "It is very generally objected," he explains, "that the size of your dictionary, & the manner in which it is to be published, & the sum required, are not ascertained."

Webster had hoped to fund his research and writing by collecting subscriptions—advance payments from those pledged to buy a copy of the book. At that time subscriptions were a common way for writers to support themselves, but Wolcott questions whether the money will be forthcoming in this case. He writes, "My experience of the world has satisfied me that it is in vain to reason with the greatest part of mankind, if they have to pay ten dollars in consequence of being convinced. If as I presume a considerable sum is wanted, I cannot encourage you to expect success."[33] Wolcott was right. Only a handful of Webster's friends and well-wishers sent money in advance. Their contributions, even when combined with the small but regular profits from his book sales, would not be enough to feed him, his wife, and his seven children while he worked.

Webster was determined to find a way. He believed the project was important enough to be worth the risk. Besides, it might well be a greater success than most of his friends thought. As he points out in a letter to Joel Barlow, nearly everyone except Barlow discouraged him from attempting a spelling book in 1783. Yet more than 200,000 copies were now selling annually. He tells Barlow that he intends nothing less than to lay the foundation of "a more correct practice of writing and speaking." Sounding the old theme, he adds, "It is time for us to begin to think for ourselves. Great Britain is probably in her wane."[34]

As one way to save money, the Websters moved from New Haven to the small farming town of Amherst, Massachusetts. In this rural area they were able to live more frugally while Webster continued to work doggedly on his dictionary project. He spent most of his days shut up in his second-floor study. He worked standing up at a two-foot-wide table shaped like a hollow circle. (He considered sitting at a desk a lazy habit.) To research a word, he began at one side of the table and walked around along its edge, consulting one volume after another from the piled stacks of dictionaries and other reference books. At fifty-four, Webster was still upright and slender, and sturdy enough to spend all day on his feet.

The work progressed slowly for several reasons. One was the sheer amount of research involved. Another major factor was Webster's decision to detour into the treacherous territory of language origins. Although he still admired Horne Tooke, he now thought that many of Horne Tooke's word histories were inaccurate. That left him frustrated in his aim to provide more complete etymologies than other dictionaries offered. As he explains in his dictionary's preface, "I found myself embarrassed at every step for want of a knowledge of the origin of words which . . . other authors do not afford the means of obtaining."[35] After completing the letters A and B, he stopped work on the dictionary proper to focus on this side project.

A new worldview was partly responsible for Webster's conclusion that Horne Tooke was mistaken. In 1808 Webster and most of his family joined the thousands of Americans caught up in the religious revival known as the Second Great Awakening. During most of his life, Webster had not been deeply religious. Now he dedicated himself to strict Calvinist principles.

His newfound religious faith ignited a fresh interest in the events of the Old Testament. These gave him a starting point for his word origins research. Beginning with the story of Noah and his descendants, Webster traced the spread of languages around the world. The result was *A Synopsis of Words in Twenty Languages*. In the *Synopsis* Webster compares a variety of European and Middle Eastern languages and makes etymological connections between words that he believes are related. About half the size of the eventual dictionary, the book took nearly ten years to complete. However, it would turn out to have little practical value.

The *Synopsis* suffers from the same shortcomings as the *Diversions of Purley* and other word histories of the period.

Webster connected words based on free association and superficial resemblances rather than verifiable linguistic facts. His knowledge of most of the languages involved was sketchy. Also, his reliance on the Bible as his main source led him astray. Because of his beliefs about how humans repopulated the world after the Flood, he assumed that English and other European languages had to be related to ancient Middle Eastern tongues like Hebrew and Aramaic. Modern linguists have demonstrated that Middle Eastern and European languages belong in two different groups.

In the end Webster did not have much to show for his ten years of work. He had hoped to include the *Synopsis* as the dictionary's third volume, but had to abandon the idea. Printing it would have entailed extensive use of non-Western typefaces, making the cost prohibitive. He then tried collecting enough subscriptions to bring out the volume as a separate book, but didn't find any takers. He eventually settled for incorporating some of the material into the dictionary entries, along with writing an essay on language origins for the dictionary's preface.

Webster's work on his dictionary project was also slow because he took time out for political activities. Although he no longer edited a Federalist newspaper, he remained politically engaged. In 1814 he lent his support and writing skills to the Hartford Convention, a gathering of Federalists opposed to "Mr. Madison's War" of 1812 against the English. He also served in the Connecticut and Massachusetts legislatures and ran unsuccessfully more than once for the House of Representatives.

He was involved in his local community as well. He served as a justice of the peace, and helped found Amherst Academy, a private school that later became Amherst College. He also started work on a revision of the King James Bible. Concerned with grammar as always, he tidied up its archaic usages. He also replaced obsolete words and substituted euphemisms for potentially offensive words and phrases. (For instance, he avoided *womb* by using indirect phrases like *made fruitful* or *made barren*.) Webster's Bible, sometimes known as the Common Version, would be published in 1833.

In 1817, as he was wrapping up the *Synopsis,* Webster at last achieved the financial security that had eluded him during most of his life. After many years of selling the rights to his speller piecemeal—and seeing printers reap the largest share of the profits—he sold the exclusive right to publish the *American Spelling Book* to the Hartford firm of Hudson & Co. In exchange, he was to receive $3,000 a year for fourteen years (the life of the copyright), beginning in 1818. Short of cash as usual, Webster later renegotiated this agreement. In 1817 he received an advance of $3,000 and the next year a $20,000 lump sum payment. Although it was only about half of what he would have made under the original contract, $23,000 was enough to relieve him of money worries. He returned to his work on the dictionary with renewed zest.

As Webster neared the end of his labors, he decided that to be thorough, he needed to consult certain books only available in Europe. After resettling Rebecca in New Haven, where she could be near her two married daughters, he set out for Paris in the summer of 1824, bringing along his twenty-two-year-old son William. Webster stayed in Paris for several weeks, but the French material proved disappointing. He and William moved on to England.

By the end of September, Webster was writing Rebecca to say that they were in Cambridge, "settled very snugly at lodgings for the winter." Besides a bedroom each, they rented a parlor. A room of about fifteen feet square, it was comfortably furnished with two tables, a sofa, and a few chairs. In this room, seated at one of the tables, Webster progressed steadily through the last pages of his great work, although he wrote to his wife that his right thumb was "almost exhausted." Early in the new year, he finished writing the entry for *zygomatic* and laid down his pen. Later, he wrote a memorandum recalling the moment: "I finished writing my Dictionary in January 1825. . . . When I had come to the last word, I was seized with a trembling which made it somewhat difficult to hold my pen steady for writing. . . . I summoned the strength to finish the last word, and then walking about the room a few minutes, I recovered."[36]

When Noah Webster finished *An American Dictionary of the English Language* he was sixty-six years old. He had been writing about American English for the past forty-two years. All the issues he cared about were packed into his dictionary's two hefty volumes—linguistic patriotism, etymology, natural grammar rules, simplified spelling. Even his religious beliefs were incorporated. He based his language origins essay on the biblical book of Genesis. He also omitted what he termed "vulgar and obscene words," even those included in most dictionaries of the time.[37] (*Fart* is one example.)

The dictionary was Webster's final attempt to convince Americans to stake a claim in their own speech. He hoped they would use his book to take their language in a more informed direction. Over the years, as Webster had observed popular democracy in action, his political views had grown more conservative. He was friendlier toward the mother country and much less impressed with his fellow citizens. He strongly disapproved of Andrew Jackson, who would be their choice for president three years later. In spite of his new political outlook, he remained committed to American speech. As he explains in the dictionary's preface, "It is not only important, but in a degree necessary, that the people of this country should have *an American Dictionary of the English Language;* for although the body of the language is the same as in England, and it is desirable to perpetuate that sameness, yet some differences must exist."[38]

Among Webster's purposes in traveling to England had been the hope of discovering how much the two languages agreed on matters of pronunciation and grammar. Yet he realized that cultural and physical differences between the two countries—in forms of government, customs, terrain, plants, and animals—called for a specifically American dictionary. "No person in this country will be satisfied with the English definitions of *congress*, *senate*, and *assembly*," he says.

Some people were concerned that by including American word inventions, Webster was allowing coarse, low-class language into the dictionary. He didn't see it that way. As he wrote to his brother-in-law while in the planning stages, "Americanisms must be admitted, for they form an essential part of our language." Anyway, he thinks they're entirely legitimate. "What is the difference, in point of authenticity, between respectable American usage and respectable English usage?" he demands staunchly.[39]

Webster's *American Dictionary* was a monumental achievement. It listed seventy thousand words, including twelve thousand not recorded elsewhere. Webster had also added between thirty thousand and forty thousand new definitions.[40] He mined the American language for "words of common use." These included new verbs—*revolutionize, electioneer*—and new items—*parachute, safety-valve*. He added or updated dozens of scientific and legal words. He also added religious definitions to words not normally in that category. Among the definitions of *life*, for instance, is "eternal happiness in heaven."

Once again, however, Webster discovered that imposing scholarship was not enough to make a book desirable to publishers—or to the public. After trying unsuccessfully to find a London publisher, Webster returned home to New Haven to search for one there. After several months, Sherman Converse, editor of the New Haven *Connecticut Journal*, agreed to handle the publishing and printing. Then began the long, fraught process of proofreading and revision. Webster himself carried out this task to a large extent, although he hired other readers for some of the material. Not until November of 1828 was the book—in two enormous volumes—at long last printed. Webster had just turned seventy. The first edition consisted of 2,500 copies, priced at $20. Soon afterward, Webster found a London publisher who printed 3,000 copies for the English market, after removing the word *American* from the title.

The book's early reception was promising. The *Western Recorder,* announcing the book shortly after it appeared, does not offer a review but says, "This work is spoken of in the highest terms." Most reviewers agreed that the number of new words was impressive. "The vocabulary is enlarged by the addition of many thousand words . . . not found in other dictionaries," says one, and furthermore, these are words "for the precise meaning of which the general reader is most frequently at a loss." Yet another reviewer remarks, "Dr. Webster, besides adding very largely to the number of definitions, has given to them, in great degree, the precision of modern science."[41]

The *North American Review* devotes forty-eight pages to a well-informed examination of the dictionary. The reviewer uses more than half of those pages to describe Webster's etymological discoveries, taking issue with some of his conclusions, but generally approving his methods. He praises Webster's new definitions as covering "the most common and important senses of words, according to the best usage of the present day." The new scientific and technical words also add to the dictionary's value. He even approves of the inserted *Philosophical and Practical Grammar,* believing that it contains "many improvements on those which preceded it."

The reviewer ends by predicting that "the author's labors, in the cause of language of his country" will soon produce a good effect on how Americans use their native tongue. "It will be seen in the better understanding of authors," he says, and "in the more correct use of words." The dictionary will also, he hopes, add to the respect "with which the author will be viewed, for his talents, learning, and persevering industry."[42] These predictions went largely unfulfilled.

Many prominent men did admire the book. Webster wrote to his son-in-law William Fowler in 1829, "My great book seems to command a good deal of attention. Mr. Quincy, now president of Harvard . . . assures me the book will be well reviewed. . . . It is considered as a national work."[43]

Others were unwilling to accept its quirks. Webster's innovative spellings were the biggest stumbling block. Most people agreed with his dropping the *u* from words like *honour* and *colour,* and the *k* from words like *publick* and *musick.* These practices were already widespread. They were less happy with oddities like *bridegoom* for *bridegroom* and *ieland* for *island.*

Webster's most persistent critic was a rival spelling-book author named Lyman Cobb. Cobb wrote several articles challenging Webster's spellings, eventually bundling his criticisms into a fifty-six-page pamphlet called *A Critical Review of the Orthography of Dr. Webster's Series of Books for Systematick Instruction in the English Language.* Cobb's use of a final *k* to spell *Systematick* makes his attitude plain.

Cobb's main complaint is that Webster's claim to have made English spelling more uniform is false. He examines the spellers and dictionaries minutely, one at a time, to uncover Webster's inconsistencies. Webster has dropped the *k* from *garlick* and *physick,* but not from *lock* and *attack.* He omits the *u* from *labour* and *vigour,* but keeps them in *curious* and *generous.* Cobb argues that Webster has not followed his own rules, and that those rules are misguided anyway. The pamphlet ends with a several-page table that compares selected words across Webster's books and shows how the spellings have changed from one place to the other.

Cobb attacked Webster personally as well as intellectually. In the introduction, he derides the notion that Webster's dictionary provides Americans with a new standard—if such a thing is even necessary. He suggests that the only reason any of Webster's books sell at all is because he and his publishers relentlessly market them. As for the new dictionary, it has gained undeserved recognition because "the most unwearied pains have been taken by Mr. Webster and his friends to puff it in newspapers and periodicals." Also, "by personally applying to Members of Congress and others, he has been able to procure the recommendations of many men."[44]

Cobb had a personal motive for his aggrieved tone. Webster and his publishers had responded to his previous attacks by publicly pointing out that Cobb was himself a textbook writer with a vested interest in seeing Webster's books fail. Cobb was not alone, however, in concluding that Webster's spelling reforms left something to be desired. Many people with no axe to grind nonetheless felt that Webster's ideas were too radical. Another problem for the dictionary was its price. At $20—about $500 in modern purchasing power—it was just too expensive for most households. Nearly a decade would pass before the last of the 2,500 American copies sold. Once again, Webster's hard work had not paid off as he hoped. He decided that he needed to bring out a cheaper, more compact edition.

In 1829 Webster consulted his publisher, Sherman Converse, about producing an abridged edition of the *American Dictionary*. After two decades of unremitting hard work on the dictionary, Webster felt unequal to editing it himself. Converse hired a Yale graduate named Joseph Worcester to undertake the task. Worcester had recently edited an American version of Samuel Johnson's pioneering 1755 dictionary. Also, unbeknownst to Webster, he was compiling a dictionary of his own that would compete with Webster's when it appeared a year later.

To supervise Worcester's work, Webster enlisted his son-in-law Chauncey Goodrich. Goodrich, married to Webster's daughter Julia, was a professor of rhetoric at Yale. He was also an astute businessman. Goodrich realized that the dictionary's unconventional spellings, convoluted etymologies, and other idiosyncratic features made it less appealing to the general public than it could have been. A more standardized volume would be bound to sell much better.

Goodrich's solution was to ruthlessly strip the dictionary of nearly everything that made it unique. Since the main point of the abridgment was to produce a shorter book, he naturally cut extraneous items like the essay on language origins and the condensed *Philosophical and Practical Grammar.* Then, without consulting his father-in-law, Goodrich normalized most of the spellings. As the preface euphemistically explains, in "disputed" cases "the old orthography takes the lead."[45] Some variant word pairs, like *acre* and *aker,* are listed under both spellings. Many others, like *bridegoom* and *bridegroom,* are listed only under the orthodox spelling, with Webster's version of the word relegated to a parenthesis.

Worcester, who had strong views on what dictionaries should look like, added his own spin to what were already significant revisions. He rewrote definitions and deleted pronunciation advice that he considered questionable. He also contributed new material. "The vocabulary has been considerably enlarged," the preface tells readers. Some of the words that Worcester added were suggested by Webster himself, but most came from Worcester's edited version of Johnson's dictionary.

When the abridged dictionary came out and Webster realized how severely Goodrich had pruned it, he was furious. The spelling and pronunciation changes made it appear that Webster no longer believed in his own reforms. The etymologies that he had labored over so meticulously were drastically reduced, and his grammar guidelines completely erased. The book also included many words and definitions that Webster himself hadn't written.

He was so distressed over the changes that he rushed to dissociate himself from the book. Shortly after it appeared, he sold the copyright to Goodrich. Then he cut the Goodriches out of his will, saying they would benefit enough from money made on the abridgment. Whether or not Webster genuinely believed this prediction, it would turn out to be true. Priced at $6, the abridged dictionary sold briskly from the first. It was not the dictionary that Webster envisioned, but it was more compatible with American tastes.

Webster lived another fifteen years after publishing his great dictionary. He remained healthy and energetic. An acquaintance meeting him in 1840, when he was eighty-one, noted that "his mind was strong, clear and active as ever; his conversation was full of . . . spirit and vivacity."[46] Webster's activities included a trip to Washington, D.C., in 1830 to speak before Congress in favor of a bill extending the term of copyright to twenty-eight years. The bill passed shortly afterward. While he was there, he lobbied to get his dictionary accepted as the country's standard for spelling.

Webster continued writing until the last, but not about grammar. After the fiasco of the abridgment, he did his own editing to create a short dictionary for schools. Several years later, he embarked on an update of the original dictionary, mortgaging his house to finance the publication, much to his family's dismay. The second edition appeared in 1841. In 1843 he published his final book, a collection of his articles on political subjects. Webster died in April of that year, at the age of eighty-four.

Shortly after his death, the publishers George and Charles Merriam bought the copyright to Webster's original dictionary, hiring Goodrich to make revisions for a new edition. The *Merriam-Webster Dictionary*, now denuded of all unorthodox features, appeared in 1847. The Merriam brothers' dictionary would be the version that made Webster's name lastingly famous. The Merriams soon outmarketed rival dictionaries, including Joseph Worcester's, which had been in fierce competition with Webster's since its appearance in 1830. Many educators preferred Worcester's conservative approach to spelling and pronunciation. Nonetheless, by the 1850s, the Merriams had cornered the school dictionary market and were on their way to dominating the home market.

While Webster's name was becoming synonymous with dictionaries, his writings on American usage and grammar were forgotten. By the time of his death, his grammar books had virtually disappeared. Fowle's claim that he could not find a copy of *A Philosophical and Practical Grammar* anywhere in Boston in the 1820s suggests that the demand for it by then was almost nil. *Dissertations* was never reprinted. The *Institute, Part II* had long ago been superseded, as Webster himself noted, by Murray and others.

The grammar books of Fowle and his fellow reformers also failed. Fowle continued teaching and writing until 1860, when he retired and moved to the Massachusetts countryside. He died in 1865, aged sixty-nine. Fowle never abandoned his grammatical principles. In 1842 he brought out *Common School Grammar*, intended for preparatory schools. In the preface he makes it clear that he hasn't repented of his earlier views. He still believes that writers like Lowth and Murray "sought to adapt our grammar to other languages . . . and to destroy every feature of it that can be called natural."[47] He's still hoping that his book will provide an antidote.

By the time Fowle died, Lindley Murray's popularity was also waning. The books that replaced his, however, were nothing like Fowle's. They were much closer to Murray's. One of the more popular volumes was *The Principles of English Grammar* by Rev. Peter Bullions. Reverend Bullions announces in the preface that the aim of his book is to improve on Murray's *English Grammar*— "correcting what is erroneous, . . . compressing what is prolix, elucidating what is obscure." He has no thought of developing any original theories. "Utility, not novelty" is his goal and Murray is still the benchmark.[48]

Bullions rephrases and reorganizes, but all the familiar rules and definitions remain intact. He's content to list the same parts of speech as Murray offered. He tells students, as Murray did, that "double comparatives and superlatives are improper." He agrees that "one negative destroys another, or is equivalent to an affirmative," and that "a sentence should not be concluded with a preposition." *It is me* is still wrong. The rules of composition that Bullions lays out—purity, propriety, and precision—are the same ones that Murray suggested several decades earlier.[49]

By the mid-nineteenth century, contention over grammatical issues was entering a new phase. Arguments over usage and style would shift to the public sphere and be aimed not at learners, but at educated adults. A new type of expert would enter the scene—the verbal critic.

Verbal critics were not so much grammarians as guardians of elegant upper-class speech. While earlier grammarians had aimed to educate upwardly aspiring Americans, verbal critics concentrated on making distinctions between the ladies and gentlemen in the top echelons and everyone else. These arbiters of proper speech did not abandon the grammatical strictures of Lowth and Murray—they simply added another layer of refinement. They didn't really need to repeat the basic rules found in eighteenth-century grammar books. These had by now become an uncontroversial fact of American life.

5.

Grammar and Gentility

In his 1870 book *Words and Their Uses,* influential verbal critic Richard Grant White vividly recalls his first clash with the forces of proper grammar. The time was nearly fifty years earlier. The scene was "an upper chamber of a gloomy brick house," where the five-year-old White stood in despair before the schoolmaster. He was failing his grammar lesson. When asked about prepositions governing nouns, the young boy answered, "I don't know," and when quizzed on subject-verb agreement, he had to admit, "I can't tell." This ignorance brought down on him a terrible punishment. "You are a stupid, idle boy, sir, and have neglected your task," his teacher told him. He then proceeded to grab White's hand and smack it with a ruler until it was reduced "as nearly to a jelly as was thought . . . to be beneficial."[1]

This first dreadful experience with grammar studies also became his last. White reports that his father, on hearing the story, removed his son to a more progressive school. "Thereafter," he says, "I studied English . . . only in the works of its great masters and unconsciously in the speech of daily companions, who spoke it with remarkable but spontaneous excellence."[2] As a result, he confesses, he has remained ignorant of the rules found in grammar books. However, he does not consider this gap in his education to be a problem. In White's view, English is almost a "grammarless" tongue, if grammar means the kinds of word variations that signal different noun cases and verb tenses in languages like Latin and Greek. Except for possessives, English nouns don't show evidence of case. Only a handful of irregular verbs like *go/went* change their basic form. White, like Webster, Fowle, and others before him, has concluded that forcing children to memorize lists of artificially labeled, mostly unvarying nouns and verbs is pointless.

White disliked Murray as much as the reforming grammarians did. In *Words and Their Uses*—a review of his fellow citizens' crimes against English—he claims that Murray's rule regarding possessives is uninterpretable. It is "truly an awful and mysterious utterance," he declares. He also attacks Murray in a later book, *Every-Day English*. He writes, "The first great English grammar, the one by which school-boydom has been chiefly oppressed, was written by an 'American,' Lindley Murray. . . . The influence of this book and its imitations in our country has not been happy. Our English has suffered from it."[3] Like many other people of the time, White considered *Murray* synonymous with grammar, but for him the name had decidedly negative connotations. His childhood experience with grammar study obviously still stung.

White's opinion of traditional grammar books suggests kinship with Webster and the radicals of the 1820s, but his perspective on the subject was very different. The radicals rejected the bulk of standard grammar rules because these don't reflect the way ordinary people talk. They urged instead greater acceptance of Americans' natural speech habits. White, on the other hand, believed that Americans' natural speech habits were ruining English. He just didn't think that grammar books were relevant to reversing that trend.

Unlike the grammar reformers of earlier days, White condemned not only Murray, but all grammar books. Webster, Fowle, and Cardell didn't question the value of grammar study itself, only the content and teaching methods of traditional text-books. White went further. He says in *Words and Their Uses*, "Of the rules given in the books called English Grammars, some are absurd, and the most are superfluous."[4] People don't need to be taught how to speak their native tongue, he argues. Even if they did, the vague, inaccurate formulations in grammar books wouldn't help them. At least, grammar books wouldn't help them acquire the English of "remarkable, but spontaneous excellence" that he heard as a boy. In White's opinion, that kind of English can't be taught.

White was a new type of language advisor—not a teacher, but a purveyor of superior English. As he explains in the preface to *Words and Their Uses*, his aim is not to teach the "entirely unin-structed" how to speak correctly (hardly possible anyway). Rather, he wants to bring order to the current linguistic chaos. He will condemn innovations that are damaging to the language and encourage preservation of what's worthwhile. He hopes his remarks will be helpful to "intelligent, thoughtful, educated per-sons, who are interested in . . . the protection of [English] against pedants on the one side and coarse libertines in language on the other."[5]

He tells readers that if any of them hope to acquire a good speaking style by studying either typical grammar books or ad-vice books such as his, "they will be grievously disappointed." Language skills come through "native ability and general cul-ture."[6] In other words, the only sure way to sound well educated and upper class is to actually be well educated and upper class. As the anecdote about White's school days suggests, he thought good speech habits were acquired by associating with the well spoken.

This idea sharply contradicted most Americans' cherished be-lief that grammar books were essential for self-improvement. In the late eighteenth and early nineteenth centuries, thousands of

Americans—including illustrious men such as Abraham Lincoln—had turned to grammars to raise themselves to a higher cultural and economic plane. Now the most prominent usage arbiter of the time was saying that elevation to the upper ranks was not that straightforward. Speaking like a member of the elite was more than a matter of learning noun declensions.

White's own social position was unassailable. His ancestors included several generations of impeccably respectable New Englanders, beginning with John White, who helped found Cambridge, Massachusetts, in 1635 and was later among the first settlers of Hartford. White's grandfather, who graduated from Yale, was a minister and divinity scholar and an unbending Tory. White's father was a prosperous New York shipping merchant who was able to afford a privileged education for his son. After his early false start, the young Richard attended the prestigious Grammar and Preparatory School associated with Manhattan's Columbia College (now Columbia University). He then graduated to Columbia College itself. Presumably it was at the grammar school that he learned proper English by listening to those around him.

After college, White first apprenticed himself to a doctor, but later switched to the study of law. He passed the New York bar exam in 1845 at the age of twenty-four. In the meantime, however, White's father lost his fortune in a catastrophic business failure. The senior White died shortly afterward, leaving his son as the sole support of two as-yet-unmarried younger sisters. Needing to earn money immediately, the young man abandoned the idea of building a law practice. Instead he turned to journalism, where he enjoyed quick success. White first wrote music criticism—he was passionate about music and had considered making it his profession—then branched out into art, literature, and politics. Besides writing critical essays, he edited a twelve-volume edition of Shakespeare's works, later published as *The Riverside Shakespeare.*

White's career as a verbal critic began in the late 1860s with regular columns on American English in *Galaxy* magazine and *The New York Times.* These were later collected into *Words and Their Uses, Past and Present,* published in 1870, and the sequel, *Every-Day English,* which appeared in 1880. A tall, stern-looking man with luxuriant side-whiskers, White employed a writing style that was as Victorian as his looks. His work—formal, learned, and discursive—includes a generous scattering of literary allusions and lengthy, untranslated Latin quotations. White was not writing for the masses, but for people of his own sort. He expected his audience to be well-read.

Although White envisioned a select audience, his steady book sales indicate that he struck a chord with a broad range of people. His books were not bestsellers on the scale of Webster's speller or Murray's grammar, but they were very successful. By 1899 *Words and Their Uses* had been reprinted thirty-six times. The publisher's note on the 1899 copyright page stated that the demand for the book has been "so large and so constant" that new plates were needed for that edition. It was still in print in 1927. *Every-Day English* also went through numerous printings, staying in print until the early twentieth century. Most of White's large number of readers must have come from outside the upper-class circles that he was addressing. They surely bought his books expecting to improve their speech, in spite of his warnings to the contrary.

White's goal in *Words and Their Uses* is to expose the absurdities of speech that he hears daily on the streets and reads in newspapers. He argues that using words in inaccurate or novel ways is a serious social problem. It leads to breakdowns in communication, loss of time and money, and a "sore trial of patience."

He bluntly sums up by declaring that the failure to preserve established distinctions in word meaning constitutes nothing less than "a return toward barbarism."[7] If allowed to continue, it could irreversibly damage American English.

He blames this impending disaster on the "superficially" educated—those whose reading is limited mostly to newspapers, "hastily written by men also very insufficiently educated." The honestly ignorant lower classes, he says, know better than to attempt refined speech. It's the half-educated upstarts, with their "pretentious ignorance and aggressive vulgarity," who are responsible for corrupting the language. He believes that commentary such as his is necessary to defend English "against the assaults of presuming half-knowledge."[8]

White realizes that languages inevitably evolve over time. Nonetheless, those who care about the integrity of English should resist unnecessary usage changes that come about through carelessness or ignorance. Just because a word or expression is fashionable, or a nonstandard form is becoming more common, that doesn't mean it should be accepted as correct.

White believes that the ultimate test of whether a word or phrase is acceptable is whether it makes good sense. In any conflict between logic and grammatical standards, he claims, logic is always victorious. He writes, "Speech, the product of reason, tends more and more to conform itself to reason." Mere general usage cannot be the final arbiter of correct speech. All sorts of "mean and monstrous colloquial phrases" would automatically become a permanent part of the language, just because they were in common use.

Nor do words and phrases become acceptable just because they are found in the works of great writers. Like the early grammarians, who used quotations from Shakespeare and the Bible as examples of false syntax, White has often found questionable usages in literary works. "There is a misuse of words which can be jus-

tified by no authority, however great," he insists, and "by no usage, however general."[9]

White rejects words mainly for their lack of logic, overlap in
meaning with other words, vulgarity, pretentiousness, and excessive gentility. He is contemptuous of euphemisms that arise
from squeamishness, such as calling a leg a limb. Other terms
offend him because they are needlessly pretentious—*initiate* for
start, repudiate for *reject, manufacturer* for *maker.* These words,
often Latin in origin, are even more problematic when they are
slightly misused. *Portion* really signifies a measured-out amount,
but many people think it's a synonym for *part.* Worse than pretentious words are coarse slang terms like *gents* for *gentlemen*
and *pants* for *trousers.* "The one always wears the other," sneers
White.[10]

White's approach to linguistic critique started a trend that still
has many followers. People today often use the phrase "bad grammar" when they really mean questionable word choice. Slight
word misuse—substituting *infer* for *imply,* for instance—is a major annoyance for today's verbal critics. They also tend to cite
the same offenses against correct speech that White named—
sloppiness, ignorance, and an apparent lack of logic. Like him,
they often criticize certain uses that fly in the face of tradition or
fail to preserve a word's "true" meaning. They insist, for example,
that *decimate,* which originated in a Roman military practice,
should mean putting to death one in ten people in a group, rather
than its modern meaning of wiping out a large number.

Modern sticklers for correct usage might agree with the general tone of White's critique, but they would probably be puz-
zled by the words and word uses that offended him. Some—like
using *aggravate* with the meaning of "irritate" instead of its original meaning of "make worse," or confusing *lie* and *lay*—are still
contentious issues. Most of the usages he mentions, however, are
now either uncontroversial or obsolete.

White complains, for example, that women use the noun *dress* to mean *gown* when it rightly refers to all apparel for both women and men. Sounding a little like Horne Tooke, he tells readers, "*dress*, the verb, means simply to set right, to put in order. . . . The kitchen dresser is so called because upon it dishes are put in order. As to the body, dress is that which puts it in order, in a condition . . . suitable to the circumstances." (*Dress* derives from an Old French word that means "arrange," and ultimately from a Latin word meaning "straighten" or "guide.") White voices the same sort of objection to the word *obnoxious* being used to mean offensive. He explains, "Its root is the [Latin] verb *noceo*, to harm . . . and therefore *obnoxious* means liable or exposed to harm," as in *obnoxious to disasters*. This use was already rare by White's day, but he thinks it's worth preserving. "We do not need both *offensive* and *obnoxious* with but one meaning between them," he says.[11]

He criticizes many new word coinages because they are illogical or unnecessary. He calls these "words that are not words." The list includes *practitioner, gubernatorial, presidential, jeopardize, reliable, donate,* and several other words that are now part of standard English. He objects to *practitioner* because there is no such word as *practition* and to *gubernatorial* because there is no such word as *gubernator*. *Presidential* logically ought to be *presidental*. *Donate* has been formed by the questionable method of chopping off *donation* and turning the result into a verb, a pointless proceeding since English speakers can already choose from *give, present, endow, bequeath,* and various other possibilities.

Jeopardize, which he calls "a foolish and intolerable word," is problematic because the *–ize* ending is normally added to nouns or adjectives to form a verb, as in *equal/equalize, civil/civilize, patron/patronize*. In the case of *jeopardize* the ending has instead been added to *jeopard*, a verb—all but obsolete by 1870—meaning "to put in peril." *Jeopardize* was not a recent coinage. The word was familiar to Webster, who also disapproved of it. His response was the opposite of White's however. He chose to include the term in his 1828 dictionary in spite of his personal dislike because respectable American writers used it. To Webster's mind, established usage meant that *jeopardize* was unarguably part of the American vocabulary. For White, forty years as a common word wasn't enough to make it acceptable.

Some of the word uses White objects to would turn out to be passing fads. Taverns are no longer called sample rooms and people seldom say *allow* when they mean believe or use *fellowship* as a verb (as in *Next Sunday we will fellowship with neighboring churches*). Much more often, usages that were a problem for White have become uncontroversial. *Affable* to mean "friendly," *bountiful* to mean "generous," *recollect* as a synonym for *remember, ice water* rather than *iced water*—these and many other locutions that disgusted White are now standard. The same is true for the word inventions that he stigmatizes as "not words." Even the most linguistically sensitive twenty-first-century Americans would find it hard to explain what's wrong with *practitioner, gubernatorial,* or *jeopardize.*

It's not surprising that most of White's commentary is now irrelevant. Languages are constantly evolving and the vocabulary changes more obviously than other linguistic features. Drifts in meaning, as happened with *dress* and *obnoxious,* new words created out of old ones, like *donate* from *donation,* and abandoned words like *jeopard* are common over the history of a language. Once these changes get under way they can rarely if ever be reversed. What's more remarkable is that several grammatical usages first condemned in late-eighteenth-century grammar books were still considered problems when White was writing. Some continue to be live issues today.

White repeatedly emphasizes in his writings that good style

can't be taught and that grammar books are useless. Nonetheless, he can't resist discussing a few troublesome forms that he thinks educated people might benefit from studying. One peeve is the common misuse of *shall* and *will*. This issue also troubled eighteenth-century grammar book authors and, for once, White shares their view. Like them, he has noticed that *will* is replacing *shall* in many people's speech. He thinks it's important for *shall* to be preserved.

White reiterates the *shall/will* rules first detailed in Lowth and other early grammars. Simple statements of future actions use *shall* with first-person pronouns and *will* with second and third person. The opposite is true for statements of determination, promises, or threats—*I will go!* but *You shall obey me!* He realizes that many people will label this distinction a "verbal quibble." That's true of any distinction "to persons too ignorant, too dull, or too careless for its apprehension."[12]

Another problem that White points out is the common confusion between *like* and *as*. White writes that he has noticed many people using *like* to introduce sentences, as in *He talked like he was crazy*. He reminds people of the standard rule—still current in modern usage guides—that *like* compares things, while *as* compares actions or states of being. A verb should never follow *like*.

A third problem is using *they* with a singular antecedent. White describes an example that a reader of his column has sent in—*If a person wishes to sleep, they mustn't eat cheese for supper*. The reader surmises that while the sentence is technically incorrect, it's what most people would say. White disagrees. He replies, "A speaker of common sense and common mastery of English would say, 'If a man wishes to sleep, he must not eat cheese at supper,' where *man* . . . is used in a general sense for the species."[13] He suggests that sympathizers with the Women's Rights Convention replace *a man* with *one*. (He also points out in passing that the correct preposition is *at supper,* not *for supper,* unless the entire supper consists of cheese.)

The persistence of these rules—and the fact that White felt the need to mention them—suggests that traditional grammar books still retained their old power. Unlike many of the evolving word uses that White discusses, the nonstandard versions of these grammatical forms never became completely acceptable. Although *shall* has long been rare in American speech except for questions like *Shall we go,* the *shall/will* rule remained enshrined in grammar books until at least the mid-twentieth century. The *like/as* rule and the ban on singular *they* are still contentious topics. Grammar book writers and style arbiters like White made sure that these rules continued to be part of what constitutes standard grammar, even though speakers then and now break them all the time.

White's dismissal of formal grammar study was not meant to be taken as permission to use nonstandard forms. He expected speakers of superior English to say *It is I,* to avoid double negatives, and to follow all the usual rules. He believed, however, that anyone who spoke good English would have absorbed these rules unconsciously while learning how to talk. People who missed that opportunity were unlikely to be able to compensate for it by memorizing a grammar book. White was writing for those who were already beyond Murray. His goal was to keep his readers informed of bad new words and usages so they could avoid them.

To White and other verbal critics, the chaotic state of the American language mirrored the chaotic state of the country. When *Words and Their Uses* appeared in 1870, Americans were still struggling with the political and economic upheavals of the Civil War. Social boundaries began shifting in unsettling ways.

African Americans were voting for the first time, as well as running for office. Women were demanding that they, too, have the right to vote. Adding to the tumult, millions of immigrants were pouring into the country, many of them non-English speaking. All of them—Irish, German, Scandinavian, Chinese—hoped to gain a foothold on the ladder of financial and social advancement.

The United States was on the verge of the Gilded Age, the only era in American history to be labeled with a negative nickname. It was a time of unparalleled opportunism. Mark Twain, who gave the era its name with an 1873 book of that title, claimed that the "chief end" of most of the population was to get rich—"dishonestly if we can, honestly if we must." In reality, rags-to-riches stories were the exception rather than the rule. Still, enough people made fortunes to give the impression that general prosperity was on the rise, and with it social mobility.

The country's freshly gilded surface hid a tawdry interior. Political corruption openly flourished. President Grant's administration was so riddled with fraud, bribery, and kickback schemes that newspapers began using *Grantism* as a term for shameless government dishonesty. At the local level, "machine" politicians like New York's William "Boss" Tweed took over state and city offices, then used their power to squeeze money out of local business people. As organized political graft took hold in the cities, "carpetbaggers"—northerners bent on exploiting Reconstruction—headed South to milk as much profit as they could out of government rebuilding programs.

The Gilded Age was the era of the instant millionaire. Heavy industry was booming in the East and Midwest, while in the West fortunes were made from railroad building and large-scale cattle ranching. Those lacking the capital for big money-making operations could try their hand at stock market speculation or hope to strike it rich with entrepreneurial schemes. Some of the era's wealthiest men rose from modest backgrounds. Andrew Carnegie, the steel industry giant, had arrived in the country as the child of working-class Scottish parents. John D. Rockefeller, founder of Standard Oil, was the son of a traveling salesman. Cornelius Vanderbilt, who used cutthroat competition to corner the shipping industry, started out working on his father's ferry.

The newly rich quickly adopted aristocratic lifestyles. They built luxurious homes in exclusive neighborhoods and vacationed in upper-class enclaves like Newport, Rhode Island. They joined select clubs and sent their children to Ivy League schools. Even those lower down the economic scale had the means to vastly improve their standard of living. New consumer goods were constantly coming on the market—everything from bottled ketchup to machine-made clothing. Most items could now be shipped anywhere in the country by steamship or rail. People who didn't live in large cities just ordered what they wanted from the Montgomery Ward catalog.

These suddenly well-off social climbers were the people Richard Grant White had in mind when he wrote about the "superficially educated" who were damaging the language with their "pretentious ignorance and aggressive vulgarity." White and other cultural commentators worried that a dangerous social leveling was taking place. Former slum dwellers now lived in the same neighborhoods as old established families. Even Americans in the middling classes now had the buying power to dress well, furnish their homes grandly, and entertain on a more lavish scale than in previous times.

Americans with new money were only part of the problem though. Many people, including a majority of immigrants, were as poor as they had ever been. They were nonetheless beginning to acquire the same manners as their economic betters and even more scandalously, assume an attitude of social equality. The age-old differences in behavior and dress that identified different social classes were starting to disappear.

Both these groups fell short, however, when it came to language. They tended to use words like *gents* and *pants,* or erred in the other direction with over-genteel or pompous word choices like *retire* for *go to bed* and *intoxicated* for *drunk.* Grammar books—the traditional route to self-betterment—didn't teach people how to make subtle word choices. White and other verbal critics believed that the established upper classes could still maintain a distinction between themselves and their social inferiors through careful speech. One purpose of their books was to explain how.

While the grammarians of earlier days came mainly from the ranks of schoolteachers, the verbal critics were often writers—either journalists like White or professional men concerned about language use. Like White, they believed that superior speech habits were largely a matter of good background—in White's words, of "social culture which began at the cradle." William Mathews, a professor of rhetoric at the University of Chicago, whose book *Words: Their Use and Abuse* sold 25,000 copies, expresses it this way: "Man's language is a part of his character . . . the words he uses are an index to his mind and heart."[14]

Their concerns about social leveling led to much fraught discussion about the overuse of *lady* and *gentleman.* White complains in *Every-Day English* that the two terms are now too vague to have any generally accepted meaning. "There are some people," he says, "whose idea of a perfect gentleman is one who pays his bills without question the first time they are presented." He knows a woman whose idea of a perfect gentleman is a man who takes off his hat when he speaks to her in the street. White's fellow critics have similar complaints. "Perhaps no honorable term in the language has been more debased than 'gentleman,'" says Mathews. The term has sunk so low that it's now applied to "the vilest criminals and the most contemptible miscreants, as well as to the poorest and most illiterate persons in the community."[15]

As for *lady,* it had become even more debased. Edward S. Gould, a fiction writer who also wrote books critiquing his fellow verbal critics' prose, points out in *Good English, or Popular Errors in Language* that *lady* has become a "snobbish vulgarism." In some circles it is used as a substitute for wife—"Mr. Somebody and *Lady.*" As with *gentleman,* it can refer to anyone of the appropriate sex. Alfred Ayres, author of *The Verbalist,* tells readers that using *lady* as a general label for any adult female is in the worst possible taste. "Gentlemen and ladies establish their claims to being called such by their bearing, and not by arrogating to themselves, *even indirectly,* the titles," he says.[16]

True ladies, Ayres declares—that is, women of taste, education, and refinement—are satisfied with being referred to as women. Only those in the lower classes, such as young women who work in shops, insist on being called by such terms as "saleslady." It's a way of demanding status that they're not rightly entitled to. In *Every-Day English,* White scornfully describes "the gentlemanly conductor" who asks passengers "to move up in the bulging streetcar and 'let in this lady,' as Bridget McQuean, smelling slightly of pipe and poteen, struggles at the car door with her basket of clothes."[17]

White's example of Bridget McQuean is not random. He often singled out the Irish for linguistic ridicule. More than a million Irish immigrants had crowded into New York and other large eastern cities since the mid-nineteenth century, many escaping the famine that hit when Ireland's potato crop was stricken with blight. They were largely unskilled laborers who took the most miserable, poorly paid jobs on offer (such as laundress).

Their distinctive brand of English nonetheless made an impact on the American language. Although they contributed only a few vocabulary words (*smithereens* and *hooligan* are two), they

influenced usage in ways that White felt were unfortunate. For instance, the Irish were thought to be responsible for the disappearance of *shall*. White writes of suffering "a smart little verbal shock when the Irish servant says, 'Will I put some more coal on the fire?' "[18] He was also unhappy with their nonstandard use of *adopt* to mean *be adopted*. He cites a personals ad reading: "A lady having two boys would like to adopt one." He assumes that "this lady, quite surely an Irish emigrant peasant woman, wished to rid herself of one of her children."[19] The Irish were also blamed for introducing *them* as a noun modifier, as in *them boys over there*.

Another character frequently held up for White's scorn was the "gentleman from Muzzouruh." Elevated to high society because of his "suddenly acquired" wealth, he had a tendency to express himself with inflated vocabulary words. He said *allow* to mean "assert" or "believe," as in, "He was mightily took with her, and allowed she was the handsomest lady in Muzzouruh." He also said *locate in* when he meant "move to" or "settle in." White considered this usage "insufferable to ears at all sensitive."[20]

White and his fellow critics all believed that faulty education—especially the superficial "half-knowledge" of the self-educated—was at the root of America's linguistic problems. In *Good English*, Gould explains how corrupt words enter the language. It begins, he says, when an educated man invents a word, perhaps improvising from a foreign source or an Anglo-Saxon root. He may also discover a new meaning for an established word. If the word is useful, then others adopt it as well. So far, so good. The glitch occurs when an ignorant man encounters the word, but only half learns it, reproducing it "in a wrong shape or with a wrong meaning." Other half-educated people pick it up in its new, corrupt form. Soon this "spuriously fabricated" word has found a permanent home in the American vocabulary.[21]

The fact that a word was widely used in its new sense did not make it legitimate. Nor did its adoption by the best writers. Mathews complains that modern-day writers coin so many new terms that even Noah Webster, "boundless as was his charity for new words," must be turning in his grave. Gould concurs. He believes that authors of "vapid, trashy, 'sensation' novels" are much to blame, but even the best writers have a tendency to spread new usages without considering the damage they may cause.

The critics coalesced around the same problematic terms—*jeopardize, donate, editorial* as a noun, *in our midst* instead of *in the midst of, inaugurate* for *begin, patronize* in the sense of buying goods. Their complaints usually centered on slight misuses or confusion between two words with similar meanings—for example, *demean* and *debase*. Although most of the uses they deprecated have since become standard, others still spark heated arguments—*aggravate* for *irritate, decimate* to mean *wipe out* instead of *reduce by one-tenth, due to* meaning *owing to, different than* instead of *different from, less* instead of *fewer* with count nouns.

They also agreed in condemning verbal prissiness. Mathews writes, "In the seventeenth century, certain fanatics in England ran about without clothes, crying: 'We are the naked Truth.' Had they lived in this age of refinement . . . they would have said, 'We are Verity in a nude condition.'" Gould scorns the word *casket* for *coffin,* which he has recently noticed in an obituary by a "sensational" writer. He wonders whether the writer imagines that "a man in a 'casket' is not quite so dead as a man in a coffin."[22] The critics favored calling things by their unvarnished Anglo-Saxon names.

The shift in attention from grammatical structure to word use indicates the post–Civil War verbal critics' changed focus. Unlike the grammarians of earlier times, they weren't interested in teaching good speaking and writing habits. Their aim was to draw a clear line between well-educated, refined, truly ladylike and gentlemanly people and those in the lower echelons. Their underlying message was the same one often heard today—the half-educated, with their slang, misguided word inventions, and misunderstood terms, were wrecking the language.

The verbal critics were fighting on two fronts. On one side they railed against slang and cant, coarseness, and trendy new word inventions, which they believed degraded the language. On the other side they attacked pretentious bombast and excessive gentility. These stemmed from a lack of social confidence and were as bad as coarseness. Those who wanted to practice the best usage would avoid both extremes. The best speech was clear, precise, unembellished, and respectful of linguistic tradition. It used plain, forceful, mostly Anglo-Saxon words.

The worst offenders in both the slang and the bombast categories were the cheap daily papers. Americans had always been avid newspaper readers—by 1790 over 250 papers were in circulation—but before the 1830s newspapers were too expensive for many people.[23] Instead, they were passed from reader to reader. Laboring men and others on limited budgets shared a single subscription or visited coffeehouses to read the copies provided for customers.

The situation changed dramatically with the advent of the penny press. Advances in printing technology during the early nineteenth century made cheap newspapers feasible for the first time. In 1833 a young New York printer named Benjamin Day brought out a daily paper called the *Sun* (motto: "It shines for all") that could be purchased for a penny. Since the average newspaper sold for six cents, the *Sun* attracted an immediate audience. Other mass circulation dailies followed. Besides their cheap price, newspapers like the *Sun* drew readers with a titillating mix of sensational news, political exposé, crime stories, and scandal. By the 1870s their circulation outpaced that of traditional dailies like *The New York Times* and their influence was at least as great.

In contrast to the *Times* and other staid, high-class newspapers, the penny papers gloried in colorful prose. They used slang expressions like *fork over* and *sound as a nut.* They made up bizarre word combinations like *charmfulness, hostilize,* and *councilmanic.* They also excelled in heavily ornamented vocabulary. Complained one critic, "The newspaper writers never allow us to go anywhere, we always *proceed.* . . . We never eat, but always *partake.* . . . No man ever shows any feeling, but always *evinces* it." One newspaper reported on a military skirmish along the Potomac by saying that "the thousand-toned artillery duel progresses magnificently at this hour, the howling shell bursting in wild profusion in camp and battery, and among the trembling pines."[24]

Penny papers also used slang to give their stories some extra zip. The *New York Herald* jocularly titled a piece about a public séance "The War of the Ghouls." The piece begins "Irving Hall last evening was the scene of some high old times . . . Spiritualists were on the warpath and the goblins played the very mischief." The papers could be painfully blunt as well. An article about the business dealings of the notorious robber baron "Diamond" Jim Fisk is headlined "The Great American Grabber."[25]

To the minds of the verbal critics, newspapers like the *Herald* epitomized all that had gone appallingly wrong with current language use. Gould remarks in *Good English,* "Among writers, those who do the most mischief are the original fabricators of error, to wit: the men generally who write for the newspapers." White's chapter on newspapers is titled "Newspaper English. Big Words for Small Thoughts." He considers newspapers the worst purveyors of pretentious nonsense. "The curse and peril of language in this day," he claims, "is that it is at the mercy of men who, instead of being content to use it well according to their honest ignorance, use it ill according to their affected knowledge."

Even worse, they infect their readers with the disease. White writes of encountering a policeman while walking past an unfamiliar building and inquiring of him what the building was. The policeman replied, according to White, "That is an institootion inaugurated under the auspices of the sisters of Mercy, for the reformation of them young females what has deviated from the paths of rectitood." White does not blame him for this pomposity because he knows that the man reads similar sentences every day in the penny papers. To buttress his case, he quotes a reporter's recent description of a murderer's arrest—"a policeman went to his residence, and there secured the clothes that he wore," which were "so smeared by blood as to incarnadine the water of the tub in which they were deposited." White surmises that to say the clothes were "so bloody that they reddened the water into which they had been thrown" would be far too plain a statement for the newspaper.[26]

Even fellow editors from the high-end newspapers criticized the language of the penny press. An 1865 issue of *The Nation* includes an article titled "The English of the Newspapers." It condemns "the solecisms, the barbarisms, and the vulgar phraseology which the readers of many public journals are fated to encounter." The paper agrees with the verbal critics that coarse language implies a coarse mind. "He who constantly obtrudes printed slipslop upon the public can hardly have either the feelings or the manners of an educated gentleman," the article's author comments sternly. He then reviews various "verbal absurdities" found in lesser newspapers, such as saying *pluvial* instead of *rainy*. *The Nation* doesn't mean to be finicky. The editors simply believe that "the loose and irregular methods of employing words which obtain in some newspapers . . . are of dangerous import to the purity of our tongue."[27]

Horace Greeley, obstreperous editor of the high-profile *New York Tribune,* couldn't have disagreed more. His approach to editorial writing was to come out swinging. The *Tribune* avoided the jaunty slang and sensationalism of papers like the *Sun* and the *Herald,* but was fully committed to bluntness, especially when writing about politics. "We defy the Father of lies himself to crowd more stupendous falsehoods into a paragraph than this contains," he writes in response to a rival paper's article. An opinion piece advocating for pensions for Mexican War veterans begins, "Uncle Sam! you bedazzled old hedge-hog!" Of a persistent opponent, Greeley says, "We ought not to notice this old villain again."[28] (Greeley used *villain* as an insult so often that his political enemies nicknamed him Old Villain-You-Lie.)

Greeley had begun his journalism career much differently from White. The child of a poor day laborer, Greeley was born in Amherst, New Hampshire, in 1811, but his family moved frequently in search of a living. His scanty education ended when he was fourteen. Most of what he knew he picked up by reading library books and working at odd jobs in various small-town newspaper offices. In 1831, at the age of twenty, he left his parents' home in Erie, Pennsylvania, and set out for New York City with $10 in his pocket and all his other belongings tied up in a handkerchief. He later described himself at that time as having an "unmistakably rustic manner and address."[29]

Over the next ten years Greeley worked his way up in the journalism world with a succession of jobs, beginning with typesetting. Soon he was writing for magazines and newspapers, including the *Daily Whig.* In 1840 the Whig Party hired him to edit presidential candidate William Henry Harrison's campaign weekly, the *Log Cabin.* After the election the *Log Cabin* ceased publication and Greeley launched the *New York Tribune,* a pro-Whig penny daily. Greeley's goal, he later wrote, was to found a newspaper "removed alike from servile partisanship on the one hand, and from gagged, mincing neutrality on the other."[30]

Greeley was never neutral and certainly never mincing. A man of deeply felt convictions, he expressed his views in forthright, pungent language. (He is best known today for the editorial advice, "Go west young man, and grow up with the country.")[31] Greeley's attitudes were radical, occasionally bordering on eccentric. He wrote forcefully against slavery and was among the first to join the newly formed Republican Party when the Whigs split apart over the issue. He supported labor unions and opposed capital punishment. He also advocated Fourierism, based on the French philosopher Charles Fourier's idea of organizing society into cooperative communities called phalanxes.

He believed in saying what he thought and, when criticized, vigorously defended his right to do so. In 1868 he wrote an opinion piece titled "Gov. Seymour as a Liar," attacking Democratic presidential candidate and former New York governor Horatio Seymour for vastly overstating the amount of federal money being spent on Reconstruction. "Of all the evil-doers," Greeley tells readers, "the Political Liar . . . is among the basest and most wicked." After comparing Seymour's numbers with the actual government figures, he ends the article by asking, "Is not the infamy of Horatio Seymour unspeakable?"[32]

The article provoked an outcry among the city's more conservative editors. *The Round Table,* a weekly collection of financial and political news and literary reviews, printed a column titled "Mr. Greeley as a Gentleman." It begins, "Mr. Horace Greeley has just disgraced himself, his newspaper, and the American press." The writer informs Greeley that the language he has employed in his article "is such as to unfit him for the society of

gentlemen" and advises him to take up the study of deport-
ment.[33]

The New York Times also scolded Greeley for lack of professional courtesy. Whether or not Greeley's accusations are true,
says the Times, using "low" language to express them does not
help his case. Greeley's language has been "the language exclusively of blackguards and brutes . . . as is only used by persons
of coarse natures." It would justify a response in words that would
make Greeley's sound "tame and mealy-mouthed." The Times
writer winds up his lecture by opining that "if the whole Press
of the country . . . adopted the teachings or followed the example of The Tribune . . . it would be quite as unfortunate for that
journal as for the reputation of the country at large."[34]

Greeley responds by inviting The New York Times to do its
worst. "We would have The Times use such terms as most forcibly express its ideas," he writes. "We especially beg it not to be
'mealy-mouthed.' So far from deeming it 'unfortunate' for us that
other journals should be abusive, we insist that no one is ever
harmed by any bad language except his own."[35] Greeley points
out that while the Times article has been polite, the writer has
failed to show that anything he said about Seymour was untrue.

By the time White and other verbal critics began mounting
attacks on newspaper style, Greeley's editing days were nearly
over. Disappointed in the corrupt Grant administration, Greeley allowed himself to be drafted into running against the president in the 1872 election. He suffered a devastating defeat,
carrying only six states. To add to his distress, his wife had died
of tuberculosis just one month earlier. Greeley received yet another blow when he returned to the Tribune after the election.
He discovered that during his long absence on the campaign trail,
the newspaper, which was now owned by stockholders, had
handed his editorial duties to others. Overwhelmed by these

repeated shocks, Greeley's physical and mental health failed and he died shortly afterward.

If Horace Greeley stood for fearless plain speaking, Sarah Josepha Hale represented the opposite end of the spectrum. Mrs. Hale, longtime editor of the popular women's magazine *Godey's Lady's Book* (or editress, as she called herself), unabashedly promoted genteel speech. Through her magazine editorials and other writings, she introduced tens of thousands of women at all social levels to the idea that proper language use was an essential part of gracious living.

Hale was a remarkable woman. Born Sarah Josepha Buell in 1788, she grew up on a Newport, New Hampshire, farm. Sarah was unusually well educated. Besides the typical school subjects available to girls, she learned Latin and philosophy from her older brother. When she was twenty-five she married Newport lawyer David Hale, who encouraged her to continue educating herself. He also supported her first writing attempts—poems and articles that she submitted to local newspapers. Sarah Hale's hobby turned into a career in 1822 when David Hale died suddenly, leaving her with five small children. The thirty-four-year-old widow decided to begin writing seriously with a view to earning money. Her first publication was a volume of poems. Over her long life Hale published nearly forty books, including poetry, novels, edited letters, anthologies, gift books, cookbooks, and advice books. Her most lastingly famous composition is the children's poem that begins "Mary had a little lamb."

Hale made her greatest mark as a magazine editor. In 1828 she became the first woman to hold such a position when the Boston-based *Ladies Magazine* offered her the job. Nine years later Philadelphia publisher Louis Godey bought the *Ladies Magazine* and merged it with his *Lady's Book*. He kept Hale on as editor. She ran *Godey's Lady's Book* for the next forty years, writing her final editorial for the December 1877 issue when she was eighty-nine, only sixteen months before she died. During her tenure, the monthly magazine gained readers every year. By 1860 the number of subscribers had risen to 150,000 and Godey could boast that the *Book* was sent to "every State in the Union and to every Territory."[36]

Godey's Lady's Book blends the educational, the inspirational, and the practical. A typical issue features several poems and short stories, including many by well-known authors; color plates of the latest fashions; knitting and sewing patterns; piano music; recipes and household hints; and book notices and reviews. Tucked into the spaces between the longer pieces are uplifting quotations and snippets of advice. One paragraph of advice begins, "Another rule for living happily with others is to avoid having stock subjects of disputation." Another reminds readers, "Never suffer your children to advance in years before you attend to their education." A short entry titled "A Word for Grumblers" offers the consoling observation, "In every man's cup, how so ever bitter, . . . there are some cordial drops . . . which if wisely extracted, are sufficient to make him contented."

Hale's voice is clearest in a section called "The Editor's Table." Here she offers opinion pieces and discussions of current events, focusing especially on women's place in society. Although Hale championed women's education—she was instrumental in the founding of Vassar, the first women's college—and argued for women as teachers and health care providers, she firmly opposed the organized women's movement of the time. Instead she believed that women should wield their influence as the moral and cultural arbiters of the home. Through her columns she gently shepherded *Lady's Book* readers toward high principles, appropriate behavior, and refined taste.

Hale's advice often covered language use. In her 1866 etiquette book, *Manners: Or, Happy Homes and Good Society All the Year Round,* she explains the importance of understanding the "true meaning" of everyday words. Although a knowledge of words is not enough in itself to guarantee clear thought processes, she believes that "the study of correctness is a great help to mental activity." Furthermore, "as women are the first teachers of every human being, it follows that women must be well instructed in their own language." Later in the book, she underlines the importance of correct language use, saying, "Words are things of mighty influence. The manner of speech indicates the habit of mind."[37]

Hale shared some of the same concerns as White and other language arbiters. One issue that offended all of them was the increasing use of *male* and *female* to refer to human beings. While indiscriminate use of *lady* and *gentleman* put people on an artificially equal footing, referring to them as males and females went to the opposite extreme. It seemed to bring people down to the same level as animals. White says of *female,* "The use of this word for *woman* is one of the most unpleasant and inexcusable of the common perversions of language." Mathews also remarks disapprovingly on this so-called "modern improvement" in speech, insisting that *woman* is a "more elegant and more distinctive title" than *female.*[38]

Hale heartily agrees. The expanded use of *male* and *female* that has crept into English has "injured its precision, weakened its power, and fatally corrupted its delicacy," she writes in an article titled "Grammatical Errors." She repeats this criticism in her etiquette book, saying "The practice of using the term 'female' as a synonym for 'woman' is vulgarizing our style of writing and our mode of speech." She says she has been writing against this "serious error" for years in the hopes of correcting it.[39]

On other points, Hale and the verbal critics part ways. Although she warns her readers to avoid using fancy words that they don't completely understand, she disagrees with White's strictures against vocabulary derived from Latin. She notes that Mr. White denounces *initiate* as a long, pretentious word for *begin,* but argues that the two terms provide different shades of meaning. She points out that English is full of word pairs such as *fatherly* and *paternal* or *ripe* and *mature,* with broadly similar but not exactly synonymous connotations. In general, she says, "Anglo-Saxon gives vigor . . . and Latin adds learning." "Fastidious scholars" might choose to limit themselves to simple Anglo-Saxon words, while "self-taught writers" might be tempted to search out the most elaborate terms, but the best writer is the one who "has the largest stock of words at his command, and knows how to use them accurately."[40]

Hale also takes a stand in favor of euphemisms. "There are many colloquial expressions, used by the best writers and speakers," she says, "which do not accord with the strict laws of etymology or grammar, but which it would be highly unjust to term underbred." She defends words that White stigmatizes as inaccurate or affected. She believes, for example, that the new meaning of *obnoxious* is acceptable because it is less harsh than saying that someone is offensive. She also approves of *persuasion* for *sect, avocation* for *employment,* and *party* for *person.* Their use "proceeds from a sentiment which is the very essence of good breeding—the desire to spare the feelings of others." In Hale's view, courtesy encompassed knowing how to choose the right euphemism when one was called for.

Although concerned with delicacy and tact, she was broader minded than White when it came to accepting useful new words. In an essay titled "Words under Ban" she defends *reliable, donate,* and several other terms that White rejects. She concludes, "The language cannot afford to lose any word, however uncouth, which expresses an idea."[41]

Hale was especially firm in defending terms that had been

feminized with the *-ess* ending, such as *authoress, editress, po-etess,* and *actress.* The verbal critics felt that these forms crossed the line into overrefinement. White calls the words distasteful, although he admits that *mistress, prioress, deaconess,* and similar terms are well established and therefore *-ess* words generally should probably be allowed into the vocabulary. Gould reacts more strongly, calling them "spurious words." He, too, recognizes the need for traditional feminine titles like *princess, baroness,* and *countess,* as well as feminine forms of words "suggestive of men"—priest, ambassador, governor, hunter—but otherwise thinks the ending is superfluous. Hale saw feminized labels differently. To her they expressed respect for a woman's unique cultural position. "Why should the cumbrous paraphrase, *female author,* be used," she asks, "when *authoress* would more properly and elegantly express the meaning?"[42]

As the guiding spirit of American women's favorite magazine, Hale wielded enormous influence. She used it partly to reinforce the notion that correct language use was a moral virtue. Women who wanted to appear well bred took care to sidestep the twin faults of vulgarity and ostentation, and to keep their language free from grammatical errors.

Although the verbal critics were dismissive of formal grammar study, it remained as relevant as ever for most people. Spurred on by the critiques of White and others, educators debated whether grammar should continue to be taught—a few advanced school districts even deleted it from the curriculum—but the grammar-book-using public was largely unaware of any controversy. Most children still studied grammar in school and adults consulted grammar books at home, just as they'd always done.

Etiquette books—a burgeoning form of literature aimed at the rising middle class—always included a section on proper speech.

A typical example, *American Etiquette and Rules of Politeness,* advises, "To use correct language in conversation is another matter of very great importance. It is exceedingly unpleasant to hear the English language butchered by bad grammar." The author goes on to recommend simplicity and purity in speech. Echoing the verbal critics, he says, "It is the uneducated and those who are only half-educated that use long words and high-sounding phrases." Vulgarisms and slang—like *good gracious* and *immensely jolly*—should likewise be avoided.[43]

The verbal critics themselves felt the necessity to touch on grammar at least briefly in their books. Besides the issues that White addresses, like incorrect use of *shall,* the critics were especially bothered by the kinds of mistakes that arise from trying too hard to be correct. They pointed out, for instance, the use of *whom* as an embedded subject, as in *I don't know whom else is expected,* and the appearance of nominative pronouns after a verb or preposition, as in *It's pointless for you and I to quarrel.*

These usages were not new. Early grammar book authors occasionally note them, along with examples of their appearance in Shakespeare, Milton, or the Bible. Murray discusses the incorrect use of nominative pronouns and *whom.* Frequently, however, eighteenth-century grammarians either didn't discuss these issues at all or limited them to a footnote. Presumably, most grammarians of that time didn't consider them serious errors. That attitude was now beginning to change. "Split" infinitives, which were not a concern for eighteenth-century grammar book writers, also began to draw attention. By the turn of the twentieth century inserting an adverb between *to* and a verb would emerge as a full-blown grammatical outrage.

Grammar teaching had also changed since the early days. New grammar books in the 1870s were designed to elicit the principles of grammar naturally rather than asking students to memorize the rules. William Swinton's popular *New Language Lessons* is an example of this approach to grammar teaching. The author explains in his preface that his object is to help children acquire good grammar by "practice and habit" rather than the study of rules and definitions. He tells teachers, "the bristling array of classifications, nomenclatures, and paradigms has been wholly discarded." Pupils are encouraged to "deal with speech" and "handle sentences" so they can see correct grammar in action.[44]

Yet Murray cast a long shadow. Swinton's students may have started out traveling a different path from those long-ago children who memorized Murray's *English Grammar,* but in the end they arrived at the same place. The book's first section, "Classes of Words," begins with a list of sentences in which the nouns are italicized. The sentences are followed by analysis—"The word 'Columbus' is the name of a person; the word 'America' is the name of a place;" and so on, until all the nouns have been identified. After the analysis comes the explanation—"Words that are used as names of persons, places, things, actions, or qualities . . . are called nouns." These familiar words are followed by a definition that reaches even further into the past. Swinton's "A noun is the name of anything existing or conceived by the mind" closely paraphrases Murray's (originally Lowth's) "a noun is the name of any thing conceived to subsist, or of which we have any notion."[45]

A Practical Grammar of the English Language by Thomas Harvey, first published in 1868, is more conventional than Swinton. Harvey divides his book into the time-honored four sections of orthography, etymology, syntax, and prosody. Although many definitions are modernized, the usual parts of speech make their appearance, along with the typical verb conjugations, parsing exercises, and examples of false syntax.

Harvey includes all the standard usage rules as well. "Avoid the use of two negatives to express negative," he tells students, and "a noun or pronoun, used as the predicate of a proposition, is in the nominative case." *It is me* is just as wrong as it was in the days of Murray. So are sentence-final prepositions. Harvey warns, "Such expressions as 'Whom are you talking to?' are inelegant, if not ungrammatical." More recent concerns also make an appearance. The author explains in detail the rules for using *shall* and *will*, and includes the ban on separating *to* from the infinitive verb.[46]

Gone are the literary examples of grammar mistakes, the improving fables, and the biblical excerpts. Otherwise, *A Practical Grammar* could easily have found a place in Noah Webster's first schoolroom. Yet the last edition of Harvey's book appeared in 1906. More than 130 years after Lowth's *Short Introduction to English Grammar* arrived on American shores, grammar students were still ingesting Lowth's rules with very few changes.

By the late 1870s the ideal of educated word use was well entrenched. At the same time, grammar rules remained as firmly fixed as ever, at least in most classrooms. Newspapers and magazines featured regular columns on proper speech and linguistic advice books continued to sell well. That included traditional grammar books. Although their format had evolved over the years, their basic message remained the same—educated people followed the rules.

Verbal purists had not yet won the day, however. They were beginning to come under attack from a new direction—the expanding field of linguistic science. Armed with new discoveries and up-to-date methods, practitioners in this field were exploring English usage from a whole new perspective. Their conclusions were significantly different from those of White and his fellow critics. As serious academic scholars, the linguists considered themselves professionals, while they saw the verbal critics as ignorant amateurs. The two groups were headed for an explosive collision.

6.

The Science of Grammar

The title of Richard Grant White's June 1871 *Galaxy* article—
"Words and Their Uses: The Author's Humble Apology for Having Written His Book"—must have startled his regular readers.
A quick scan of the first paragraph, however, would have reassured them. The "apology" was actually a determined defense
of his work. White seldom needed to take such a step. As he explains in the article, his book has provoked much "intelligent and
decided" discussion, nearly all of it positive. A glaring exception
has recently come to his notice—a series of hostile articles that
appeared in the Yale *College Courant* from November 19, 1870,
through January 28, 1871.

The articles were signed "X," but White knew they were written by a Yale professor named Thomas Lounsbury, with substantial input from his colleague William Dwight Whitney. With
mock humility, White tells his *Galaxy* readers that he takes it as
a great compliment that "two of that famous faculty felt that it
was prudent for them to unite their forces for the demolition of
the work of a poor dabbler . . . like me."[1]

"Demolition" is a strong word, but it's not an exaggeration. The
professors had not merely given White's book a poor review. They
had spent ten weeks and several thousand words blasting away
at it. (Why Lounsbury and Whitney chose to use a pseudonym
for their articles is unclear. Signing controversial commentary

with a false name—usually Roman or Greek—was common practice earlier in the century, but unusual by the 1870s.)

The *College Courant* articles opened a new front in America's ongoing usage war. Grammarians in the late eighteenth and early nineteenth centuries, whatever their differences, agreed on their basic goals. While they might quibble over details—and radicals like Webster and Fowle might reject certain traditional rules and labels—they all believed that an ideal of elegant English existed and could be captured in the right kind of grammar book. In the end, they all produced familiar-looking volumes that combined precedent with their own judgment and taste.

The *Courant* authors viewed grammar from a far different vantage point. Unlike earlier generations of usage warriors, they were not schoolteachers or popular writers. They were scholars of language. Lounsbury was a professor of English literature with a comprehensive knowledge of early English and Whitney was a professor in the new field of philology—the systematic study of language. Lounsbury and Whitney's approach to grammar and usage was one of scientific inquiry. They didn't believe that personal taste had any place in grammar discussions.

The professors were not against grammar teaching—several years after the *Courant* articles appeared Whitney himself would author a grammar book—but they believed in researching the history and development of words and phrases before making pronouncements on their use. White relied on reason and his own preferences to decide what was correct. He passed judgment on usage standards, while Lounsbury and Whitney explored actual use.

The clash between the verbal critic and the professors drew the battle lines for a fight over the nature of grammar that's still going strong. In the beginning, the debate played out mostly in the pages of magazines. Nineteenth-century periodicals often gave generous space to scholarly controversies, printing lengthy attacks and detailed responses, supplemented by heated letters from readers. *The Galaxy* provided White with lavish room for his columns, *The Nation* frequently published Whitney's commentary, and Lounsbury's articles appeared regularly in *Harper's*.

Today the battle has moved to the Internet. Dueling blog posts from language specialists and grammar critics trigger furious arguments and rebuttals. Heated posts to the comments section take the place of letters to the editor. In spite of the new format, the content and general tone of these discussions has not changed much over time. White and his antagonists would no doubt recognize the basic arguments.

The *College Courant* was an unlikely venue for Lounsbury and Whitney's attack. A weekly newspaper for Yale students, faculty, and graduates, the *Courant* filled most of its pages with a mix of school news, alumni announcements, book notices, and brief excerpts from other periodicals. Although the paper kept two columns free for submissions from faculty and alumni, a ten-part series devoted to reviewing one book was something out of the ordinary. Evidently the topic was deemed compelling enough to keep subscribers engaged for two and a half months.

In Part I the authors ease into their theme by noting that nearly everyone is sensitive to the possibility of making an error in language use. This feeling, they write, is widespread and powerful, extending through all classes of society. It's no wonder, then, that so many books have appeared lately with the aim of correcting common usage mistakes. "Certainly," they remark, "the rapid sales of these shows how general is the desire for information. Unfortunately, their contents show how extensive is the ignorance of those who set out to supply it." While the authors concede that most usage books include a few helpful observations, "these are so mingled with unsupported assertions and ill-considered statements" that they are "as likely to mislead as to correct." Such books seldom lay down any objective principles for deciding what's right.

The authors' description of typical verbal criticism could easily apply to a majority of grammar discussions before and since. They note "a certain arrogance of tone which jars unpleasantly upon the reader's feelings," and comment that the "denunciatory style" is more appropriate "for a prophet warning sinners . . . than for a scholar discussing disputed points of grammar and expression." Usage rules are passionately asserted rather than supported with evidence. For, the authors say, "owing to some yet unexplained reason, a contest in grammar is only a little less bitter than a contest in theology."[2]

Although they start out speaking in general terms, and briefly mention other recent books, they quickly zero in on White. He is the most prominent of those offering verbal advice, and moreover, he has a reputation as a Shakespearean scholar. They believe that White's audience had a right to expect a better than average usage book. In their opinion, *Words and Their Uses* has been a disappointment. It "abounds with statements so reckless, with blunders so gross, and with ideas so confused, that it will be a dangerous guide to anyone who is disposed to regard it as an authority."

The professors challenge White's insistence that general usage—even the usage of respected authors—doesn't count when deciding whether a certain word or grammatical construction is correct. In *Words and Their Uses,* White claims that "there is a misuse of words which can be justified by no authority, however great, by no usage, however general." He argues that logic is the highest arbiter of correct speech. When "formal grammar" and reason collide, he declares, English will always shift in the direction of reason. New words and word uses that go against logic, or that blur established meanings, are wrong, according to White. They should be rooted out of the language, even if most people now use them.[3]

Lounsbury and Whitney intend to demonstrate that, contrary to White's assertions, general usage is the only possible measure of linguistic correctness. Correctness cannot be based on reason, they argue, because "reason is very much like conscience; from the same fact it may lead two men to draw directly opposite conclusions." Nor can a word's acceptability be based on its historical meaning, for the simple reason that very few English speakers know the histories of the words they use. Everyone, including White, uses words and grammatical forms that were once new or that meant something different. The relevant meaning of a word is what it means now. White only believes otherwise, they say, because he is ignorant of how language really works.

Echoing the long-ago conclusions of Noah Webster, they state, "It is the duty of the grammarian simply to collect, digest, and enroll the laws which the users of language have established; it has been too much their practice to fancy themselves legislators where they are only recorders." Verbal critics like White follow eighteenth-century grammarians in assuming that great writers sometimes made usage mistakes—the "false syntax" examples of traditional grammar books. Lounsbury and Whitney take the opposite view. They assume that if a word or grammatical form appears regularly in the writings of respected authors, it can safely be considered a standard usage. "Of all the delusions into which purists and grammarians fall," they remark, "none is wilder than the belief that a great literary artist is not as particular in the details of his art as the critics who sit in judgment upon him."[4]

The professors demonstrate the difference between their attitude and White's with an example of an unquestionably nonstandard use—the substitution of past participles for simple past, as in *I seen* for *I saw* and *I done* for *I did*. Although such forms are heard among the lowest classes, they say, educated people universally consider them unacceptable. Could such a usage ever become proper under any circumstances?

They predict that White would answer no. He would presumably argue that *I seen, I done,* and similar forms offend against basic principles of logic and linguistic tradition. The authors themselves, however, take a contrary position. They believe that if *did* were to disappear from the language and "all the best speakers . . . invariably said *I done, . . . done* would be the legitimate imperfect [past tense] of *do,* and it would be the merest pedantry to persist in condemning the new form."

Interestingly, that's exactly what happened historically with a number of Anglo-Saxon verbs, for instance *speak* and *break.* Everyone now says *spoke* and *broke*—probably shortened forms of the past participles *spoken* and *broken*—while the old past tense forms *spake* and *brake* have become obsolete. In other cases the opposite has occurred. The past tense of certain verbs is now used as the past participle. "We, for instance," they tell readers, "in our low-minded and vulgar manner of speaking, say *I have stood,* or *I have understood,* while Mr. White, in obedience to a higher law, doubtless says *I have stonden* or *I have understonden.*" After all, they point out, those forms were correct in earlier varieties of English.[5] To underline their point, they plan to explore the history and evolution of English verbs through the next several essays.

A rush of erudition follows. The authors of the *Courant* articles outline the classification of Anglo-Saxon verbs, explaining the different verb conjugations, tracking their evolution down to present-day English, and offering examples from literary works of different periods. They compile a list of verb forms that were once acceptable but are now considered wrong. In particular, they give several examples of *drunk* used as simple past, including one from the collection of Shakespeare's plays that White edited—

"*Falstaff*: I am a rogue if I drunk today [*King Henry IV, Part 1*, act 2, scene 4]." They point out that White has complained in his book about the form *I drunk* (rather than *I drank*) even though he must realize that it was acceptable in Shakespeare's time. That means he can't be ruling it ungrammatical on the grounds of tradition or logic. The only reason *I drunk* is wrong in 1870 is that general usage has changed.

The professors apply the same treatment to several of the usages that White condemns, burying White's arguments under a heavy bombardment of scholarship. For instance, White has been reckless enough to speculate that the use of *me* in the "not entirely vulgar" phrase *It is me* can be traced back to an Anglo-Saxon form of the pronoun. They respond, "No one who has any respectable knowledge of Anglo-Saxon or early English" could ever hold that opinion. Someone who has made a genuine study of the language would know that the Anglo-Saxons used a different idiom altogether (a phrase that translates as *I am it*).

Then they pile on details. They refer to instances of *I am it* in "Semi-Saxon" and early English. They provide late examples from Chaucer. They discuss evidence that nominative and objective pronouns began to be confused around the fourteenth-century Middle English period, when *It is me* first appeared. They note that occurrences before the fifteenth century "are exceedingly few and scattered."[6]

By this point it's clear that White's attackers are much more at home with the history, logic, usage, and original meanings of English pronouns than their victim. The implication is that his views on the vulgarity or otherwise of *It is me* are nothing more than his uninformed personal opinion. (They don't offer their own judgment on this usage. Whitney notes in his 1877 grammar book that it's become so common that "it is even regarded as good English by respectable authorities," so they probably found it at least marginally acceptable.)[7]

The writing is laced with sarcasm. Exclaiming breathlessly on the "wonder-working power" of applying reason over usage, the authors marvel that "in the course of two pages, Mr. White's remorseless logic has knocked the life out of some fifty common English words."[8] In another place they express surprise that White, who is a man of sense "when his mind is not perverted by what he fancies to be learning," has accepted the ban on *female* to refer to women. They show the flimsiness of the usual argument against it by saying, "A cow, or a sow, or any she-brute, we are constantly told, is a female; therefore how can we know that a woman is meant? . . . All that is necessary to reply to this profound observation is that all who have brains will understand it."[9]

The professors wrap up their *Courant* series by explaining why they have trounced so hard on White's book. They have devoted so much space to it, they say, "because books constructed upon the essentially vicious principles upon which this is constructed are becoming far too common. Setting out to reform, they end by originating more errors than they correct." Besides, "they render respectable and inoffensive people unhappy by leading them to doubt the correctness of the most common and legitimate words and idioms."

The authors say that they would be happy to see a trustworthy work on disputed usages. However, to be of value, it would need to be based on "the principle that correct usage is not something to be proved by processes of logic, or something to be evolved from the depths of one's consciousness, but something to be found out by the patient, and careful, and wide-reaching study of the language itself." They doubt that such a book will appear soon. Writing it would take time-consuming "labor, and thought, and research." Also, as White and other verbal critics became more knowledgeable about English, they would inevitably be less inclined to critique it as they do now.[10]

White, always feisty, responds defiantly to this bludgeoning in his *Galaxy* article, published several months later. He realizes that the purpose of these attacks is to expose him as "a shallow pretender to knowledge which I did not possess." This criticism gives him little concern. It has never been his intention, he says, to lay claim to philological scholarship—he makes no pretensions to learning. He feels compelled to point out, however, that all except one of the many Anglo-Saxon examples scattered through the *Courant* articles are familiar to him. He has no doubt that he could find just as many others that would support his own position rather than theirs.

These are minor issues. White devotes most of his attention to answering the heart of their criticism—his position that reason always trumps illogical forms, even those adopted by eminent writers. Here White remains adamant. He says, "I believe, assert, and endeavor to maintain that in language, as in morals, there is a higher law than mere usage. . . . This is the law of reason."

He argues that producing examples of certain usages from Chaucer and Shakespeare, as his opponents have done, is beside the point. They obviously believe that eminent writers give a word or phrase authority, but he doesn't, so there is really no basis for discussion. He goes further—"This citing of poets as authority on the *correct* use of language is to me one of the most amazing of the aberrations of the professorial mind. . . . There is no monstrosity, no extravagance in the use of words, no verbal outrage of the laws of reason . . . that could not be justified by their example." He still firmly believes that great writers sometimes make usage mistakes.[11]

Not unnaturally, White felt deeply insulted by the contemptuous tone of the *Courant* articles. He describes one comment as "at best rather worthy of a cheap and lively newspaper than of a Yale professor." Of another criticism he says, "If this is a fair mode of argument or attack at Yale, I am very glad that I was bred in another school." He calls the articles "a fine example" of "malicious . . . and destructive criticism." Nonetheless the authors have not shaken White from his point of view. He remains tenaciously committed to the claims in his book in spite of all the arguments against them that the *Courant* articles provide. He doesn't accept Lounsbury and Whitney's premises, so their conclusions are irrelevant to him. White and his critics are traveling along paths too widely divergent ever to intersect.[12]

The clash between White and the Yale professors is similar in some ways to earlier grammar conflicts. Previous disagreements between orthodox grammarians and their critics also hinged on issues such as the histories of words and the legitimacy of popular usages. Nearly one hundred years before the *College Courant* articles appeared, Webster was lambasting other grammarians for their dismissal of Horne Tooke's etymologies, as well as attacking them for their refusal to accept common locutions like *Who did she speak to?* Nor was it remarkable that Lounsbury and Whitney justified their position by claiming to be more knowledgeable and more sensible than their opponent. Nearly every grammar book writer after Lowth made some such statement in his preface.

The Yale professors, however, gave this familiar attitude a new spin. They didn't just attack White's conclusions—they questioned his right to speak on the subject at all. Throughout the *Courant* articles, they repeatedly suggest that White's errors stem from straying outside his area of expertise. Unlike them he has not studied or taught philology, nor has he done extensive research on the history and structure of English. They imply that he bases his linguistic judgments on his own reasoning abilities because it's easier than the "long and patient study" required to master his subject. In other words, he is an amateur, while they are professionals.

Lounsbury and Whitney were pioneering a new way of analyzing English, one that owed more to the natural sciences than the grammar writings of earlier eras. The trend toward scientific classification that influenced the rational grammarians in the 1820s had grown stronger in recent decades, especially after the 1859 publication of Charles Darwin's *On the Origin of Species*. Scientific rigor was the new order of the day. Language scholars were now beginning to see how scientific principles of careful observation and description could also benefit grammar and usage studies. These new methods called for specialized knowledge, however. The Yale professors had it and White did not.

Thirty-two-year-old Thomas Lounsbury, an 1859 graduate of Yale, had recently been appointed a professor of English language and literature at that institution. Lounsbury was a burly, bearded man who resembled a soldier more than a staid college professor—he was a Union army officer during the Civil War—but the scope of his learning was impressive. His specialties ranged from Chaucer and Shakespeare to the history of the English language. As the *Courant* articles make clear, Anglo-Saxon English was one of his strengths. Later in his career, Lounsbury's interests would expand further into spelling and pronunciation issues, as well as usage standards. Among his prolific writings are books on all three topics.

William Dwight Whitney came to philology from science rather than literature. He grew up intensely interested in the natural world. As a young man, he shot and mounted a collection of New England birds that he later presented to Yale. He also accompanied his older brother Josiah (after whom California's Mount Whitney is named) on an 1849 geological survey of the area around Lake Superior. William originally planned a career in medicine, but on the first day of his apprenticeship in a doctor's office, he contracted measles. By the time he completed his convalescence, a chance discovery had sent him in a new direction. Browsing among the volumes in Josiah's library one day, William found a book about Sanskrit, the language of traditional Hindu religious and literary texts. Intrigued, he began to read it. Before long he was engrossed in the details of Sanskrit grammar, and had transferred his fascination with classifying from nature to languages.

In 1849 Whitney began training for his new career. First he enrolled in Yale for a year to study with one of the few Sanskrit specialists living in the United States. Next he traveled to Germany to learn from eminent language scholars there. Sanskrit eventually led him to comparative language studies—a key component of philology—and the historical study of English. He made quick strides in his chosen field. In 1854, when he was twenty-seven, Yale offered him a professorship of Sanskrit and related language studies.

A man of medium height who wore a long beard during most of his life, Whitney looked more like a college professor than Lounsbury and had equally impressive scholarly credentials. By 1870, when he and Lounsbury launched their attack on White, he was widely respected both for his work on Sanskrit and his writings on language study generally. In 1867 he published *Language and the Study of Language,* which introduced the latest discoveries of philology to a broad audience. In 1869 he helped found the American Philological Association and became its first president. White was familiar with Whitney's work—he cited Whitney's 1867 book admiringly in *Words and Their Uses* for its negative remarks about cheap newspapers. It was one of the two men's few areas of agreement.

The path from Sanskrit to English usage rules may not seem clear-cut, but in the early decades of the nineteenth century this ancient Indian tongue became the catalyst for a profoundly new approach to analyzing languages. Before then, Sanskrit had been nearly unknown to Europeans. One of the first westerners to learn it was a colonial Indian judge named Sir William Jones. A gifted language scholar, Jones was already fluent in several languages when he arrived in Kolkata (Calcutta) in 1783. He was eager to learn Sanskrit, partly because the literature attracted him, but even more because Sanskrit was the language of the Hindu law code. Most British judges in India relied on interpreters when hearing cases. Sir William wanted to read the laws for himself.

After a few months of lessons, Jones began to notice striking similarities between Sanskrit and the two classical languages of Europe, Latin and Greek. He discovered dozens of words that are similar in form and mean the same thing—Sanskrit *mātar,* Latin *māter,* Greek *mētēr,* "mother"; Sanskrit *pitar,* Latin *pater,* Greek *patēr,* "father"; *pat, pēs, pous,* "foot"; *mam, mē, me,* "me"; and many others. Chance resemblances can occur between words in any two languages, but the similarities in this case were too numerous to make that explanation probable. Furthermore, the words came from the most basic sections of the vocabulary— names for relatives, body parts, numbers, pronouns. Cultures rarely borrow such terms. If those words correspond closely in two languages, the languages are probably historically related.

Sir William also noticed that Sanskrit, Latin, and Greek show similarities in their grammar. For instance, they conjugate verbs in a similar way. The verb *to be* is irregular in all three languages, with forms that look remarkably alike. Sanskrit *asmi, asi, asti*

("I am, you are, he/she is") matches Latin *sum, es, est* and Greek *eimi, ei, esti*. The odds against three unrelated languages displaying such a pattern by chance are astronomical, especially when the languages share many other common features as well.

Describing Sanskrit in a 1786 presentation to fellow members of Kolkata's Asiatic Society, Sir William declared it to be "more perfect than the Greek, more copious than the Latin, and more exquisitely refined than either, yet bearing to both of them a stronger affinity, both in the roots of verbs and in the forms of grammar, than could possibly have been produced by accident." He went on to surmise that the three languages were "sprung from some common source, which, perhaps, no longer exists." He also speculated—correctly, as it would turn out—that Persian, Irish, and Gothic (an extinct German language) belonged in the same group.[13]

Sir William's discovery created a sensation in scientific circles. Others before him had noted that Latin and Greek share many common features, but most people attributed these resemblances to the linguistic intermingling that occurred during centuries of trade and conquest. This explanation didn't work when Sanskrit was added to the mix. Sanskrit speakers would have had little if any contact with the two western cultures of classical times, so vocabulary exchange was extremely unlikely. The simplest explanation for the host of similarities is that Sanskrit, Latin, and Greek are all offshoots of a single much older tongue.

When word of Sir William's theory spread, language scholars were inspired to examine other European languages using his method. They began systematically comparing broad swaths of vocabulary in search of cross-linguistic patterns. Eventually scholars would conclude that most of the languages of Europe and western Asia are related—descended from a "common source" that scholars would name Indo-European. Indo-European originated several thousand years ago, probably in the Russian steppes or somewhere nearby. As its speakers migrated east and west, their once unified language splintered into many distinct languages, but traces of common ancestry are still apparent in the vocabulary and grammar of the descendants. English is a member of this vast language family, part of the Germanic sub-group that also includes German, Dutch, Norwegian, Danish, and Swedish.

Even more inspiring than the discovery of this hidden linguistic relationship was the way that Sir William had reached his conclusions. Word historians of the past like Horne Tooke and Webster usually proceeded with their etymologies word by word, often speculating about a word's origin, then looking for evidence to support their ideas. Sir William's method was closer to comparative anatomy. He looked at the languages in question as systems, and searched for widespread patterns rather than resemblances between specific words. Looking for broad patterns is a surer way to discover linguistic relationships than considering words one at a time because the changes that occur in languages tend to affect certain sounds or grammatical features, not just random words.

When comparing two languages for signs of a connection, the patterns of differences can be as revealing as the similarities. For instance, Latin *pater* and English *father* mean the same thing and are similar enough to be related, but with slightly mismatched sounds, such as the initial *p* and *f*. Comparing a whole range of Latin and English word pairs reveals that the *p/f* mismatch is not unique to *pater* and *father*. It shows up in many word pairs— *pēs/foot, piscis/fish, pūlex/flea, pluit/flow.*

Rather than weakening the case for a historical connection between English and Latin, this difference strengthens the likelihood that they're related. The best explanation is that *pater/ father* and the other pairs each evolved out of a single Indo-European word with the initial sound *p*. (Indo-European words are reconstructed by comparing related words in the descendant languages to determine the most likely original form.) Over time, as English and Latin grew into two distinct languages, the *p* of Indo-European evolved into an English *f*.[14]

The comparative method can also help reveal the history of a single language. A nineteenth-century philologist looking for the origins of *from*, for instance, would use the comparative method to carefully trace versions of the word back through English documents of earlier times, and then through records of other Indo-European languages. He would discover related words in the Germanic languages—Anglo-Saxon *fram*, Old German *fram*, Old Norse *frá*. He would also find the apparently related Latin word *prō*, yet another example of the *p/f* pattern.

This new way of constructing word histories was a clear departure from the Horne Tooke style of free-form theorizing. The study of word histories and language relationships—once a pursuit for individual enthusiasts—grew into an organized discipline with established guidelines and well-researched conclusions. From now on, no one could get away with declaring, as Horne Tooke had once done, that *from* came from a noun that meant "beginning" without providing historical evidence to back up the claim.

Comparative linguistics was slow to arrive in the United States. Part of the reason was simply the sluggish pace of all communications at that time. Sir William's 1786 talk did not appear in print until 1790. Then the print version had to make its way out of India by sail, arriving in Europe some months later before eventually traveling to America. Another roadblock was the devotion of many American language scholars to the writings of Horne Tooke, or in Webster's case, to his own theories. Webster was aware of Jones's work, but skeptical of it. He writes in the introduction to his 1828 dictionary, "It is obvious that Sir W. Jones had given very little attention to the subject [of etymology], and that some of its most common and obvious principles had escaped his observation."[15] As always, Webster preferred his own methods.

By 1870 American scholars were beginning to embrace this new field, although only a few universities, such as Yale, offered classes in the subject. Lounsbury and Whitney were among the earliest American philologists. As they and their colleagues applied the comparative method to the various stages of English, they realized that many of the "rules" proposed by Lowth and later grammarians either weren't based on any historical norm—as in the ban on double negatives—or tried to preserve usages that were becoming obsolete—as in the case of *shall*.

White's verbal analysis, in Lounsbury and Whitney's view, showed the same weaknesses. What he insisted were logical principles seemed to them to be disguised personal preferences. When White talked about word histories—typically while defending his ideas of linguistic purity—he still leaned on the old-fashioned eighteenth-century intuitive method. The two philologists considered his "feel" for English a poor substitute for an informed understanding of its history and development.

White and other popular commentators condemned many reasonable usages based on their own notions of linguistic elegance. Nineteenth-century philologists, like their spiritual forebears the rational grammarians, believed that usage standards should be based on the real structure of English. Lounsbury and Whitney were fighting the same battles that Webster and Fowle had fought decades earlier, but their detailed research into the history of the language provided them with more potent ammunition.

White's position came under attack from more than one direction. In 1872, only a year after the *College Courant* articles appeared, he endured a more prolonged and vicious assault from Fitzedward Hall, an American philologist living in England. Hall's slender book, titled *Recent Exemplifications of False Philology,* is devoted almost entirely to attacking White. Like the *Courant* articles, *False Philology* reflects a new way of thinking about language use.

Fitzedward Hall arrived at philology by an adventurous route. Hall was born in Troy, New York, in 1825, the oldest of six children. As the son of a prosperous lawyer, he received a conventional education. Although the origins of English words always intrigued him, he concentrated on studying mathematics and science, earning a civil engineering degree at the age of seventeen. Four years later he enrolled at Harvard for further education, but before he could begin classes, his younger brother threw the family into an uproar by running away to sea. As the oldest child, twenty-one-year-old Fitzedward was delegated to go after him. He sailed from Boston in the spring of 1846, bound for Kolkata.

Hall's ship wrecked as it sailed into the mouth of the Ganges River, an accident that changed the course of his life. As he was now stranded in Kolkata for the near future, he decided to fill in time by learning Hindustani and Persian (a common second language in nineteenth-century India). He later added lessons in Bengali and Sanskrit. Hall never found his brother, but he did discover a passion for language studies.

Hall stayed in India for over ten years. While there, he married an Englishwoman living in Delhi, taught Sanskrit and English at Government College in Benares, became an inspector of public instruction for the colonial British government, and fought alongside the British during the Indian Rebellion of 1857. All the time, he continued to perfect his knowledge of Sanskrit. He was the first American to edit a Sanskrit text. He also learned as much as he could about philology and the history of English.

When Hall finally left India, he did not return home to the United States, but settled with his family in London. For a while, his life assumed a more conventional shape. He held a professorship of Sanskrit, Hindustani, and Indian jurisprudence at King's College, as well as the post of librarian at the India Office, which oversaw British Indian affairs. Then in 1869 events took another strange turn.

Hall was dismissed from his post of India Office librarian and ejected from the London Philological Society after a controversy concerning the loan of valuable manuscripts in his charge. The details of the scandal are murky. Long after the events, Hall described his firing to an acquaintance by saying that the India Office had wrongly accused him of being a hopeless drunkard and a foreign spy. The public record from the time consists mainly of a series of elliptical letters in the *Atheneaum* from Hall and others, hinting at devious maneuvers and subtle counterploys. After it was all over, Hall escaped to the Suffolk village of Marlesford. A few years later, his marriage broke up. He stayed on in Marlesford alone, resentful and increasingly reclusive.

In this bitter frame of mind, Hall turned to writing about his own language. *Recent Exemplifications of False Philology* is an extended attack on what he terms "the rabble of verbal critics" currently pontificating about English with little knowledge of their subject. Although his book covers many of the same points as Lounsbury and Whitney, their criticisms seem politely reserved compared with Hall.

Hall's writing style manages to be both arcane and outrageous at the same time. He describes the work of White and his like this way: "The criticaster [inferior critic], having looked for a given expression . . . in his dictionary, but without finding it there, or even without this preliminary toil, conceives it to be novel, unauthorized, contrary to analogy, vulgar, superfluous, or what not. Flushed with his precious discovery, he explodes it before the public." Hall intends to expose the fallacies of this "style and temper of philologizing."[16]

Hall starts by examining the ill-considered grammatical comments of several well-known authors, including Coleridge. He takes the same approach as Lounsbury and Whitney, refuting these authors' statements with copious literary examples to the contrary. He presents these mostly in the form of long footnotes. For instance, he refutes Coleridge's criticism of writers who use *whose* for nonhumans (instead of *of which*) by stating that *whose* "has had the support of high authorities for several hundred years." He reinforces this claim with a footnote nearly a page long—a relentless list of quotations that starts with a fifteenth-century manuscript and ends with Samuel Johnson.[17] Hall believes with his fellow philologists that common usage is the only reasonable way to determine whether a word or phrase is acceptable.

After these preliminaries Hall turns to his main business—taking down White. He announces that he intends to review the weaknesses of *Words and Their Uses* in detail in order to show what happens to "one who puts his faith over-confidingly in dictionaries and intuition." Hall has no more patience with intuition than the *College Courant* authors. His way of critiquing White is to quote one of White's usage strictures and then show that it's based on a lack of knowledge about English.

For example, White has pronounced against using *experience* as a verb, claiming that a diligent search turned up only one example of the word in an authoritative source. Hall snaps, "Since 'diligent search' may mean, with Mr. White, industry in turning over the pages of dictionaries, one can scarcely wonder" at his faulty conclusions. Hall's own results have been somewhat different. He says, "How long we have possessed the verb *experience* I cannot say, but as long ago as 1531 it was used by Sir

Thomas Elyot." He follows up with an onslaught of quotations from giants of English literature.[18]

The remainder of the book—nearly one hundred pages—proceeds along similar lines. Like Lounsbury and Whitney, Hall has been struck by White's judgment that "there is a misuse of words which can be justified by . . . no usage, however general." Like them, he considers it nonsensical. He brushes aside White's style judgments with the comment, "His animadversions where original are, I believe, in almost every case, founded either on caprice, on defective information, or on both." Unfortunately, Hall fears that White's writing style is calculated to appeal to the masses. His dogmatism and positiveness, says Hall, are "of that peremptory stamp which insures the prompt submission of the unthinking multitude."[19]

He calls White's belief that speech is the product of reason and logic an "incoherent fiction," pointing out the same problem that the *Courant* authors notice—identical facts may lead people to different conclusions. He phrases it in more colorful terms though. "It is not given to everyone," he sneers, "to enjoy those intimate relations with reason which have been vouchsafed to Mr. White as one of the elect."[20]

Hall sums up his problem with White this way: "Reduced to its simplest expression, the principle on which Mr. White criticizes our language is whim. The very fundamentals of true philology he has still to acquire." In fact, Hall's complaint is the same as Lounsbury and Whitney's—White is not qualified to write about English. Not only do his rules and guidelines contradict normal usage, they show an ignorance of etymology. In order to write a serious book about language use, "it is by no means enough to trust to memory and to pore over dictionaries," says Hall. It's also necessary to read widely and "with the eye of a philologist." Hall surmises that "success in one department of letters has emboldened him to venture his cunning in another department, and one in which he is totally incapable of distinguishing himself."[21]

Hall ends with the unconvincing declaration that he does not feel any personal hostility toward White. His reason for attacking *Words and Their Uses* is the same as Lounsbury and Whitney's—the book has spread grammatical confusion among the uninformed. Otherwise, he insists, White's mistakes "would never have moved me to write in a polemic spirit." He has only done so because they provided a way of offering a few hints on the necessity of "patient inquiry, cautious reflection, and dispassionate judgment" when attempting to practice philology.[22]

Reviews for *False Philology* were mixed. One magazine review begins, "This is a curiously scornful and acrid discussion of questions about the derivation, meaning, and use of words, accompanied with the impalement . . . of Mr. Richard Grant White." The reviewer nonetheless finds the book "stimulating, learned, useful, and almost always correct." Another review is more flattering, suggesting that Hall wrote with "genuine modesty and zeal, for the sake of our old mother tongue." The reviewer praises him for his lack of linguistic extremism, which gives some idea of the intemperate tone of most usage commentary.[23]

The Nation featured a review by William Dwight Whitney, which he used mainly to fight another round of his own with White. Whitney remarks approvingly on the term "false philology," which he thinks accurately describes the "dreary and barren" field of verbal criticism. Of course he also approves of Hall's "pungent and able" criticisms. He spends most of the review, however, skewering the second edition of *Words and Their Uses*, released after Hall wrote *False Philology*. Whitney scoffs at White's new preface, in which White defends himself against Whitney's and other people's previous attacks by saying that he has never made any claim to be a philologist. Whitney doesn't accept this excuse. "In these days of philological light and knowledge," he declares, "no man has the right to come forward and lecture the community on the proprieties of speech, and then try to creep away from adverse criticism under cover of the plea that he is 'no philologist.'"

As far as Whitney can ascertain, White's second edition is merely a longer version of his first edition, "in which the author defends at greater length his old dogma that usage does not govern language." White, just as wrongheaded as ever, still apparently believes in the superiority of his own linguistic judgments. Whitney says ruefully, "If, then, Dr. Hall imagined that his criticisms would have any real effect on his antagonist, he has probably by this time seen his error."[24]

Obviously, White could not allow Hall's attack to pass unnoticed. His answer was a vitriolic three-part *Galaxy* essay of several thousand words titled "Punishing a Pundit." This scathing rejoinder had a twofold aim. White wanted to show that Hall's scholarship was not nearly as impressive as Hall believed it to be, but he also wanted to argue that scholarship isn't what counts when writing about usage. White thought that Hall, like Lounsbury and Whitney, fundamentally misunderstood what it takes to practice verbal criticism. Good taste, good judgment, and a feel for linguistic style are what matter, according to White. He considered Hall lacking in all three, therefore not really qualified to write about the subject.

White's *Galaxy* articles are mostly devoted to picking apart Hall's arguments. Before getting down to cases, however, White takes some time to insult "Dr. Hall" personally. He implies that Hall's decision to live in England even though he's an American has something disreputable about it. He also belittles Hall's scholarly credentials. An English university has seen fit to award Hall a doctorate, but White is "sufficiently familiar with the scholastic essentials to the honorary dignity borne by him not to be unduly impressed by it." He himself saw through the author at a glance, he says, "for even a millstone may be seen through if it has a hole in the middle."

Hall, a man born "without a sense of decency," is nothing more than a verbal critic himself, says White, but one who has the remarkable gall to criticize better writers than he is. White accuses Hall of writing a book not to improve or protect the English language—"not to help his readers to understand it, or to use it with simplicity, clearness and force—but merely to show that he knows everything knowable about it. . . . He, Fitzedward Hall, formerly Vermont Yankee, now British resident . . . Professor of Sanskrit, and Pundit by brevet . . ." He had originally planned to ignore the book, which he felt was beneath his notice. However, since a respectable journal like *The Nation* has thought it appropriate to devote column space to a glowing review, he feels that it's his duty to discuss Hall's book after all.[25]

Hall's excesses offer a tempting target and White scores some bull's-eyes. He jeers at Hall's weakness for ornate words and phrases, writing, "Upon his pages swarm such words as *provection, neoterism, antithet*," and such phrases as "criterion of grammaticalness." White feels that anyone with "a loving sense of real English" would shrink from these pedantic absurdities. He considers Hall's long lists of example quotations pointless, calling them "mere repetitions of this or that word, which are of little or no significance." They are just a way for Dr. Hall to show off.

White also complains with some justification of the "sourness of temper" that leads Hall to "speak injuriously of men for the mere sake of saying something to hurt them." He treats with contempt Hall's assertion that Hall has not attacked White out of vindictiveness. He points out that Hall has searched *Words and Their Uses* "with the eye of a mosquito," even attacking what he must have realized were typographical errors.[26]

White trained an equally intense gaze on Hall's book. He uses most of his two remaining articles making copiously detailed critiques of Hall's arguments and writing style, and pointing out his limitations as a scholar. He uses descriptions like "amazing pretence" and "pompous ignorance." White also makes it clear that he stands by everything he said in *Words and Their Uses*. For instance, he devotes three pages to defending his condemnation of the new word *jeopardize,* even adding to his original arguments.

At the end of this furious assault, White seems satisfied that he has adequately destroyed his enemy's position and can afford to offer one or two backhanded compliments. He gives Hall credit for having "every accomplishment in English except the faculty of understanding and the ability to write it." Hall's learning is considerable, says White, even though he has no "true philological instinct." Finally, White announces that he forgives Hall for his splenetic attack and now, having exposed his critic as a "mere etymologist," is ready to turn his attention to some worthier topic.[27]

In fact, neither White nor Hall showed any sign of retreating from the field. Both remained active partisans in the ongoing conflict between philologists and verbal critics—a conflict that never got any closer to being resolved because neither side could accept the other's basic premises. The two positions may be irreconcilable. Quarrels over the value of specialist's knowledge versus educated taste still blow up regularly, with the issues no nearer to being resolved than they were in Hall and White's day.

The closing paragraphs of White's answer to Hall show how far apart the critics and the philologists really were. White clearly felt that he was making a devastating criticism by calling Hall a "mere etymologist" without literary taste or skill. Hall would not have interpreted that word the same way. From Hall's perspective, etymologists—trained scholars of language—were far more qualified to comment on usage than an amateur like White, however literary he might be. That was the whole point of his attack in *False Philology*. White refused to accept that idea. He considered education and taste the only qualifications necessary for making linguistic judgments. The fact that Hall knew a lot more than he did about the structure of English didn't impress him at all.

None of the 1870s participants in the usage debates ever budged from their original opinions. White's confidence in his own judgment remained unshaken in spite of repeated batterings at the hands of philologists. During the two years following his clash with Hall, he wrote five linked *Galaxy* articles with the title "Linguistic and Literary Notes and Queries." These consist mainly of responses to the many letters he received asking for his opinion on disputed words and grammatical structures. His replies indicate that his linguistic attitudes were as rigid as ever.

White still disapproved of grammar as a subject of formal study. "I wish that so many of my correspondents were not so anxious on the subject," he writes, "so disturbed because sentences won't 'parse,' so solicitous to find a 'rule.'" He reiterates his belief that the best way to learn good English is to "read the best authors and talk with the most cultivated people."[28] White also still believed in applying the criterion of logic to new coinages. Several letter writers have asked him about the word *scientist*, a recent coinage that was becoming popular. He replies that he finds the word "intolerable both as being unlovely in itself and improper in its formation." If anything, the word should be *sciencist*. Even that, however, illogically combines a word derived from Latin (*science*) with a Greek ending (*–ist*). It would be more appropriate to say *man of science*.

He still rejected widespread use as an argument for accepting certain words and phrases. When one correspondent asks him to weigh in on the increasingly agitated "split infinitive" debate, he agrees with the man's description of the usage as a "barbarism of speech." He says, "The examples which [the letter writer] gives are in themselves a condemnation." Then he adds, "Distinguished precedent might be shown for this construction, as for many other bad uses of language; but it is eminently unenglish."[29] For White, a long pedigree was not enough to render a usage respectable English, in spite of what Hall or his colleagues might argue.

White steadily produced books and articles, not only on language, but on Shakespeare, music criticism, and other topics, until shortly before he died in 1885. His second collection of *Galaxy* columns, *Every-Day English,* published in 1880, confirms his unhesitating commitment to his earlier work. Writing about *Words and Their Uses* in the preface, he says, "The views taken in the book in question . . . seem . . . to need no apology or modification; at least I have none to offer."[30] Both books would remain popular with the public well into the twentieth century. Although White encouraged his readers to polish their speech habits by reading good authors and associating with literate people, many obviously considered his books a faster route to achieving their linguistic aims.

Hall also remained in the fray throughout his career. He spent most of his time editing and translating Indian literature and writing on scholarly philological topics, but that didn't stifle his urge to spar with verbal critics. His attacks were not limited to White. In 1880 he published an article in *The Nineteenth Century* magazine titled "English Rational and Irrational." It is a choleric blast against "would-be philologists who collect waifs and strays of antipathies and prejudices, amplify the worthless hoard by their own whimseys, and . . . digest the whole into essays and volumes."[31] The piece doesn't mention White. Instead it attacks several popular writers who have been foolish enough to voice an opinion on word use.

He also engaged in extended combat with Ralph Olmsted

Williams, author of a book about dictionaries. For several years, they traded criticisms and rejoinders in the pages of *The Dial* and *Modern Language Notes*. Most of their discussions concern such nitpicky issues as whether *part from* or *part with* is more correct, with neither man giving much ground.

Hall devoted his last years mainly to unpaid work on Oxford University's new dictionary project. Still hale and energetic, he spent at least four hours a day reading and correcting page proofs and providing example quotations culled from his extensive reading and his own memory. By the time he died in 1901 at the age of seventy-five, he had contributed several thousand quotations to the still unfinished *Oxford English Dictionary*. These included over two thousand examples from the dialect spoken in his adopted home of Suffolk.

Whitney also continued to write about usage, although he concentrated on scholarly work. He produced grammars of Sanskrit, German, and French, as well as a second book of modern linguistic thought titled *The Life and Growth of Language*. He also edited *The Century Dictionary*, an important resource for later dictionary makers, including the editors of the *Oxford English Dictionary*. Illness forced him to retire in 1886 and he died eight years later, aged sixty-seven.

Seven years after the *Courant* articles appeared, Whitney published a textbook called *Essentials of English Grammar*. The book is an unusual melding of modern linguistic insights with traditional notions of proper speech. In his opening remarks, Whitney says, "It has been my constant endeavor to bear in mind the true position of the grammarian . . . that he is simply a recorder and arranger of the usages of language, and in no manner or degree a lawgiver."[32] He notes that he has provided only a very few "set rules." He believes that the point of studying a grammar of one's own language is to gain an understanding of the linguistic principles involved. Rote memorization won't help students toward that goal. Throughout the book Whitney makes an effort to explain the why as well as the how of English usage.

He explains that the point of grammar books is to help students recognize the difference between "good English" and "bad English." He defines good English as "those words, . . . and those ways of putting them together, which are used by the best speakers, the people of best education." Bad English is whatever those speakers avoid. Whitney reminds students that "grammar does not at all make rules and laws for language. It only reports the facts of good language." Grammar books, he suggests, should be used more as reference guides than instructional manuals.[33]

Whitney's advice here almost echoes White's plea to his readers to be less "solicitous to find 'a rule.'" Both men believed in a standard for English and both thought it should be based on "the best speakers." The difference lay in how they determined the best speech. Whitney looked to the common everyday usages of reasonably educated people, especially when those usages were backed up by literary precedent. White proposed standards based mainly on his own feelings about individual words and grammatical constructions, without regard for how well established or widespread they were.

In practice, Whitney was almost as conventional as White. In his book he lists the usual parts of speech with familiar definitions—a noun is "the name of anything." He also includes parsing exercises that are recognizably related to those found in earlier books, although with more linguistic explanation. For instance, *brother* in one example sentence is parsed as "a noun, because it is the name of something . . . ; a common noun, because it belongs alike to every individual of a class; . . . masculine, because it denotes only a male being."

Although he doesn't give students "set rules" to memorize, he doesn't invite them to break the rules, either. All his grammar choices are orthodox. He identifies noun cases by their old-fashioned names, including dative and vocative. His examples feature the pronouns of standard grammar, such as nominatives in comparative phrases—*he is a better man than I.* He uses *whom* and keeps it with its preposition—*To whom did you speak?* rather than the more colloquial *Who did you speak to?* In any event, *Essentials of English Grammar* must have seemed conventional enough overall to appeal to a significant number of teachers. It went through eighteen editions between 1877 and 1903.[34]

Lounsbury, Whitney's onetime collaborator, enjoyed a long and versatile career, remaining active until his sudden death in 1915 at the age of seventy-seven. Like Whitney, he continued to write about usage while focusing on other scholarship. He wrote books about several authors, including Chaucer, Shakespeare, and James Fenimore Cooper. He became increasingly interested in American spelling and served as president of the Simplified Spelling Board beginning in 1907. He also wrote numerous language-related articles for *Harper's.* In 1908, several of these would be collected into a book, thus hurtling nineteenth-century grammatical controversies into the twentieth century with no loss of momentum.

All the participants in the usage debates routinely garnered admiring reviews. Equal respect did not lead to equal sales figures, however—the verbal critics were incomparably more popular with the book-buying public. While Whitney's textbook sold reasonably well, its sales numbers didn't begin to touch those for White's books. Both *Words and Their Uses* and *Every-Day English* went through printing after printing and were still available in the 1920s. Other word use books—for instance, *The Verbalist* by Alfred Ayres—were also reprinted dozens of times. In contrast, *Recent Exemplifications of False Philology* never rated a second printing.

The philologists complained that White and other verbal critics didn't provide objective standards or a broader context for judging good usage. Most readers, however, thought the critics offered something much better—specific instructions for what to say or not say. Hall was right in predicting that White's "dogmatism and positiveness" would make a deeper impression on the minds of the grammatically insecure than the cogent, but subtle, arguments of the philologists.

At the turn of the nineteenth century, working-class Americans memorized Murray's grammar to give themselves linguistic confidence as they climbed the social ladder. White's books fulfilled a similar purpose for their post–Civil War descendants. For those people, maintaining a solid social position meant heeding White's pronouncements on split infinitives and other slippery usage issues.

Meanwhile, far from the linguistic front lines, grammar teaching proceeded much as it had always done. Public fights about what constituted standard English didn't filter down into the classroom. Although some schools experimented with new ways of teaching grammar, or with not teaching the subject at all, most still felt the need of a conventional textbook. In 1878, one year after Whitney brought out *Essentials of English Grammar,* a book appeared that was destined to have a much more lasting impact on the course of grammar studies than either Whitney and his fellow linguists or their adversaries the verbal critics.

Higher Lessons in English by Alonzo Reed and Brainerd Kellogg signaled a new era in the classroom. The book incorporates some popular teaching trends of the time. The authors discourage rote memorization and only define parts of speech after describing them and giving examples. They emphasize inductive reasoning, feeding students information a little at a time. For instance, they begin their lesson on sentences by explaining that sentences express a thought. Then they encourage students to explore the concept of sentences, leading them eventually to the idea that a sentence consists of two main parts—a word or phrase about which something is said, and what is said about it. Only then do they provide definitions for the terms *sentence, subject,* and *predicate.*

The book made its strongest impact with a novel idea for identifying the pieces of a sentence. To help students visualize the relationships between the various words and phrases, Reed and Kellogg introduced a technique called sentence diagramming. Sentence diagrams indicate the connections between words—subject, direct object, modifier, and so on—using a system of horizontal, vertical, and slanted lines. Diagramming is a comparatively fast and uncomplicated way to analyze sentences. Instead of tediously writing out the information that a word is a noun, the subject of a particular verb, and so on, students could simply draw a horizontal line under the subject and the verb and then draw a short, straight vertical line to separate the two. Other lines would connect modifiers to the main subject and verb. Once completed, the diagram gave students a clear picture of a sentence's internal structure.[35]

Although Reed and Kellogg's book added a new twist to grammar lessons, its grammatical information was safely orthodox. The authors issue their rules in the form of cautions, but the content is still the same. Their caution for negating sentences is stated, "Unless you wish to *affirm,* do not use two negative words so that they shall contradict each other." When discussing adverbs, they write, "Caution. . . . They should not stand between *to* and the infinitive." In their section on pronouns, they explain in a footnote that while some people have defended *It is me,* "a course of reading will satisfy any one that the best writers and speakers in England are not in the habit of using such expressions . . . and that they are almost, if not quite, unknown in American literature."[36] (The latter assertion is questionable. Webster had noted nearly a century earlier that *It is me* was common in America, at least in spoken speech. While the usage was obviously still deprecated among grammar sticklers, it's doubtful whether it was any less common in 1878.)

Grammar teachers enthusiastically adopted this innovative teaching tool. Well into the next century, grade-school students would be put to work diagramming sentences, with *Higher Lessons in English* going through twenty-one editions between 1878 and 1913. At the same time, all the traditional grammar rules remained firmly in place. Reed-Kellogg diagrams have never completely gone away. Although sentence diagramming has not been part of the standard curriculum in recent decades, some teachers still introduce their students to diagrams, drawing on lessons from their own school days. Online parsers can also be found that will generate diagrams automatically.[37]

By the early decades of the twentieth century, philologists, grammar teachers, and verbal critics inhabited separate worlds. Philology—soon to be called linguistics—prospered as a scholarly discipline. At the same time, it nearly disappeared from the public conversation about language use. While specialists in university linguistics departments explored the history and structure of English, grade-school students absorbed the same grammar rules that their parents and grandparents had learned. Double negatives and sentence-ending prepositions were still absolutely wrong in most people's minds.

Adults who needed usage advice continued to turn to popular magazines and style guides such as White's. The "antipathies and prejudices" that Hall castigated changed from year to year—*jeopardize* and *pants* soon entered the standard vocabulary—but they never disappeared. Seekers after linguistic wisdom could always find some list of questionable words or grammar mistakes to avoid. Lowth and Murray had weathered their most powerful challenge yet and come through largely unscathed.

7.

Grammar for a New Century

On March 4, 1905, seventy-six years after Andrew Jackson was inaugurated as the "people's president," the east lawn of the Capitol was once again the scene of tumultuous celebration. By early morning, thousands of festive, jostling men, women, and children had gathered around the inaugural platform in front of the building's East Portico. The crowd stretched back nearly to the Library of Congress a block away. More people thronged nearby Pennsylvania Avenue. According to one witness, people were wedged together so tightly that "only the tops of their heads could be seen."

The mood was jubilant. Even the biting winds and threat of a shower didn't dim the crowd's enthusiasm. They were here to cheer on their hero, Theodore Roosevelt—or Teddy, as they called him. They had just elected him president and were waiting to see him take the oath of office later in the day.[1]

Roosevelt had already served as president for nearly four years. As William McKinley's vice president, he stepped into the presidency when McKinley was assassinated by an anarchist in 1901. President Roosevelt was a success from the start. When the 1904 election came around, voters swept him back into office, in the words of *The New York Times,* "with a degree of acclamation such as was never before given to a candidate for the Presidency."[2] Roosevelt won by the widest popular vote margin since Madison ran unopposed in 1820 and the largest majority of electoral votes since Andrew Jackson crushed Henry Clay in 1832.

Voters took to Roosevelt for some of the same reasons that an earlier generation had loved Jackson. Like Jackson, Roosevelt was a war hero. Americans thrilled to his daring exploits with the Rough Riders during the recent Spanish-American War, including the famous charge up Cuba's San Juan Hill. Although Roosevelt was not a born frontiersman like Jackson, he seemed like one. He had owned a ranch in the Dakota Territory and hunted buffalo and other big game. He was as tough and skilled in the outdoors as Jackson had been in his day.

The two men shared another important trait as well. They spoke to the voters in down-to-earth language that was unpolished but compelling. Old Hickory had not gone in much for fancy rhetoric, and neither did Teddy. Although Republican Party insiders considered Roosevelt too volatile, ordinary Americans loved his robust ways and forceful, slangy speech.

At ten o'clock on inauguration day, Roosevelt's open carriage, drawn by four matched bays, started on its journey from the White House to the Capitol. As the carriage with its honor guard of Rough Riders rolled down Pennsylvania Avenue, the multitudes lining the street let out a roar loud enough to be heard by those waiting on the east lawn almost a mile away. Men threw their hats into the air and women waved handkerchiefs. Another three hours would pass before the actual swearing in. Preliminary ceremonies, including the swearing in of Vice President Charles Fairbanks, were scheduled to take place in the relative privacy of the Senate chamber. In the meantime, the crowd milled around, munching sandwiches and watching the weather.

Another ear-splitting cheer went up shortly before one o'clock, when Roosevelt finally strode out of the East Portico onto the inaugural platform. The president emanated vitality, with a stocky, muscular body, military moustache, and square, white teeth that were a gift to political cartoonists. By this time, the morning's clouds had given way to bright sunshine. "Roosevelt weather," everyone agreed—"Roosevelt's luck."

After the brief oath-taking ceremony, Roosevelt gave his inaugural address, one of the shortest on record. The blustery winds carried most of the words away from the crowd, but it really didn't matter. The content of Roosevelt's message—a call to commit to the duties of citizenship—wasn't as important as the style of delivery. One spectator who stood close to the platform later commented that he only heard eight words of the speech. He did receive a clear impression of the speaker though—"a strong man in dead earnest saying the things that he believed from the bottom of his heart."[3]

Even Roosevelt's supporters agreed that he was not a born orator. He spoke in a high-pitched shout and jumped from topic to topic. "It does not seem to me . . . that Mr. Roosevelt is a persuasive speaker," opines the author of an article on political speechmaking. "He always gets an uproarious response; but this is not a tribute to his oratory, it is awarded the man."[4]

Roosevelt was not overcareful about grammar, either, any more than Jackson had been. One journalist remarks on his "too great use, perhaps, of the split infinitive, an ambiguous use of pronouns or participles, or some other carelessness in syntactical matters." Another commentator marvels at Roosevelt's ability to get away with all kinds of "blunders and mistakes, errors of judgment and of taste," including many "absurdities of language." He complains that Roosevelt "dismisses subjects of gravity and importance with a last word in the slang of the streets. He is 'delighted' to see people, he has 'corking' good times, and his enemies and opponents he 'beats to a frazzle,' 'pounds to a pulp' or 'wipes off the map.'"[5]

These critics missed the point. To most of Roosevelt's supporters, his taste for slang and punchy metaphors was not a problem—it was a plus. They thought that his knack for producing just the right memorable word or phrase more than compensated for any weaknesses as a formal speaker. The Roosevelt era, like the age of Jackson, was a moment when slang and casual speech came into their own. Americans' love of inventive colloquial language seemed close to overcoming their commitment to grammar and proper word use.

Roosevelt embraced this trend with gusto. His speeches were peppered with dramatic terminology. Those whose points of view he disdained were labeled *muckrakers, parlor Bolsheviks,* or *the lunatic fringe.* He summarized his approach to foreign policy with the pithy advice, "Speak softly and carry a big stick." His colorfully aggressive speech—slang-whanging, Jackson's friend David Crockett would have called it—captured the American public's imagination. As with Crockett's backwoods idioms, it made a much more lasting impression than carefully grammatical formal phrases would have done.

Roosevelt's background and early life could hardly have been more different from Jackson's. While Jackson hailed from the Tennessee backwoods, Roosevelt was born in a spacious New York brownstone to a wealthy and old-established family. Growing up, he was privately tutored until he entered Harvard at seventeen. Unlike Jackson, who never picked up a book for pleasure, Roosevelt read constantly. He even carried books on hunting trips. He was fascinated with natural history and considered a career as a scholar in that field.

Roosevelt also wrote easily and prolifically—books and articles spilled off his pen almost continuously throughout his life. He published his first piece of writing while still at Harvard—a pamphlet cataloging the summer birds of the Adirondacks. He authored over forty books on a wide range of subjects, from hunting memoirs to a history of the War of 1812. Perhaps his best-known work, the four-volume *Winning of the West,* appeared a few years before his election to the vice presidency.

Roosevelt also wrote dozens of articles about topics as varied as the art of Frederick Remington, wolf hunting in Oklahoma, and the meaning of American citizenship. After he left the presidency, he became a contributing editor to *The Outlook.* Even while in office, he wrote articles for *The Outlook, Scribner's,* and other magazines. (Although it's not obvious from his finished writing, he did struggle with spelling, as had Jackson. He supported the Simplified Spelling Board and tried unsuccessfully while president to require that all government documents be written in simplified spelling.)[6]

Several of Roosevelt's favorite words and expressions have become part of America's political vernacular. He frequently used *bully,* which had acquired the slang meaning of admirable or first rate around the middle of the nineteenth century (as in the congratulatory *Bully for you*). More than once Roosevelt pointed out to friends that the presidency provided "a bully pulpit"—that is, a first-rate platform—for airing his views. The term evidently made a deep impression on those who heard him use it. Several mentioned it in later reminiscences. One close associate, for instance, remembered gathering in Roosevelt's office with half a dozen others while the president read out the draft of a forthcoming speech. After one tub-thumping paragraph, Roosevelt paused. The narrator recalled that the president swung around in his swivel chair to look at his audience while remarking, "I suppose my critics will call that preaching, but I have got such a bully pulpit."[7]

Another of Roosevelt's expressions that outlasted his time is *malefactors of great wealth.* He invented the term to describe corporations or wealthy individuals who behaved unethically, and used it in both speeches and writing. During a 1907 address, for example, he spoke of the government's continued determination "to punish certain malefactors of great wealth." In an *Outlook* editorial, Roosevelt attacked "the big newspaper, owned or controlled by Wall Street, . . . which is quite willing to hound politicians for their misdeeds, but which . . . defends all the malefactors of great wealth."[8] The president found that this and other trenchant coinages were highly effective at getting his point across.

Roosevelt made his final contributions to the political vocabulary during his unsuccessful 1912 attempt to retake the presidency. In the excitement of his 1904 victory, Roosevelt had rashly declared that because he had already served nearly four years as McKinley's replacement, he wouldn't run again. Instead, he handpicked a successor, Secretary of War William Taft. Taft and Roosevelt were close friends and allies at that time. Unfortunately, the good will didn't last. Roosevelt believed that his friend had betrayed his policies and the two men parted ways. As the 1912 election drew near, Roosevelt decided that in spite of his promise, he should run once more.

Typically, he announced his intention with a striking metaphor. When a reporter asked him if he had decided yet whether to run, he answered with language from his boxing days—"My hat is in the ring!" he cried. "The fight is on and I am stripped to the buff." Throwing a hat in the ring had been an actual boxing activity since the early nineteenth century. Professional boxers earned money by traveling to county fairs and other venues and offering to take on all comers. A man interested in accepting the challenge threw his hat into the boxing ring, presumably because a shout or raised hand might not have been noticed in the ringside chaos. Before 1912, *hat in the ring* appeared frequently in magazine and newspaper descriptions of fights. Now it exists entirely as a political metaphor, thanks to Roosevelt.

Roosevelt, who still commanded legions of followers, won the majority of the primaries—there were only about a dozen in those days. However, Taft controlled the Republican Party machinery.

He made sure that state nominating conventions committed all their delegates to him, guaranteeing him the nomination. Roosevelt ran as the candidate of the breakaway Bull Moose Party, named for his boast that he was as strong as a bull moose. During the campaign, the former president, obviously fighting fit, continued his habit of hurling pungent language at opponents. He excoriated Taft as a "fathead" with brains "less than a guinea pig." He likened Democratic candidate Woodrow Wilson's demeanor to that of "an apothecary's clerk." One journalist described Roosevelt's campaign speeches as "a fierce onslaught.... He is not there to persuade his antagonists, but to break their heads."[9]

Wilson, a former president of Princeton, spoke in a very different style. "Mr. Wilson has long been known as an exquisite master of English prose," gushes one political writer. He adds that in spite of Wilson's "classical habit of language," he uses "simple words and strong words, but seldom slang." Roosevelt thought Wilson's measured rhetoric masked bad intentions. Later, when President Wilson hesitated to bring the United States into World War I, Roosevelt accused him of misleading Americans with "a shadow dance of words." Roosevelt declared, "He has covered his fear of standing for the right behind a veil of rhetorical phrases."[10]

Many 1912 voters no doubt preferred Roosevelt's fiery, if roughedged, oratory over Wilson's careful phrases, but the political logistics were against him. Republican Party loyalists who would ordinarily have supported Roosevelt voted for Taft as the party's nominee. The resulting split in Republican votes assured Wilson's victory. After the 1912 election, Roosevelt retired from public life and Americans had to adjust to presidential language that was much more sedate. He left behind a legacy of political words and expressions that still resonate today.

Part of Roosevelt's political genius was to recognize voters' enjoyment of lively, piquant language. Although often warring with a desire to speak correctly, this appreciation has remained an enduring aspect of American culture. Grammar books could never entirely root it out. In the early nineteenth century, David Crockett rose to fame on the strength of his Tennessee folk speech. At the beginning of the twentieth century, Roosevelt used "the slang of the streets" to get to the White House.

The Roosevelt era was a good time for slang users. Casual language was more widespread and more accepted than ever before. One reason was the proliferation of popular novels and magazine stories that pepped up their dialogue with slang, jargon, and regional speech. These included the form of mass entertainment known as the "dime novel."

Dime novels had been available since the 1860s. Cheaply printed and flimsily bound, these magazine-like volumes were intended to appeal to a broad audience. In spite of the name, many of the books cost only a nickel, making them affordable for working-class people. Readers of all classes and ages enjoyed them, though, from school-age children to educated adults. The most popular sold in the tens of thousands and were reissued multiple times. Although dime novels reached their sales floodtide during the late 1800s, they were still a favored choice of reading matter at the turn of the century.

Dime novels specialized in stories of adventure, romance, and suspense. Many of the books appeared in series. The series recounting the adventures of schoolboy Frank Merriwell was among the most popular. Two other bestselling series featured private detective Nick Carter and famous rodeo star Buffalo Bill. Dime-novel genres included westerns, detective stories, school stories for boys, spy stories, and travel tales, complete with sensational cover illustrations and highly colored double titles, such as *Frank Merriwell in Gorilla Land, or the Search for the Missing Link.*

Part of what made these books so entertaining was their jaunty dialogue. *Frank Merriwell in Gorilla Land* includes such catch phrases as *dead as a door-nail* and *my blood freezes.* Characters behave badly by "cutting out" a rival and "kicking up" trouble. Frank's sidekick is a Vermonter named Ephraim Gallup, whose regional dialect runs to down-home phrases such as *gol dern it, by gum,* and *dinged ef that don't beat all.* A Nick Carter story titled "The Call of Death, or Nick Carter's Clever Assistant" is rich with crime jargon. Nick tosses around terms such as *mug shot, easy mark, bad egg,* and *the straight goods.* He says dismissively of an unsuccessful crook, "He could not frame up and pull off a job of any size . . . if his life depended on it."[11]

More serious authors also added color to their narratives with slang and local speech. Mark Twain's stories are full of western and southern regionalisms, folksy expressions, and uneducated usages. His most famous character, Huckleberry Finn, narrates his adventures in his own distinctive idiom. Huck says *ain't* and *clumb,* and *real swell,* and uses *set* for *sit* and *learn* for *teach.* He also makes lavish use of double negatives—*It warn't no use, I didn't mean no harm.* Not only were Twain's stories popular with the reading public, most reviewers were charmed by his effective portrayal of colloquial speech. Only one or two deplored his linguistic "coarseness."

The realist author William Dean Howells, although less known than Mark Twain today, was another respected writer of the 1880s whose characters often expressed themselves informally. In his 1889 novel *A Hazard of New Fortunes,* an unsophisticated young woman from a natural-gas boomtown in the Midwest startles New Yorkers with expressions such as *I reckon* and *as cross as two sticks.* She drops the –g in words like *goun', dyun', meetun'.* She describes her hometown of Moffitt as "a real live town." A magazine writer of her acquaintance wonders whether he dare represent the young woman in a story, "just as she is, with all her slang and brag," and decides that she would have to be toned down to be believable.[12] Another character, an entrepreneur named Fulkerson, energizes his speech with racy expressions like *from the word go, first rate, natural-born,* and *Ta ta!*

In the turn-of-the-century works of George Ade, slang vaulted from a supporting role to stardom. Ade is now obscure, but his stories and plays drew enthusiastic audiences when they were new. Originally from Indiana, Ade moved to Chicago in 1890 and began writing for the *Morning News.* He loved to roam the Chicago streets, chatting with all sorts of people from shopgirls to newsboys to policemen on the beat. He soaked up jargon and cant expressions and turned them into literary gold.

Ade began writing very short stories that he called "slang fables." These preserved the formal tone of real fables, but replaced their archaic language with current slang. The lengthy titles are reminiscent of dime novels—"The Fable of the Kid Who Shifted His Ideal," "The Fable of Paducah's Favorite Comedians and the Mildewed Stunt," "The Fable of the Copper and the Jovial Undergrads."

"The Fable of the Preacher Who Flew His Kite, but not because He Wished to Do So" is typical of Ade's stories. It opens with the line, "A certain preacher became wise to the fact that he was not making a hit with his congregation. . . . He suspected that they were rapping him on the quiet." The preacher concludes that his congregation is unimpressed with his straightforward sermons because he doesn't use enough fancy Latin words and arcane biblical allusions. He decides that to prove "he was a nobby and boss minister, he would have to hand out a little guff." He duly dresses up his sermons with quotations from fake Icelandic poets and other made-up sources. Sure enough, the pew holders think it is "hot stuff." The story ends with the preacher's parishioners "boosting" his salary in appreciation.[13]

Besides his slang fables, Ade also wrote plays. His built his plots around homey topics like football, small-town politics, and college life. All the plays feature liberal doses of casual speech—terms like *gee whiz, pinhead, rube, done for,* and *ain't.* Ade's slang-filled extravaganzas drew packed houses week after week. It seemed that Americans couldn't get enough of their native tongue at its most vulgar. Ade's skill at manipulating the speech of the streets allowed him to retire a rich man.

While writers were taking advantage of colloquial words and phrases to amuse their audiences, language scholars were beginning to study nonstandard language and regional dialects more seriously. In 1889 a group of English and linguistics professors, writers, and other interested people met at Harvard to organize the American Dialect Society. Their purpose was "the investigation of the English dialects in America, with regard to pronunciation, grammar, vocabulary, phraseology, and geographical distribution." The organization drew 140 members the first year.

Dialect Society members believed that "the real life of language is found only in the folk dialects." They turned the traditional thinking about language on its head by declaring that dialects are not "corruptions," as were previously thought, but "the native and natural growths" of everyday speech. From their perspective, it is the standard that's "semi-artificial." A 1912 leaflet explaining the Society's position notes that "most persons are prone to look upon [dialectal] variations as . . . 'bad grammar.' . . . The truth is, however, that these variations represent one of the most important groups or classes of facts on which the scientific study of language rests."[14]

Society members launched an ambitious program of language collection and began planning a dictionary of American words. In the meantime, they published their findings in the periodical *Dialect Notes.* A typical issue of *Dialect Notes* might include a list of several dozen college slang terms; lists of colloquial expressions, vocabulary words, and pronunciations unique to a specific region; the jargon of fringe groups like hobos and circus people; and historical vocabulary from pioneer diaries or obscure folk songs. A volume from 1908, for example, features a list of regionalisms from East Alabama, including the nonstandard verbs *brung, et, drownded, cotched,* and *used to could;* local words like *y'all, yonder,* and *bodacious;* and metaphorical expressions like *sit on the anxious bench* (be nervous).

Many of the words and expressions that the Society assiduously recorded were appearing in print for the first time. In some cases they were retrieved as they were disappearing from daily speech. Grammarians and language experts of earlier days would only have recorded such nonstandard forms to warn their readers against using them. More likely, however, they wouldn't have felt a need to mention these words at all—everyone knew they constituted bad English and should be avoided.

The Dialect Society sought this language out. Members combed old documents, newspapers, letters and diaries, and out-of-print novels in search of America's submerged linguistic past. They sent out hundreds of questionnaires to colleges around the country. They advertised for speakers willing to give interviews. For the first time, the language that fell outside the boundaries of grammar books was being treated with respect. (The American Dialect Society is still going strong today. Its early regional word lists are incorporated in the recently completed five-volume *Dictionary of American Regional English.*)

Slang was gaining a newfound respectability even among those fierce cultural monitors, the editors of mainstream magazines. A 1909 *Scribner's* editorial, discussing a bill in the New York legislature that outlaws "joy riding," offers the opinion that "the wealth of language comes from below." Some readers might feel concern at the legislature's enshrinement of the term *joy riding,* but the author of the editorial approves. Speaking of slang, he says, "This enrichment of the American tongue is probably reckless, but certainly picturesque and often approaches the higher realms of poetry and philosophy."[15]

An *Atlantic* writer concurs. "All language which grows out of a man's instinct . . . is beautifully interesting, wholesome, and spirited," he says. Forcing people into an artificial linguistic formality is generally a mistake, in this writer's view. "Everybody talks well when he talks in the way he likes . . . the rest is effort and pretense," he argues. Some people use more elevated words naturally, and there is nothing wrong with that. If a man speaks naturally of "trousers," well and good. However, the author declares, "The man who says 'trousers' when he wants to say 'pants' is a craven and a truckler."[16]

The editors of *The Living Age* tell readers that a letter writer has scolded them for using the word *swashbuckling*. They admit that the word is slang, but point out in their defense that many of the words that the best speakers now take for granted started out as nonstandard innovations. If the word is coming into common use, that must mean there's a demand for it. They remind their disgruntled correspondent, "All language is but the invention of man for his own convenience. . . . We should be the poorer if we kept out all ill-formed words."[17]

Naturally, some writers dissented from this enlightened stance. Ambrose Bierce offers "Some Sober Words on Slang" in a 1907 commentary for *Cosmopolitan*. Slang, he explains, once defined the jargon used by thieves, peddlers, vagabonds, and other lowlifes. Now it means something different and "more offensive"— the "intolerable diction of respectable persons who obey all laws but those of taste." Although often originating among the lower and criminal classes, these words and expressions become part of the normal vocabulary. They may even be formerly ordinary words that have acquired new, "extravagantly metaphorical" meanings. "It is not altogether comprehensible how a sane intelligence can choose to utter itself in that kind of speech," muses

Bierce. Then he voices the still-common concern that nonetheless, "speech of that kind seems almost to be driving good English out of popular use."

Bierce is especially outraged by the continued popularity of George Ade's *Fables in Slang,* which he denigrates as "unspeakable stuff." He complains that slang has taken the place of wit, and writing such as Ade's has replaced more intelligently satirical essays. He continues, "Slang has as many hateful qualities as a dog bad habits, but its essential vice is its hideous lack of originality." A piece of slang may sound clever the first time it's used, but after that it becomes repetitive and boring.

Bierce ends his comment by relating in scandalized tones the story of a learned professor who has recently suggested that if the author of the Scriptures were alive in the early twentieth century, he would no doubt enliven his writing with current slang. He might, for instance, replace "possessed of a devil" with "bats in the belfry." Bierce remarks stiffly, "I should not care for his Revised Edition."[18]

Others agreed with Bierce. One article writer repines, "We read of the Stone Age, the Gospel Age, the Golden Age to Come . . . but that we are today living in what may pertinently be termed the Slang Age is an undeniable fact. The fearful inroads that are being made on pure English by this wily intruder is . . . deplorable in the extreme." A short piece in another magazine presents a list of words and phrases including *beat it, sure, classy, it's a cinch, peachy,* and *nutty,* with the recommendation that anyone using them be liable for a prison sentence.

A periodical aimed at young people also suggests that slang users be punished, although more mildly. The editors advise girls to form "diary clubs" and meet once a week or so to read their diaries out loud. A public airing of their writing will encourage them to avoid low expressions like *she don't* and *I haven't got any.* If these and similar phrases creep in by accident, the guilty one can pay a small fine that will later be used to buy refreshments for all the club members.[19]

In spite of Americans' increased pride in their vernacular, large numbers of people still worried about correct usage. Like slang, the topic was controversial. As America's endless grammar discussion crossed into the new century, it began taking on the familiar contours still apparent today. On one side were the linguists, who focused on recording American English and describing it from a specialist's point of view. On the other side were the usage critics, worried that linguists' neutral approach to the language would open the door to a grammatical free-for-all and the death of old standards.

Thomas Lounsbury, now retired after thirty-five years of teaching, was still writing about usage for the subscribers to *Harper's* magazine. In 1908 he collected several of his *Harper's* articles in a book titled *The Standard of Usage in English,* a volume that would no doubt have infuriated Richard Grant White had he been around to read it. In the preface, Lounsbury reaffirms the principles that he laid down in his *College Courant* essays nearly four decades earlier. When it comes to deciding how to speak, he still believes that the "authority of great writers" counts for more than the "confident assertions of the more or less imperfectly trained . . . persons who profess to show us what we are to do and what we are to refrain from doing." He also still thinks that as a grammarian he should be a "historian," not an "advocate."[20]

Lounsbury's attacks on language reactionaries in *The Standard of Usage in English* have a recognizably modern flavor. Although grammar radicals of earlier times were equally committed to refuting what they saw as linguistic nonsense, they weren't above indulging their own prejudices. Much of Webster's advice about proper pronunciation and word use was based on nothing more solid than his belief in the superiority of the New England dialect. He also relied on his own fanciful notions of etymology when classifying parts of speech.

Lounsbury aimed for a higher standard of objectivity. He rarely admitted to any personal grammatical tastes. Nor did he try to imagine how English would change in the future or offer suggestions for its improvement. He restricted himself to analyzing the language based on its known history and current actual use. His main goal was to counter widespread linguistic myths with demonstrable facts.

The book's first chapter, titled "Is English Becoming Corrupt?" takes on the perennial belief that the language is in a state of collapse and failing fast. Both Lounsbury's outline of the problem and his counterarguments still sound familiar. He starts by describing the "grammatical sentinels . . . on the watch-towers, ready to raise the cry of warning or alarm" at the first sign of linguistic corruption. There is nothing new about "these foretellers of calamity," he assures readers. They have always been with us and he suspects that they always will be.[21] (Lounsbury's prediction is true so far. Concerns about the disintegration of English still pop up regularly in twenty-first-century newspapers and grammar blogs.)

What's more, he says, this sort of fretting displays a kind of sameness over time. Grammatical worriers always start with the assumption that English enjoyed a golden age that's now in the past. They always blame the same culprits for recent linguistic decline—slang, unnecessary new words, ungrammatical locutions, foreign phrases. They declare that slipshod speech is becoming more acceptable, not only in daily life but in published writing. They inevitably attribute this sorry state of things to ignorance and moral decline.

Lounsbury concedes that in the past the "foretellers of calamity" had some excuse for their wailings because little was known about the forces that affect language. With the discoveries of modern philology, the situation has changed. We now know, he explains, that language is constantly evolving. Words gain or lose meanings or disappear from the language entirely. Grammatical forms shift, or become more or less acceptable. It's not possible to freeze a language in some perfect state unless, like Latin, nobody speaks it anymore. In any case, Lounsbury says, attempts to rescue English are pointless. Verbal critics of earlier times had no effect on language-use trends. Words and expressions that they deplored (like *scientist*) became standard anyway, while words that they championed (like *jeopard*) slipped out of use. He doubts that today's critics will have any better luck.

Lounsbury then moves on to a critique of traditional grammar books that, except for its slightly old-fashioned wording, might have been written by a linguist today. "Since the middle of the eighteenth century," he writes, when grammar books "first began to . . . exert distinct influence, far the larger proportion of them have been produced by men who had little acquaintance with . . . the history and development of grammatical forms and constructions." Because of their lack of knowledge, they substituted artificial rules for informed descriptions of actual usage. Later grammar arbiters repeated these rules in their books and eventually, he concludes, "a fictitious standard of usage" was established.[22]

In Lounsbury's view, the real danger to English doesn't lie in any potential tendency toward grammatical lawlessness and corruption. Instead the danger comes from the "amateur champions of propriety" who wage wars of "ignorant formalism and empty precision" against the natural development of the language. Such strictures amount to nothing more than personal preferences. If "a particular individual dislikes a particular word or phrase," remarks Lounsbury tartly, "that is one of the best of reasons why he should not employ it himself; it is not a very cogent reason for inducing others to follow his example."[23]

Later in the book, Lounsbury restates his long-held position, founded on his philological training, that the only workable way to establish proper usage guidelines is by taking into account the actual speech habits of respected writers and other educated people. He repeats the idea that he first stated in the *Courant*—"good usage is not something to be evolved from one's own consciousness, or to be deduced by some process of reasoning; it is something to be ascertained." He sums up, "Whatever is in usage is right."[24]

In the early twentieth century, that sentiment was more acceptable than it would have been in Webster's day, but still far from universal. Because Lounsbury was a respected public writer on language, *The Standard of Usage* received some favorable notice from serious reviewers. One writes, "[Lounsbury's] clear analysis and sound deductions ought to make this work rank high among the productions of modern American scholarship." Another reviewer observes, "Ancient superstitions die hard. . . . There was a call for a book . . . which should declare that English . . . does not need a guardian."[25]

A third reviewer, however, has a contrary perspective. All in all, he considers the book "excellent reading as well as sound doctrine," but he is disappointed by Lounsbury's unconcern for "the ultimate fate of 'shall' and 'will.'" He characterizes the professor's attitude as "Let usage determine; he remains a calm looker-on." All very well, the reviewer complains, but "what was once a clearly defined and useful distinction will soon be obliterated." Evidently, the reviewer didn't notice—or was not convinced by—Lounsbury's contention that verbal critics and even linguists are helpless to stop such changes.[26] Later usage sticklers would continue to reject that argument. Linguists are still occasionally accused of standing idly by while cherished standards collapse.

One reader of Lounsbury's book believed that he was not only wasting time while the language decayed, but actively contributing to the problem. Leila Sprague Learned, author of an *Atlantic* article titled "A Defense of Purism in English," wrings her hands over "the ever-increasing tendency to slang and to colloquialisms." She points to the increased use of *It is me, due to* for *owing to, everyone* followed by *their,* and similar examples of degraded speech.

It's especially deplorable, says the author, that some professors of English now positively condone such usages. Surely they are exacerbating the problem. "When a college professor expresses the idea that improprieties are excusable because of their frequent use," she comments severely, "it seems to me timely and justifiable to suggest that our teachers of English be examined for their qualifications."

Later in the article Learned critiques Lounsbury's grammar. She suggests that "sometimes Professor Lounsbury's use of language might impress the critical student as inconsistent with the rules of rhetoric." She follows up this observation with a list of infelicitous phrases from his book, along with suggestions for more elegant paraphrases. (She does the same for the "much praised" Richard Grant White. It seems that even he did not always live up to his own standards of linguistic purity.)[27]

The Nation also waded into the controversy over corrupt usage. Like Learned, the magazine blames professors for the new climate of linguistic permissiveness. In the 1870s *The Nation* welcomed Whitney's attacks on White and other verbal critics, but now the editors decry the cult of usage. A piece titled "It's Me" begins, "A notable development of present-day civilization is the tightening bond of sympathy between science and the small boy." The author explains that scientists have recently come out in favor of various formerly forbidden activities. For example, he says, "It's good for a boy to have three helpings of pie . . . because his growing organism demands it." It's also good for the small boy to say *It's me* and *It's her* "because that is the way everybody will speak a few hundred years from now."

The author attributes this upside-down state of affairs to an exaggerated respect for usage. Although the allure of usage is powerful in a democracy—"anybody can walk out into the street and pick up usage"—*The Nation* questions whether it's sufficient for judging good English. "What if . . . Shakespeare said 'Damned be him who first cries hold, enough?'" asks the author. That doesn't automatically make it correct. He suggests that "Shakespeare . . . might have slipped on the ice and broken a leg without making fractured legs an essential attribute of genius. Life is guided by norms, and not by aberrations."

A letter that appeared two weeks later points out that *It's me* is "a fact of language," in frequent use since Elizabethan times. The letter writer provides several literary examples from authors more modern than Shakespeare, including Emerson, Shelley, Thackeray, and Browning. The editors reply unrepentantly, "Perhaps this letter from a teacher of English explains in part the inability of so many college graduates to write correctly."[28]

Another topic that inspired sharp exchanges in the letters section of magazines was the use of split infinitives. From being a nonissue in the days of Lowth and Murray, split infinitives had become a grammatical hot button by the late nineteenth century. In 1895 *The Critic* published a series of letters to the editor that reveal a typical range of views. The first letter begins plaintively, "Is it too late to try to save the infinitive mood in its original simplicity?" The writer continues, "There is no such verb as 'to fully notice,' yet one of the smoothest pens that [has] run on your pages for many a day writes in the review of Zangwill's 'The Master,' 'It almost takes an artist to fully notice.'"[29]

Another reader writes in to defend the construction. Recalling the stern strictures that hedged around infinitives in his school days, he says, "We might never dare 'to fully prove' anything; we could only aspire 'fully to prove it' or 'to prove it fully.' Neither of which was exactly what we wished to do." He then suggests that perhaps it's because the reviewer in question has "one of the smoothest pens" that he decided to split an infinitive for the sake of clarity and euphony. The author of the letter thinks talented writers should be allowed the freedom to insert adverbs "where sense and emphasis require."[30]

This broad-minded attitude drew a quick response from a third reader. He writes, "It is painful to see a serious attempt to defend the so-called 'split infinitive,' but the pain gives way to blank astonishment when the defence is put on the ground of euphony." In this reader's opinion, the reason split infinitives have been banished from good usage is that the best writers have found them clunky and inelegant and therefore avoided them. He then argues that the worse a piece of writing is, the more split infinitives it will contain. As a case in point, he mentions the flyers and other ephemeral publications surrounding the recent Chicago railroad strike. These low-class pieces of writing, he claims, featured "a perfect avalanche" of split infinitives.[31]

After seeing the furor surrounding his colleague's use of this deprecated form, it's no surprise that another *Critic* writer starts off an article titled "How to Not Read" with the disclaimer, "It is bad luck, I know, to commence with a split infinitive." He excuses himself with the explanation that "how to not read" means something different from "how not to read."[32]

In *The Standard of Usage*, Lounsbury devotes a chapter to this vexed issue. He lists the most common criticisms of the form— that it's a corruption, that it's a recent innovation, that good authors avoid it—and counters them one by one. As always, he bases his case on the history and structure of English.

Lounsbury answers the corruption argument by pointing out that on the contrary, the true corruption occurred when speakers started joining *to* with what Lounsbury calls "simple" infinitives. In Anglo-Saxon English, infinitive verbs always appeared on their own, without *to* or any other introductory word. Some infinitives still do—those following *make,* for example. A sentence like *They made me to leave* sounds very strange. Other verbs present a choice. Either *I helped to cook* or *I helped cook* is possible. Given this history, the term "split infinitive" doesn't make much sense. The infinitive, properly speaking, is only the verb itself. The *to* is a later addition. "Let us imagine," jokes Lounsbury, "what must have been the feelings of the purist of the twelfth century . . . when he saw the preposition *to* . . . prefixed indiscriminatingly to the infinitive."[33] Somehow the usage caught on in spite of him.

Next, Lounsbury takes care of the argument that split infinitives are a recent innovation by noting that people have been splitting *to* and the simple infinitive almost as long as the two words have been joined together. Among the earliest examples in print are several that appear in John Wycliffe's fourteenth-century translation of the Bible. Moreover, many great writers have used the construction. Lounsbury offers a list that includes Samuel Johnson, Daniel Defoe, the poets Coleridge and Wordsworth, George Eliot, and Matthew Arnold, among others.

Lounsbury does admit that the usage has become much more common in recent years. It's happening, he believes, because English speakers have discovered that they can express a greater range of nuances if they sometimes insert an adverb between *to* and the verb. If such is the case, then no amount of condemnation on the part of critics will prevent split infinitives from becoming a permanent feature of the grammar.

He concludes, "The mere opinions of individuals, no matter how eminent, will never long carry much weight with the users of speech. If men come seriously to believe that ambiguity can be lessened or emphasis increased by changing the order of words in any given phrase, we may be sure that in time the habit of do-ing so will be adopted." Trends like these are simply part of the normal process of language change. If they were truly corruptions, says Lounsbury, "our language would have been already ruined any number of times."[34]

While the more high-toned periodicals gave space to advanced discussions of linguistic topics, popular magazines continued to offer grammar advice as if modern philology had never been invented. *The Ladies' Home Journal,* for instance, printed a regular column on correct speaking and writing. Readers wrote in requesting, "If space permits, please condemn 'localisms,'" or asking for "a *practical* rule" for deciding between *you and me* and *you and I,* or wondering what the difference is between *loan* and *lend.*

Their questions were answered with calm authority. The *Journal* editor advises that when confused about whether to use *you and me* or *you and I,* the reader should drop the *you and* to see which of the remaining pronouns sounds better. The distinction between *loan* and *lend,* she tells another correspondent, "which should be observed but which very often is not," is simply that *loan* is a noun and *lend* is a verb. A section titled "Heard in the Street" lists overheard grammatical mistakes along with their corrections. "Thank you, I will be happy to go" should be "Thank you, I shall be happy to go."[35]

The *Journal* provided straightforward advice that could easily have come from an old copy of Lindley Murray's grammar (and actually might have—late editions were still around). Its subscribers weren't looking for a historical analysis of disputed structures or guidelines for making nuanced usage choices—they wanted to know what was correct. It's doubtful that many popular magazine readers had heard of the controversies raging between linguists and traditionalists, or would have been stirred by them. They still thought of grammar as a list of memorizable rules.

By this time, more than a century had passed since the first appearance of Lindley Murray's *English Grammar* and few people remembered his name. Conversations about grammar in recent decades had advanced into territory that he could hardly have imagined. Still, his spirit lingered. In some quarters, the old beliefs were as strong as ever.

The twentieth century's answer to Murray started life modestly as a student writing aid. This forty-three-page booklet, titled *The Elements of Style,* first appeared on the shelves of Cornell University's bookstore in 1918, where it sold for a quarter. English professor William Strunk Jr. had written it specifically for his English 8 classes. Other students wandering the textbook aisles probably would have passed it by unnoticed. A diminutive five inches wide by seven high with gray board covers, *Elements* was more like a classroom handout than a real book. It was self-published and looked it. Around campus it became known as "the little book," with the emphasis on "little."

The Elements of Style appeared at the end of World War I, on the eve of America's first explosion of youth culture—the raucous decade now known as the Roaring Twenties. Soon the red-hot slang of flappers and flaming youth would take the country by storm. Youth slang was already rampant on college campuses, where young men and women bonded with their own brand of talk. The American Dialect Society even took college slang seriously enough to record it in *Dialect Notes.* Several decades would pass, however, before college students would be encouraged to write creatively in their natural voices. Those hoping to pass English 8 were still confined to conventional usage and traditional word choices.

Strunk's one-time student and future coauthor, Elwyn Brooks (E. B.) White, writing about his old professor in a 1957 *New Yorker* article, describes him as "a memorable man, friendly and funny," with a passion for clean, bold, concise writing. White took Strunk's English 8 class in 1919, so was one of the first to use *Elements*. In his article, White recalls that "Will Strunk really put his heart and soul" into the idea of tight writing. Brevity was his watchword. His lectures were so pared down, says White, "that he often seemed in the position of having shortchanged himself, a man left with nothing more to say yet with time to fill."

Strunk solved the problem, according to White, by repeating his sentences three times over. White remembers that "he leaned forward over his desk, grasped his coat lapels in his hands, and in a husky, conspiratorial voice said, 'Rule Thirteen! Omit needless words! Omit needless words! Omit needless words!'" That rule, which struck White so forcibly when he first heard it, would become the most famous command in *Elements*.[36]

Strunk's motives in writing *The Elements of Style* were similar to Lindley Murray's when he wrote the first version of his *English Grammar* for the local Quaker girls' school. Like Murray, Strunk wrote with a narrowly defined audience in mind—the students taking his advanced classes on literature study and writing technique. He hoped to save them and himself time and frustration. Over many years of teaching, he had graded hundreds of compositions and encountered the same missteps over and over. Now, with the help of his little book, students could correct their most egregious style mistakes before handing in their papers.

Like Murray, Strunk slanted his material toward his targeted readers. His purpose was not to give comprehensive or sophisticated style advice. As he makes clear in the book's introduction, his aim was more limited. He describes the book as "intended for use in English courses in which the practice of composition is combined with the study of literature." He warns his students, "The book covers only a small portion of the field of English style." He recommends several more substantial guides that they should also consult.

Strunk doesn't expect his classes to learn how to write well by studying a forty-three-page booklet. "Once past the essentials," he explains, "students profit most by individual instruction based on the problems of their own work." Furthermore, he does not advocate blind adherence even to these basic rules. "The best writers sometimes disregard the rules of rhetoric," he admits. He then adds with characteristic bluntness, "When they do so, however, the reader will usually find in the sentence some compensating merit. . . . Unless he is certain of doing as well, he will probably do best to follow the rules." He advises students to learn how to write "plain English adequate for everyday uses" before they attempt to develop an original style.[37]

Strunk organized the book for maximum ease of use. Besides the brief introductory comments, it consists of four sections, each with a numbered list of rules and accompanying comments. The table of contents lists every rule, so users can quickly find help for a particular problem. The first section after the introduction lists eight "Elementary Rules of Usage." Most of these deal with punctuation—"Form the possessive singular of nouns with 's"; "Do not join independent clauses by a comma." The rules are succinct and unadorned. As White put it, "for sheer pith . . . it probably sets a record that is not likely to be broken."[38]

Strunk realized that applying his pithy rules could be tricky, so he fleshed them out with explanatory remarks and examples. For instance, after stating the rule "Form the possessive singular of nouns with 's" he gives a list of exceptions—*Moses' laws, for righteousness' sake*. Often, rules that sound too sweeping on their own are put in context in the explanatory paragraph. Expanding on the rule "Use the active voice," Strunk says. "This rule does not, of course, mean that the writer should entirely discard the passive voice, which is frequently convenient and sometimes necessary."[39]

A section on composition follows the usage section. This part of the book offers guidelines for structuring a piece of writing. Here, too, the advice is basic and straightforward—"As a rule, begin each paragraph with a topic sentence." Several of the rules—there are eighteen in all—are reminiscent of Murray's "Perspicuity" section, where he proposed guidelines for good writing. Murray's three requirements for strong writing were "purity, propriety, precision." Strunk's principles are similar. "Put statements in positive form," he enjoins his students, don't use slangy terms like *lose out* and *kind of,* and of course, "omit needless words." Murray advised his readers to avoid ending sentences with "any inconsiderable word." Strunk tells students to "place the emphatic words of a sentence at the end." Although Strunk doesn't say so, it's safe to assume that he would have felt as reluctant as Murray to end a sentence with a preposition.[40]

The book continues with a section on form—mainly covering the accepted format for quotations and references—and ends with checklists of misused and misspelled words. Strunk describes the items on the misused list as "not so much bad English" as "careless writing." Some are standard entries in "frequently confused" lists—*affect/effect, fewer/less*—or standard usage critics' peeves, such as using *due to* to mean *because of* instead of *attributable to.* Others seem to be more personal dislikes. Strunk labels *factor* "a hackneyed word" and calls *student body* a "needless and awkward" phrase better expressed by the simple *students.*

Although Strunk mentions one or two usage issues—he tells students not to use *they* with *everybody,* for example—*The Elements of Style* is almost devoid of actual grammar advice. Rather, it reflects Strunk's preoccupations as a teacher. It addresses basic composition errors, such as poor organization, wordiness, and confusion about how to use quotations. Strunk would no doubt have been surprised if anyone had told him that his little book of writing hints would one day metamorphose into the new sticklers' Bible.

Strunk retired from teaching in 1937 and *The Elements of Style* disappeared from the Cornell bookstore's shelves. It might have disappeared entirely if not for White. White's college years were mostly taken up with editing the well-regarded *Cornell Daily Sun.* As he later admitted, he was only loosely engaged with his class-work. His English 8 class, however, was an exception. Long after leaving Cornell, he would write to Strunk's brother recalling the class as one of a handful of educational experiences that had stayed with him. "The ideal of precision, of brevity, of clarity," he wrote, "it can hardly be called an education but it has been such a help."[41]

Even so, White's memory of Strunk's book was hazy when he encountered it again. By the time it arrived in his mailbox in March 1957, White had been a *New Yorker* staff writer for three decades and was famous as the author of *Stuart Little* and *Charlotte's Web.* The book was a gift from former classmate Howard Stevenson. Stevenson, now the editor of the *Cornell Alumni News,* had discovered two copies of *Elements* in Cornell's library and somehow beguiled the librarians into parting with one so he could send it to White. It's rare for libraries to surrender their books. Cornell's librarians might have agreed to it because White was a celebrated alumnus or because the self-published book didn't seem especially valuable.

Writing about the book in *The New Yorker,* White confesses that he had nearly forgotten about it, although he must once have owned a copy. He was delighted to rediscover its virtues. White admired the book's succinctness and heartily approved of its forceful tone. He describes it as "a forty-three page summation of the case for cleanliness, accuracy, and brevity in the use of English." It is, he says, Strunk's attempt to "cut the vast tangle of English rhetoric down to size and write its rules and principles on the head of a pin."

He imagines "Sergeant Strunk" snapping orders to his platoon of student writers—"Do not join independent clauses with a comma"; "In summaries, keep to one tense." Most of all, "Omit needless words." White confides, "I have been trying to omit needless words since 1919 and although there are still many words that cry for omission, and the huge task will never be accomplished, it is exciting to me to reread the masterly Strunkian elaboration of this noble theme."[42]

Besides outlining the content of the book for *New Yorker* readers, White paints a charming picture of his former teacher, who had died eleven years earlier. He writes nostalgically, "From every line there peers out at me the puckish face of my professor, his short hair parted neatly in the middle and combed down over his forehead, his eyes blinking incessantly behind steel rimmed spectacles, . . . his smile shuttling to and fro." White assumes that Cornell's English classes now rely on much longer, fancier textbooks than *The Elements of Style*—"books with upswept tail fins and automatic verbs." Still, if faced with college students in need of writing advice, he says, "I would simply lean far out over the desk, clutch my lapels, blink my eyes, and say, 'Get the *little* book! Get the *little* book! Get the *little* book!'"[43]

White's brief essay sparked an immediate response. The same week that it appeared in *The New Yorker,* Jack Case, an editor at Macmillan Company, wrote to White expressing interest in an updated version of *The Elements of Style*. No one at the publishing house had yet seen the original, but Case and others there believed that an unadulterated shot of plain grammar advice was just what midcentury Americans craved. It would be an antidote to the unsettling linguistics-based theories of language use then making the rounds of college English departments.

White agreed to edit and enlarge the book, and his new edition appeared in the spring of 1959. Although much longer than the original, it still amounted to only seventy-one pages. Nearly all of Strunk's content remained unchanged. In White's words, he "added a bit, subtracted a bit, rearranged it in a few places, and in general . . . made small alterations."[44] The section on misused words almost doubled. White added several common usage critics' peeves—*hopefully* used as a sentence modifier, *different than* used for *different from, unique* used with modifiers like *very.* White also deleted the section on misspelled words and replaced some of Strunk's literary examples with excerpts from modern authors such as Faulkner and Hemingway.

The biggest change from the 1918 book is an added final section, "An Approach to Style." With this section, White released the book from its English 8 straitjacket and expanded it into an exploration of the writing process itself. Part inspirational essay and part practical checklist, it guides writers through the tangled thickets of composition. White explains that it's intended to provide "gentle reminders" of "what most of us know and, at times, forget."

He cautions that there is "no infallible guide to good writing." How to achieve style in its larger sense of the writer's distinctive voice is something of a mystery, and this final chapter is "a mystery story, thinly disguised." However, to keep the tone of the book consistent, White has decided to present his reminders in the form of twenty-one numbered rules, each followed by a clarifying paragraph.[45]

When formulating his rules, White adopts Strunk's tone of clipped command. Some rules are broad enough to encompass a whole writing philosophy—"Write in a way that comes naturally," while others address a specific issue—"Use orthodox spelling"—but all are short and curtly stated. White ends his style section by repeating his old professor's central dictum. Beginning writers, he says, "should err on the side of conservatism." Although he assures his readers that English is "a living stream," where "no idiom is taboo, no accent forbidden," he thinks it's best to be "armed with the rules of grammar" before venturing into new creative territory.[46]

Although *Elements* is often described as a grammar book, White's revision, like Strunk's original, contained very little grammar advice. What does exist, however, is relentlessly conservative. For instance, although White admits that "there is a precedent from the fourteenth century downward for interposing an adverb between *to* and the infinitive," he advises, "the construction is for the most part avoided by careful writers." He also upholds Strunk's position that *he* (not *he or she*) should be paired with words like *everyone,* unless the referent "is or must be feminine." *They* is never correct.[47]

Some of White's comments in the text suggest a more flexible attitude. "Style rules of this sort are, of course, somewhat a matter of individual preference," he acknowledges in his introduction, "and even the established rules of grammar are open to challenge." He prefaces the list of suggested usage guides that begins the misused words section with a remark that almost seems to echo Whitney or Lounsbury. "The shape of our language is not rigid," he says. "In questions of usage we have no lawgiver whose word is final."[48]

This theoretical openness didn't translate into a broad-mindedness about specifics. In practice, White was firmly in the purists' camp. Both he and his editor, Jack Case, were contemptuous of academic linguists, or as White called them, "the Happiness Boys," who to their minds encouraged an "anything goes" attitude toward language use. Case nonetheless understood that the book would be vulnerable to criticism if outdated rules, such as the distinction between *shall* and *will*, were allowed to stand the way Strunk had written them. He suggested in a letter that White might soften his stance by inserting the words "in formal writing" or some similar formula here and there. White answered implacably, "I don't know whether Macmillan is running scared or not, . . . but I know that I cannot, and will-shall not, attempt to adjust the unadjustable Mr. Strunk to the modern liberal of the English Department."[49]

White and Strunk both understood that language and usage evolve—as a graduate student, Strunk had studied philology as well as literature—but they believed in the traditional rules. Later in his response to Case, White explains, "No ball game [is] anything but chaotic if it lacks a mound, a box, bases, and foul lines. That's what Strunk was about, that's what I am about, and that (I hope) is what the book is about."[50] Strunk and White's foul lines were drawn very close to the ones that Lowth and Murray had laid down. They only swerved to incorporate a few later contributions from the verbal critics, such as the ban on split infinitives. If White's readers wanted to experiment with usage and grammar, they were free to do so. However, they would do it without permission from *Elements*. Strunk and White's principles would remain unapologetically conventional. As with earlier guidelines, they would harden over time into articles of faith.

Case's worries about the book's reception turned out to be unfounded. As a reference book of under one hundred pages, *Elements* didn't draw major reviews, but several magazines and newspapers printed positive notices. A reviewer for *The Rotarian* says, "This small book is immensely practical and thoroughly enjoyable. I recommend it strongly." *The Analysts Journal* assures its subscribers that business writers will "find *The Elements of Style* not only interesting but editorially profitable."[51]

New York Times writer Charles Poore devoted a "Books of the Times" column to *Elements*. E. B. White, he says, has been rummaging in our linguistic attic and "brought out a splendid trophy for all who are interested in reading and writing." Not that Poore agrees with all of White's rules. White's insistence on adding possessive *'s* to names ending in *s—Charles's tonsils,* for example—seems unnecessarily cumbersome. Nonetheless, he thinks readers can learn much from the book. "Buy it, study it, enjoy it," he says, "it's as timeless as a book can be in our age of volubility."[52]

White's own magazine, *The New Yorker,* only gave the book a brief unsigned notice, but described it in glowing terms. "Distinguished by brevity, clarity, and prickly good sense, it is, unlike most such manuals, a book as well as a tool," praises the reviewer. The notice rounds off with a warm commendation—"his old teacher would have been proud of him."[53]

Elements may have won only superficial notice from reviewers, but book buyers clamored for it. In May 1959 it was a Book-of-the-Month Club selection. By fall the book had reached the top of several bestseller lists and seemed in no danger of falling off anytime soon. A year after its first appearance, it had sold a dizzying 200,000 copies.[54] *Elements* was more like a bestselling grammar book of early America than a typical twentieth-century usage guide. These were usually steady sellers, but few if any vaulted to literary fame.

White did occasionally receive letters from readers who had noticed that the book sometimes failed to follow its own rules. For example, it includes many passive sentences even though one of the principles of composition is "Use the active voice." White answered these letters good-humoredly, pointing out that Strunk often modified his advice by saying "as a rule" or something similar. Strunk did, after all, point out in his explanatory paragraph that passive was often desirable or necessary. Answering a letter from a reader who complains that White uses *parvum opus* ("small work") although the book tells writers to avoid foreign languages, he replies, "Latin . . . isn't a foreign language, it's a dead language. To me, it's very much alive—at the root of many of our words."[55]

Much more often than not, the letters were laudatory. One woman wrote to tell White that his writing reassured her that the world is a rational place. Another wrote to let him know that she was omitting needless words. "Thanks," he responded. "So am I."[56]

Some of the popularity of *Elements* is no doubt attributable to White's status as a well-known author. The book itself, though, clearly had great appeal. A pocket-sized style guide consisting mainly of brief, numbered commands is much easier to read and consult than a detailed guide the size of a dictionary. People were no doubt attracted to *Elements* for the same reasons that colonial Americans liked the grammars of Lowth and Dilworth—it was short, straightforward, and seemed to guarantee that following the rules would result in elegant English.

Elements would go on to sell millions of copies through four more editions. It would become required reading for beginning writers and publishing professionals alike. Writing teachers would recommend it to their students. Editors would keep copies on their desks. The rules themselves would be memorized and quoted, while the mitigating comments were forgotten or ignored. *Strunk and White* would soon become shorthand for no-fail usage advice, just as *Murray* had once been another word for grammar.

The century had begun with an unprecedented embrace of slang and colloquialisms and an apparent loosening of grammatical standards, but nearly sixty years later the old grammar rules still retained a tight cultural grip. In spite of the Happiness Boys, large numbers of midcentury Americans felt the need for an old-fashioned usage guide. There wasn't much grammar in *The Elements of Style,* but what was included was strict enough to gladden the hearts of purists.

8.

The Persistence of Grammar

In 1961, 133 years after the appearance of *An American Dictionary of the English Language,* the name of Webster was once again embroiled in controversy. It began in early September when the G. & C. Merriam Company issued a press release announcing the imminent appearance of *Webster's Third New International Dictionary.* It would be the first complete overhaul of the company's venerable unabridged dictionary since the publication of *Webster's Second* in 1934.

The first hint that the new dictionary would break with tradition came with the press release issued a few weeks before publication. It promised no fewer than 100,000 new words and updated meanings, from *A-bomb* to *Zen,* but the changes would not be limited to new words. People who upgraded to *Webster's Third* could expect several "revolutionary" new features, among them a new pronunciation key and a new way of structuring definitions.

The press release highlighted the third edition's up-to-the-minute content. It quoted the dictionary's editor-in-chief, Philip B. Gove, revealing that the new volume would reflect "the informality of current usage" with "pungent, lively remarks" from "contemporary notables." Scores of illustrative examples from bygone literary figures like Dryden and Pope had been replaced by the likes of Ethel Merman, Willie Mays, novelist Mickey Spillane, and former madam turned bestselling author Polly

Adler. As yet more evidence of the current linguistic informality, Merriam's marketers featured a snippet of the new volume's unusually broad-minded entry for *ain't*.[1]

The publicity department's attempt to shake up the stuffy image of the dictionary would turn out to be a mistake. Especially unfortunate was their decision to showcase *ain't*. When newspapers reported on the forthcoming dictionary, they focused on the shock aspects of the new book.

One of the earliest mentions came in *The New York Times*. Under the lighthearted headline "Webster Soups Up Its Big Dictionary" *Times* writer McCandlish Phillips announces that the new Merriam-Webster dictionary will be "entirely renewed in content and radically altered in style." He quotes Gove's comments on the informality of American speech. Then at the end of his brief article, Phillips tosses in one last fun fact. "The use of 'ain't'," he notes, "is defended as 'used orally in most parts of the U. S. by cultivated speakers.'"[2]

This tidbit, an afterthought for Phillips, counted as big news for other journalists. A rash of facetious headlines broke out— "Saying Ain't Ain't Wrong" (*Chicago Tribune*), "It Ain't Necessarily Uncouth" (*Chicago Daily News*), "It 'Ain't' Good" (*Washington Sunday Star*), and "Say It 'Ain't' So" (*Science*). After having fun with their headlines, the papers generally gave a matter-of-fact description of the dictionary's main features, and for the most part, their reports are positive. The *Daily News*, for instance, takes issue with *Webster's* justification of *ain't*, snapping, "Cultivated, our foot," but it applauds the inclusion of new words like *A-bomb* and *beatnik*. "In the main," remarks the reviewer, "we believe it the function of an unabridged dictionary to deal realistically with a world that has, after all, buried John Dryden and Alexander Pope and elevated Mickey Spillane and Miss Adler to best-sellerdom."[3]

The first truly negative notice came from the September 8

Toronto Globe and Mail. In the somberly titled article "The Death of Meaning," the paper accuses Merriam-Webster of contributing to the degeneration of English by embracing the word *ain't.* The new dictionary, cries the reviewer in dismay, "will comfort the ignorant, confer approval upon the mediocre, and subtly imply that proper English is the tool only of the snob; but it will not assist men to speak truly to other men." The reviewer pictures a future in which civilization, helped along by the barbarities of *Webster's Third,* will regress into a primitive state. Yet the dictionary itself may prepare Americans for their fate. "In the caves," concludes the reviewer, "a grunt will do."[4] The Washington *Sunday Star* spoke up next. Opines the *Star* reviewer, "Perhaps the most shocking thing in the whole book is that it takes a rather respectful view of 'ain't.'" The reviewer prefers the dictionary's 1934 edition, "which bluntly—and correctly in our view—brands 'ain't' as a 'dialectal' and 'illiterate' expression." (The superiority of the 1934 edition would become a common theme among the dictionary's opponents, who would set up a cry of "Hang onto your *Webster's Second!*") The *Star,* like the *Globe & Mail,* sees the appearance of the new dictionary as the first step toward anarchy. It's no wonder, frets the reviewer, that the English-speaking world, "when it thus tolerates the debasement of its language," is having trouble with types like Soviet leader Nikita Khrushchev.[5]

This apocalyptic language was typical of the negative reviews that would soon proliferate. Horrified commentators reached for words like *shock, disaster, calamity, debased,* and *vulgarism.* The *New York Times* referred to the new volume as "Webster's Third (or Bolshevik) International." *The Richmond News Leader* predicts a war that will be waged "wherever men who believe in excellence find themselves in conflict with men who prefer an easy mediocrity." There is "madness in their method!" cries Garry Wills, writing for the *National Review.*[6]

In some ways, there's nothing remarkable about this outpouring of anguish. The same themes reverberate through centuries of usage arguments. Over-the-top outrage, ridicule, and scandalized disgust have dogged linguistic radicals from Noah Webster to Fitzedward Hall. As Lounsbury and Whitney noted in their first *College Courant* article, arguments about language have more in common with religion than with scholarly inquiry. Champions of linguistic orthodoxy have routinely predicted societal collapse when the old ways are challenged.

Even so, the outcry over *ain't* seems like an extravagant response to a word that, after all, had also appeared in *Webster's Second*, as well as earlier versions of the dictionary. Webster's 1828 dictionary includes an entry for *ant* (pronounced "ain't," according to the key), defined as "vulgar dialect, as in the phrases *I ant, you ant, he ant, we ant, &c.*" Although some had criticized Webster at the time for including "low" language in his dictionaries, recording colloquialisms and slang had long been standard practice among dictionary makers. It was not normally a matter for hand-wringing.

The problem with *ain't* in the eyes of *Webster's Third* critics was not so much that it was listed in the dictionary, but that it was treated with respect. As the *Sunday Star* reviewer points out, *Webster's Second* makes the low status of *ain't* clear by appending the labels "*Dial.* or *Illit.*" *Webster's Third* takes a more neutral approach. After the definition, it comments, "Though disapproved by many and more common in less educated speech, used orally in most parts of the U. S. by many cultivated speakers, especially in the phrase *ain't I*." The word is only labeled *substandard* when it's used to mean "have not" (as in *I ain't got it*).

The controversy was hotter than it might have been because the Merriam press release presented the entry for *ain't* in drastically edited form. It omitted both the phrase "disapproved by many" and the information that the "have not" meaning was considered substandard. Reviewers were left with the erroneous impression that *Webster's Third* considered *ain't* completely acceptable. Even when the dictionary entry is read in its entirety, however, the difference in slant from the second to the third editions is obvious.

Critics believed the rephrased definition of *ain't* signaled a dangerous turn toward linguistic permissiveness. *Ain't* was merely the most egregious example of what they saw as the disastrously mistaken approach to language use that permeated the whole dictionary. Reviewers objected to the inclusion of business-speak terms like *irregardless, finalize,* and the new coinages created by casually slapping on *–wise,* as in *speechwise.* They were also offended by popular slang terms like *boo-boo* and *footsie,* and beatnik lingo like *cool cats.* Besides questionable vocabulary, the dictionary gave examples of often heard, but nonstandard, grammatical formations like *whoever* in object position and *different than,* without necessarily condemning them as wrong.

Although the second edition had listed many words not normally considered part of standard English, it had conveyed subtle usage judgments with a variety of status labels—*improper, jocular, colloquial, illiterate, dialectal, erroneous.* Most of these labels were missing from the new edition. *Slang, nonstandard,* and *substandard* still appeared in *Webster's Third,* but not often. Instead, example sentences demonstrated typical uses of the word. The editors' idea was that readers would identify slang or informal speech from the context, but this subtlety escaped many dictionary users, who assumed that unlabeled words were being treated as totally acceptable.

The release of the dictionary on September 28 triggered a second round of hostile comments. *The New York Times* printed another, much colder, review in its editorial pages. It opens with a sentence concocted from words that the *Times* was disturbed to find in *Webster's*—"A passel of double-domes at the G. & C.

Merriam Company joint in Springfield, Mass. have been con-fabbing and yakking . . . and now they have finalized Web-ster's Third New International Dictionary." (Like the slogan "Hang onto your *Webster's Second!*," this ferociously jocular opening would soon become a reviewing cliché. Even though the reviewers disapproved of slang in the dictionary, they couldn't resist indulging in a little themselves.)

The editorial then gets serious. The *Times* editors accuse the Merriam Company of surrendering to "the permissive school that has been busily extending its beachhead on English instruc-tion in the schools." They complain that "intentionally or unin-tentionally," the new dictionary reinforces the notion that "good English is whatever is popular."

Although the *Times* recognizes that a deluge of new words has entered the language since 1934, it believes that the dictionary, as the "peerless authority" on American English, should have been much more restrictive in its choices and much more criti-cal of the nonstandard words that were included. The diction-ary's editors, in the *Times* editors' opinion, have dismally failed in their responsibility to the public. The review ends with a plea to the dictionary's editors not to throw out the printing plates for *Webster's Second* just yet.[7]

The dictionary's other innovations only added to reviewers' an-noyance. They grumbled that the new pronunciation symbols were confusing and the technique of writing definitions as a sin-gle phrase made entries hard to read. They thought that quot-ing movie stars rather than great British authors gave the dictionary an air of frivolity. Some were upset by Merriam's de-cision to cut encyclopedia-type materials—the biographical and geographical appendixes, foreign quotations, proverbs, famous fictional characters, and similar items—to make room for the new entries. The main target of their fury, however, remained the status granted to bad grammar and incorrect usage.

"Webster's, joining the say-as-you-go school of permissive English, has now all but abandoned any effort to distinguish between good and bad usage," laments a *Life* magazine reviewer. The reviewer accepts *ain't* as a "justifiable" contraction, but scolds the dictionary's editors for including "monstrous non-words" like *irregardless* and *finalize*. The magazine *Science*, although generally approving of the dictionary, especially its handling of scientific terms, hopes that "the next edition will distinguish more sharply . . . between illiterate and literate usage."[8]

Atlantic writer Wilson Follett published an influential review that could have been inspired by the shade of Richard Grant White. Follett identifies the book's main improvement as the plethora of new technical and scientific words. The merits of these, he says, can only be judged by specialists. On the other hand, the book's shortcomings are immediately evident to everyone. They are in the area of "standard, staple, traditional language." We can all make judgments about this area of language, declares Follett, because we all use it. Like White, Follett felt confident matching his native good taste against the expertise of specialists.

In Follett's view, the new dictionary was a catastrophe. "Webster III," he thunders, is out to destroy "every obstinate vestige of linguistic punctilio, every surviving influence that makes for the upholding of standards, every criterion for distinguishing between better usages and worse."

Follett provides a long list of nonstandard expressions—*wise up, ants in one's pants, hepcat*—that have entered the dictionary with no qualifying label to mark their problematic status. He feels that this failure to pronounce on what's correct amounts to "a large-scale abrogation" of the dictionary maker's responsibility. Dictionaries are meant to provide guidance, a ruling on what constitutes good speech. Unwary users of *Webster's Third* may get the impression that all words and phrases are equally acceptable.

Even more objectionable is the inclusion of questionable example sentences. *Due to* is used with the meaning *because of* in "abominations" such as *The event was canceled due to inclement weather*. *Different than* appears in several examples, such as *different than any other piece we've done lately* (from no less respectable a source than *Harper's*). *Like* is shown introducing embedded clauses, as in *looks like they can raise better tobacco*. The dictionary also gives examples of plural pronouns with *everybody*—*Everybody has made up their minds*—and *whomever* in subject position—*I go out to talk to whomever it is*.

Follett is appalled that *Webster's* has decided to "exert its leverage" in favor of these ungrammatical uses. The fact that people say these things does not necessarily make them worthy of inclusion in an authoritative dictionary. By confining itself to neutrally recording current English, *Webster's Third* has failed in its duty as a gatekeeper. (The dictionary actually does note in several of these instances that the usages are "disapproved by some grammarians." Either Follett didn't notice these comments or didn't consider them a forcible enough condemnation.)[9]

Chicago Daily News columnist Sydney Harris gets to the heart of what troubled Follett and others. Harris starts out with the usual jovial opening—"Lemme recommend a swell new book"— followed by a slang-filled paragraph or two. He closes the review, however, in a more serious vein. Harris tells readers, "Our attitude toward language merely reflects our attitude toward more basic matters." Sloppy word use is not terribly important in itself, but it indicates a general decay in values. "If everything is a matter of taste and preference and usage," he insists, "then we are robbing ourselves of all righteous indignation against evil."[10] The real fault of *Webster's Third,* in the view of Harris and other critics, is that it turns a blind eye toward America's linguistic sins.

To Harris, and to many like-minded people before and since, correct usage was a sign of high principles and moral virtue. By not sufficiently condemning words like *irregardless*—and the people who say them—*Webster's* seemed to be condoning immoral behavior. It was as though they were claiming that people who use words and grammar correctly are no more virtuous than people who say *ain't*.

In 1961 many formerly solid traditions were teetering on the edge of collapse. A new political era seemed to be dawning when John F. Kennedy, the youngest president ever to be elected, beat the older and more established Richard Nixon by a razor-thin margin. Dramatic social changes were also in the offing. Activist college students were striking the first blows against segregation with sit-ins and Freedom Rides throughout the South. On the cultural front, the group of writers and poets known as the Beats were challenging the pieties of mainstream American life, while the new rock 'n' roll music seemed to be tempting young people toward a looser, riskier lifestyle.

Old standards of language use appeared to be crumbling as well. Part of the reason was that modern theories about language were infiltrating the schools and universities. E. B. White may have scorned the Happiness Boys—more typically called structural linguists—but others took them more seriously. Their influence had become a nagging pain to usage conservatives.

Structural linguists were the modern descendants of the philologists. Like their nineteenth-century counterparts, they studied languages methodically. In recent decades, however, the focus had shifted from tracking the historical development of a language to describing and analyzing its current structure.

Descriptive linguists (as they were also called) studied languages with the aim of describing them as accurately and completely as possible. The acceptability or otherwise of a word or usage was merely one more fact about it, largely irrelevant to what linguists were interested in. They wanted to understand how language works. Labels like *substandard* and *slang* are not intrinsic features of language—they're about the social status of the speakers. To descriptive linguists' minds, anything that people were currently saying must be "good" or "grammatical" language in some context, even if it was rejected in others. They believed with Thomas Lounsbury that "whatever is in usage is right."

Those who defined grammar as a set of prescribed rules interpreted this neutral view of language use as permissive, or "anything goes." E. B. White and others with his outlook saw linguists as approving, or even encouraging, violations of traditional grammar. Linguists might have pointed out—as many defenders of *Webster's Third* later did—that neither they nor grammar critics can hold back language change. People who use *ain't* in normal conversation or habitually say *Who did you speak to?* were almost certain to continue saying those things, whether linguists gave them permission or not.

The descriptive approach to language was beginning to influence the way some English teachers thought about grammar. A 1952 curriculum review by the National Council of Teachers of English includes a chapter on "The Modern View of Grammar and Linguistics" that outlines the authors' interpretation of modern linguistic principles—language constantly changes; correctness can only be based on current usage; and all usage is relative.

"The contemporary linguist does not employ the terms 'good English' and 'bad English' except in a purely relative sense," explain the authors, "Good English is . . . the form of speech which is most clear, effective, and appropriate on any given linguistic occasion." Bad English is the opposite, "no matter how traditional, 'correct,' or elegant the words or phrases employed." Later, they suggest what this idea might mean in practical terms. They propose, "The teaching of correctness must shift in emphasis. . . . Instead of teaching rules for the avoidance of error, pupils must be taught to observe and understand the way in which their language operates."[11]

The possibility that schools would start teaching children to draw their own conclusions about usage was bound to upset anyone raised on old-fashioned grammar books. It invited linguistic anarchy. Even more disturbing, it opened the door to social leveling. This idea was no more appealing to usage arbiters in 1961 than it had been in the 1870s when Richard Grant White was laying down the laws of usage in his *Galaxy* column. While linguists still agreed with Lounsbury, defenders of the traditional standard continued to believe with White that "there is a misuse of words which can be justified by no authority, however great, by no usage, however general."

Reviewers attacked *Webster's Third* in doom-laden terms partly because they feared that the linguistic principles corrupting English teaching had also tainted the dictionary. Some thought their forebodings were justified when editor-in-chief Philip Gove wrote an article for the October 1961 issue of *Word Study* ominously titled "Linguistic Advances and Lexicography."

Gove's article did not in fact contain much that should have troubled traditionalists. In it he concludes that modern linguistics has not had much impact on dictionary making so far. It has not affected spelling, which has been fixed for English since the eighteenth century. Definitions, the main reason why monolingual dictionaries exist, have been only marginally affected, mainly through the redefining of a handful of grammatical terms. The biggest impact on *Webster's Third* has been in the area of pronunciation. In an effort to represent the country's multiple pronunciations with greater accuracy, the dictionary has introduced a new pronunciation key based on the technical alphabet used by linguists (called the International Phonetic Alphabet).

Gove's critics, however, were not focused on specifics. What really worried them was the editor-in-chief's attitude. Although

Gove argued that modern linguistics had hardly influenced the dictionary at all, he made it clear that he believed in its general principles. He closes the *Word Study* article by admitting that lexicography is not yet a science. It is more of an art, requiring "subjective analysis, arbitrary decisions, and intuitive reasoning." Still, that's no excuse for intellectual sloppiness. Lexicography "should have no traffic with guesswork, prejudice, or bias or with artificial notions of correctness or superiority. It must be descriptive and not prescriptive." He adds, "If the dictionary should neglect the obligation to act as a faithful recorder and interpreter of usage, . . . it cannot expect to be any longer appealed to as an authority."[12] Usage purists who had relied on the grammatical judgments in *Webster's Second* vehemently disagreed.

Gove was an unlikely candidate for linguistic radicalism. Like Noah Webster, he descended from a long line of respectable New Englanders. He was born in New Hampshire in 1902 and grew up there. At the age of sixteen Gove enrolled in Dartmouth College, majoring in English. As some reviewers later noticed, his own usage was exemplary. Gove's 1946 letter of application to Merriam reveals that he was one of a small minority of Americans in the 1940s who bothered to make the distinction between first person *shall/should* and second and third person *will/would*. The letter opens with the sentence, "I should like to know whether there is an opportunity for me to go to work for your company." Even Strunk and White could not have asked for a more meticulous style. Nonetheless, as a dictionary editor, he accepted other speaking styles as equally valid.[13]

After earning a master's degree at Harvard, Gove began a career as a college teacher that included fifteen years of directing the freshman English program at New York University. At the same time he worked toward, and eventually gained, a Ph.D. in English literature at Columbia. He spent several years collecting material on the great lexicographer Samuel Johnson before ultimately deciding to write his dissertation on the topic of imaginary voyages in literature.

With the start of World War II, Gove joined the navy. When he returned to civilian life after the war, he began to contemplate a career change away from teaching. One of the companies he queried was Merriam. Although his years of research on Johnson didn't result in a dissertation, he had learned quite a bit about the process of crafting a dictionary. Merriam hired Gove in 1946 as an assistant editor. Five years later, the company asked him to take on the task of overseeing the third edition of their unabridged dictionary.

Gove's idea that the dictionary should act as a faithful recorder of actual usage is not much different from Webster's often repeated maxim that grammar books and dictionaries should be based on the language, not the other way around, but Webster's dictionary was by this time very different from his original book. By 1951, all radical notions about language use had long since been expunged from its pages. The dictionary had grown into a bastion of conventional American speech and Gove's point of view now appeared to be an abrupt break with tradition.

As the controversy over the new dictionary gathered steam, the Merriam Company—astounded at first by the outpouring of disapproval—belatedly decided that a response was in order. A starchy letter from Gove appeared in the November 5 *New York Times*. He expresses astonishment at the slangy opening of the paper's recent editorial, "in which you pounce on nine words out of 450,000 to announce that we have been confabbing and yakking . . . to finalize a new dictionary." He continues, "The paragraph is, of course, a monstrosity. . . . It hits no mark at all.

A similar monstrosity could be contrived by jumbling together inappropriate words from formal literary language, or from the Second Edition."

Gove argues that the dictionary is merely doing its job of reflecting real American usage. The much maligned *finalize,* which had drawn scandalized comments when President Eisenhower used it a few years earlier, "turns up all over the English-speaking world" beginning in the 1920s. President Kennedy had used it only recently. It even turns up occasionally in the pages of the *Times.* Gove notes that *The New York Times* has in fact contributed several hundred quotations to *Webster's Third.* That's one of the ways the dictionary's compilers keep up with current usage.

Gove assures the *Times* editor, "We plan to continue reading and marking The Times as the number one exhibit of good standard contemporary cultivated English," even if the *Times* management urges its staff writers to continue relying on *Webster's Second.* He feels, however, that "the ultimate arbiters of our linguistic standards should not be urged to look back to artificial precepts of a bygone age. They must accept linguistic facts." He finishes by pointing out, "Whether you or I . . . like it or not, the contemporary English language of the Nineteen Sixties . . . is not the language of the Nineteen Twenties and Thirties."[14]

Gove makes some of the same points in a much shorter letter responding to the negative review in *Life* magazine. He notes that *irregardless,* which *Life* has stigmatized as a "monstrous nonword," also appeared in *Webster's Second.* Moreover, *Webster's Third* marks it as nonstandard. Other words from the third edition that *Life* condemns are likewise found in earlier editions. Gove then reiterates his position that the purpose of a dictionary is to record the language as it exists. "For us to attempt to prescribe the language," he says, "would be like *Life* reporting the news as its editors would prefer it to happen."

The *Life* editors were apparently unimpressed with this response. They appended a note to the letter, explaining that they didn't intend to give the impression that *irregardless* and the other words mentioned were not in *Webster's Second*. The point of their complaint is that the second edition labels the word "erroneous and humorous," while Gove's edition has upgraded it to merely "nonstandard." They feel that "Editor Gove is saying that if a word is misused often enough, it becomes acceptable."[15]

Gove and the *Life* editors were shouting across the same gulf that had divided linguistic radicals and conservatives since the late eighteenth century. As always, neither side was prepared to budge an inch. Philip Gove believed in actual use and the editors of *Life* believed in the rules, and no amount of arguing could change that. Like linguists and verbal critics in the 1870s, the two sides were making vastly different assumptions about language use and grammar. Descriptivists thought attempts to pervert the processes of language change were not only absurd, but useless. Those in favor of prescribed rules believed that standards could and should be imposed.

Others besides Gove came to the defense of the dictionary. Most were linguists or lexicographers, but not all. Roy H. Copperud, a journalist who would later write a book on American usage and style, was one who swam against the negative tide. In an *Editor & Publisher* column, he remarks on the "flurry of nitwitted commentary" stirred up by the publication of *Webster's Third*. He says, "They whine that the new dictionary is guilty of 'permissiveness,' reflecting the wrong-headed, though widely held . . . conviction that the business of a dictionary is to lay down the law." He adds, "Twenty minutes spent on the conclusions of any reputable linguist in the last 25 years should convince even the most obtuse that the business of a dictionary is to report how words are used, and not to prescribe or proscribe meanings." Copperud admits to personal prejudices against certain words, for instance, *finalize*. He knows, however, that it would be "both stupid and futile" for the dictionary to try to outlaw them.

Copperud also comments approvingly on some of the changes that other reviewers attacked. He thinks it's sensible of the editors to leave out encyclopedia-type material to make room for tens of thousands of new words. He finds the new pronunciation symbols baffling, but assumes that users will get accustomed to them eventually. "In general," he summarizes, "it may be said that this dictionary aims at representing English as it is used by the literate majority in this country."[16]

A handful of other reviews also support the aims and general organization of the dictionary. A brief jokey comment in *America* starts out sarcastically, "To the barricades! Man the breastworks! The dignity of the English language, at least as she is spoke by us Amuricans, is being assaulted." The editor then explains to the many reviewers who are apparently confused that the dictionary "does not *make* language; it records language's use." The St. Louis *Post Dispatch* also comments that the *Times* seems to have "an egregious misconception of what the purpose of a dictionary is." The *Reporter*, laughing at those who cling to *Webster's Second*, questions why they don't go back even further in time. After all, dictionaries of the English language have been in existence for several hundred years.[17]

Lexicographer Bergen Evans was a vocal champion of the new dictionary. Several months after Follett's savage attack, the *Atlantic* published a rejoinder by Evans. Evans also tackles the question of what purpose a dictionary is supposed to serve. In answering it, he takes on the major criticisms that have been leveled at *Webster's Third*. To begin with, he says, a dictionary is concerned with words. If the enormous increase in American vocabulary over the past three decades has compelled the editors of the dictionary to throw out the names of Greek gods, the table of weights and measures, and other extraneous information, so be it.

As for what has changed or been added, Evans reminds his readers of a basic principle of modern linguistics—correctness can only rest on usage, and usage is relative. Usage has changed enormously between 1934 and 1961. Any dictionary that didn't reflect this fact would not be doing its job. The very newspapers and magazines that have attacked *Webster's Third* include "pages that would appear, to the purist of forty years ago, unbuttoned gibberish." The issue of the *Times* in which the editors declare their loyalty to *Webster's Second* uses, by Evans's count, no fewer than 153 words and constructions not listed in that revered tome, as well as nineteen that were listed, but marked as non-standard.[18]

It is not the responsibility of dictionaries to confirm our prejudices, argues Evans. They can't pretend that certain usages or pronunciations don't exist because we find them distasteful. Evans considers *finalize*, which has been singled out for condemnation more than any word except *ain't*. He believes that *Webster's Third* has handled the word in the only way possible. To omit a word that has been common for two generations—that has been used by two presidents and a secretary-general of the United Nations—would be the true abrogation of the lexicographer's duty. Nor should the word be marked as substandard. "President Kennedy and U Thant are highly educated men," he points out, "and both are articulate and literate." *Finalize* is not even a freak form. It was created through the same linguistic process that gave the language *formalize, verbalize, standardize,* and many other *–ize* words.[19]

"Standard," says Evans, is a slippery concept, because "words are continually shifting their meanings and connotations and hence their status." People who have been used to considering a certain word or grammatical structure substandard, who then begin to hear and read it everywhere, will no doubt be distressed to finally look up the word and discover that it's listed in the dictionary with no indication that it's less than respectable. Changes of this type seem to happen rapidly in the twentieth century, "but it is no more the dictionary's business to oppose this process than to speed it up."

Evans concedes that the dictionary is not perfect. People may reasonably argue that some proper names should have been retained or that the new method of defining words has some disadvantages. One thing is certain though, he concludes roundly— "Anyone who solemnly announces in 1962 that he will be guided in matters of English usage by a dictionary published in 1934 is talking ignorant and pretentious nonsense."[20]

Evans was one of the few who drew parallels between Gove's tribulations and Noah Webster's. In a lively article for *The New York Times Magazine,* he recounts the contempt that greeted Webster's 1806 dictionary, with its odd spellings and colloquial Americanisms. He quotes the *Boston Palladium,* calling Webster's dictionary "superfluous, as we already possess the admirable lexicon of Johnson." Then he remarks in an aside, "(As we say today: 'Don't throw away your Second International!')" Webster, too, he points out, was attacked for including vulgar new words such as *advisory, presidential,* and *insubordination.* He informs readers, "*Demoralize, Americanize* and *deputize,* by the way, caused as much agitation in 1806 as *finalize* was to cause 156 years later."[21] Not much had changed in the world of usage criticism.

Months after its release, the uproar over *Webster's Third* raged unabated. In March 1962 *New Yorker* staff writer Dwight Mac-Donald wrote one of the most comprehensive reviews of the book, and probably the nastiest. Because the review is detailed, and even offers a few measured words of praise, it comes off as thoughtful, making the total effect all the more devastating. Mac-Donald got many of his facts wrong, as various responders pointed out. However, none of the rebuttals had the wide distribution or powerful impact of the review itself. Decades later, opponents of the dictionary would still be quoting it to make their case.

MacDonald starts with a sweeping condemnation of the dictionary editors' methods. "This scientific revolution," he pronounces, "has meshed gears with a trend toward permissiveness, in the name of democracy, that is debasing our language by rendering it less precise and thus less effective as literature and less effective as communication."[22] He prefers the "forthright" labels of the second edition—*colloquial, erroneous, incorrect, illiterate*—to the "fuzzier" *nonstandard* and *substandard*. He of course fulminates against *ain't*, blaming the word's wishy-washy labeling on Gove's structural linguistics tendencies.

Although MacDonald has the usual technical quibbles with the dictionary—too many major authors dropped in favor of people like Ethel Merman and the omission of encyclopedia-type material—his overarching complaint is that Gove and his staff have let the facts of American usage influence the content of entries. The problem with "the permissive approach," as MacDonald sees it, is that erroneous usages are treated as acceptable if enough people say them. The editors give one meaning of *nauseous* as "experiencing nausea," although rightly the word means "causing nausea." They allow *biweekly* to mean both "every two weeks" and "semiweekly" when only the first definition is correct. They accept *deprecate* and *depreciate* as synonyms. Mac-Donald believes that this failure to pass judgment on meanings that have traditionally been considered wrong lets the dictionary user down. "If he prefers to use *deprecate* and *depreciate* interchangeably, no dictionary can prevent him," says MacDonald, "but at least he should be warned."[23]

MacDonald takes the same view as Richard Grant White. "Deciding what is correct," he argues, "is more a matter of a feeling for language . . . than of the [usage] statistics on which Dr. Gove and his colleagues seem to have chiefly relied. . . . If nine-tenths of the citizens of the United States, including a recent President, were to use *inviduous*, the one-tenth who clung to *invidious* would still be right."[24] He might as well have said, as White did, "There is a misuse of words which can be justified . . . by no usage, however general."

Several months after MacDonald's review appeared, James Sledd, a professor of English and a notable defender of the dictionary, refuted MacDonald's charges in a conference paper presented at an American Ethnological Society meeting. In it he argues forcefully that MacDonald is ignorant of the nature of structural linguistics, does not understand how lexicographers traditionally work, and—most remarkable of all—is unfamiliar with the contents of *Webster's Second.*

Sledd notes that a number of the words and definitions that MacDonald denounces are also found in the second edition. *Webster's Second,* for example, includes the same two definitions for *biweekly* that so exasperated MacDonald when he read them in *Webster's Third.* Sledd also quotes the preface to *Webster's Second* to show that the same precepts that MacDonald attributes to the pernicious influence of structural linguistics also formed part of the operating principles of those who compiled the 1934 dictionary. For instance, the second edition was also more concerned with reflecting current usage than acting as a repository of linguistic antiquities. William Allan Neilson, editor of *Webster's Second,* had written in the preface, "More important than the retaining of time-honored methods or conventions has been the task of making the dictionary serve as an interpreter of the culture and civilization of today."

The second edition relied on usage statistics in the same way as the third. The introduction states that definitions and pronunciations "must be written only after an analysis of citations." MacDonald's idea that Gove had rejected the traditions of *Webster's Second* was simply mistaken, in Sledd's view. He suggests that to be consistent, MacDonald should "strike out both editions from his lexicographic honor roll," as they both made editorial decisions based on current American speech.[25]

Sledd's paper effectively exposed the weaknesses of MacDonald's argument. However, as a presentation at a scholarly conference, it did not reach nearly the audience of MacDonald's *New Yorker* article. MacDonald's article, with all its inaccuracies, was widely quoted at the time and remains one of the most potent pieces of ammunition in the war against *Webster's Third*.

Perhaps the strangest fallout from the *Webster's Third* controversy was the founding of the rival *American Heritage Dictionary*. James Parton, president of the American Heritage Publishing Company, first tried to buy Merriam out. Declaring that "Merriam's great scholarly reputation has become tarnished . . . through its publication of the radically different Third Edition," Parton vowed to take the dictionary out of print if he acquired the company.[26] When his takeover bid failed, he turned to the next best thing—a dictionary that would challenge *Webster's*.

The *American Heritage Dictionary* made its debut in 1969. It was not an unabridged dictionary on the scale of *Webster's Third*, but it boasted an innovation that should have endeared it to language purists—a Usage Panel. The Panel consisted of 105 journalists, prominent writers, college professors, and editors. Members included Dwight MacDonald and several other people who had written against *Webster's Third*. The dictionary's editors submitted questions about usages that troubled them and the Panel voted for or against the word or phrase, sometimes contributing supplementary comments as well.

Usage turned out to be a knottier issue than Parton might have realized when he set up his panel. Panelists frequently disagreed with each other or with the editors on the level of acceptability of a particular term. They were nearly unanimous about *ain't*—99 percent disapproved of it in writing and 84 percent in both writing and speech. For the most part, however, the *American Heritage* Usage Panel seemed no more authoritative or less random than the statistics of real usage that influenced *Webster's Third*.[27]

Gradually, the turmoil over the dictionary subsided and work at the Merriam Company continued as before. Gove and his staff began to collect and edit material for the next edition. Over the next decades, Merriam would issue several updated versions of the third edition, each with an addenda section for new words. The main text itself was reprinted without major revisions. Gove retired in 1967 and died in 1972 at the age of seventy. His obituary in *The New York Times* notes that "many of his innovations, developed for Webster's Third, have been adopted by dictionary-makers today."[28]

Dictionaries have moved on since the 1960s. The *American Heritage Dictionary* still features the judgments of its Usage Panel, but the Panel now counts several linguists among its members. *Webster's Third* has also evolved. The Merriam Company (now called Merriam-Webster and owned by Encyclopædia Britannica) took the dictionary online in 1996. In 2008 work began on the fourth edition, with updated sections posted to the site as they become available.

To some extent, grammar has also moved on. Few schools now provide the kind of formal grammar lessons that were a routine educational experience from colonial times until the mid-twentieth century. Murray and his successors have disappeared from the classroom. Grammar advisors still abound, but they tend to take a more relaxed attitude toward such classic shibboleths as nominative-case pronouns after *be* and prepositions at the end of a sentence.

"These days," writes former *New York Times Book Review* editor Patricia O'Conner, "anyone who says 'It is I' sounds like a stuffed shirt." As a practical demonstration of this view, her style guide is titled *Woe Is I*. Bryan Garner, author of *Garner's Modern American Usage,* concurs, saying, "*It is me* and *it's me* are both fully acceptable, especially in informal contexts."[29]

Sentence-final prepositions also receive a warm embrace from up-to-date usage arbiters. For instance, O'Conner calls the stricture against their use "a worn out rule" and Mignon Fogarty, also known as Grammar Girl, lists the rule as one of her top ten grammar myths. Garner labels it "spurious." Voicing a sentiment that Webster and the rational grammarians would heartily approve, he admonishes, "Latin grammar should never straitjacket English grammar."[30]

In fact, modern style guides have abandoned many of the grammatical strictures popularized by Lowth and repeated by later grammar book authors. *Shall* is generally agreed to be archaic. Double negatives, although still considered substandard in most cases, are marginally acceptable in a phrase such as *not unattractive*. Split infinitives, which Richard Grant White condemned as "a barbarism of speech," are now widely tolerated, although editors at a few publications have held out against them.[31] The idea that common, long-standing usages should be accepted as standard English is starting to seem a little less radical.

Even the rules in *The Elements of Style* are not held in the same reverence they once were. A roundup of opinions published by *The New York Times* on the fiftieth anniversary of Strunk and

White's joint publication includes as much criticism as praise. Although O'Conner considers the writing advice—omit needless words, be clear, use concrete language—"pure gold," she sees much of the grammar advice as "baloney." Writer and writing teacher Ben Yagoda calls it "a strange little book" and Mignon Fogarty suggests that " 'Strunk and White said so' is not a sure-fire defense in a style argument." Stephen Dodson, an editor who blogs at *Language Hat,* calls the book "the mangiest of stuffed owls."

The severest critic is linguist Geoffrey Pullum. He accepts the style advice as harmless, but "the uninformed grammar rules are a different matter." He points out, as others have, that Strunk and White often break their own rules, for instance, in their frequent use of passive verbs. Besides, Pullum notes, "the book's edicts contradict educated literary usage, even that of books published when Strunk was young and White was a baby." Sentences like *Everybody brought their own,* which they condemn, has been "good standard English" since the time of Jane Austen.[32]

Pullum criticizes Strunk and White at greater length in an article for *English Today.* His chief complaint is the same one that linguists Lounsbury and Whitney made against Richard Grant White and the verbal critics. Neither Strunk nor White was qualified as a grammarian. Their statements about grammar, says Pullum, "are riddled with inaccuracies, uninformed by evidence, and marred by bungled analysis." He makes his point the same way that Lounsbury and Whitney did in their *College Courant* articles—with textual evidence. For instance, he counters Strunk and White's rule "With *none,* use the singular verb" by noting that respected writers have been using *none* with the plural since at least the nineteenth century. Oscar Wilde's 1895 play *The Importance of Being Earnest* contains the line, "None of us are perfect" and Bram Stoker's *Dracula* includes several instances of *none* with plural, such as "None of us were surprised." After several examples along these lines, Pullum concludes, "*Elements* is a hopeless guide to English usage." Worse, it is harmful because it convinces educated adults that their perfectly acceptable usage is incorrect.[33]

In a response in the same journal, Michael Bulley, a professor of classics and English defends *The Elements of Style* against Pullum's criticisms. He, too, relies on classic arguments. White insisted in his response in *The Galaxy* that his feel for language was more relevant for giving usage advice than Lounsbury and Whitney's technical expertise. Similarly, Bulley writes that the basis for style choices should be "aesthetic, not technical." While Bulley shares some of Pullum's misgivings, he disapproves of Pullum's method of combing English literature for evidence that a usage is acceptable (or to put it another way, that Strunk and White's rules are wrong). Collecting examples, in his opinion, is not a substitute for employing good judgment. After all, he says, Strunk and White "wrote a style guide, not an overview of usage." They are entitled to offer their considered opinion on what constitutes elegant speech.[34]

In spite of the changed attitudes reflected in many usage guides, old-style verbal critics are still thick on the ground. New modes of communication like e-mail and Twitter have only increased anxieties about correct usage. Because people no longer have a handy copy of Murray's on their shelf, they turn to online style arbiters for guidance. Blog posts with titles such as "Top Ten Grammar Mistakes" and "Words You're Probably Using Wrong" are as plentiful as grammar advice columns were in nineteenth-century magazines. Typically they're written by bloggers with no special expertise, just an urge to speak their minds about usage. The rules they provide for the grammatically insecure often sound as if they were lifted straight from *Godey's Lady's Book*. As with many usage arbiters from earlier days, grammar bloggers tend to rely on personal taste and their memories of once-heard rules rather than an informed understanding of the structure of English.

For hard-line language purists, good taste and traditional rules still trump linguistic history and widespread usage, and they still respond with anguished cries to any changes in the linguistic status quo. An explosion of outrage greeted the 2012 announcement of the Associated Press that it would accept *hopefully* in its deprecated sense of "it is hoped." "The AP Stylebook Makes a Change—and Breaks Our Hearts," wails the subhead of a *Salon.com* article that bemoans the degradation of grammar. A *Washington Post* story about the new rule drew over six hundred comments, nearly all negative. Their tone ranged from resigned to horrified. Arguments that *hopefully* is no more problematic than other sentence-modifying adverbs like *thankfully, sadly,* and *frankly* were dismissed as irrelevant, as was the fact that the word has been in common use for decades.

Skirmishes continue to blow up between linguists and the traditionalists who blame them for the disasters befalling English. Ryan Bloom, in a blog post for *The New Yorker,* accuses irresponsible "descriptivists" of ignoring the "real-world costs" of giving people "permission to speak and write how we like." According to Bloom, Americans who've been led to think that it's okay to break usage laws—to say *who* instead of *whom,* for instance— are letting their language slide, and therefore losing out on good jobs and education. British verbal critic Lynne Truss is even more scathing in a column for *The Telegraph.* She castigates linguists and lexicographers who are "entirely concerned with looking cool and broad-minded and 'descriptive'" rather than throwing their weight behind proper usage. She is scandalized by the thought of "well-paid academics just sitting back and enjoying the show" while the language collapses around them.

Dwight MacDonald and other critics of *Webster's Third* felt much the same way about Gove. To go back further, Richard

Grant White felt much the same way about Fitzedward Hall, and various reviewers felt that way about William Fowle and the other rational grammarians. Accepting that *Who did she speak to?* is normal English for everyone except those who, in Webster's words, "learn the language by books," is still seen by some as a sign of linguistic radicalism and moral recklessness.[35]

Just as defenders of *Webster's Third* responded to critics by explaining the true purpose of a dictionary, linguists have replied to these attacks by explaining that descriptivists are not in charge of the language. Their job as researchers is to observe and analyze. Even if they tried to dictate usage, they argue, they'd be unlikely to have any better luck than traditional grammarians or verbal critics. Usage standards change over time in spite of pronouncements by experts. "Blaming descriptive linguists for children's illiteracy is like blaming physicists for children's inability to ride bikes," comments Jonathon Owen of the *Arrant Pedantry* blog. Pullum likewise points out in an essay in the *Chronicle of Higher Education* that it is not his responsibility as a linguist to prevent changes to English, even if he could, but "to formulate accurate generalizations" about how it functions.[36]

Owen explains in another post that "linguists love facts." They are therefore inclined to dismiss grammar prescriptions that are based on spurious facts and faulty assumptions. Linguists, he says, are not necessarily against prescribed rules, but those rules should be based on evidence, not personal taste.[37] Traditionalists are no more accepting of these arguments than they have ever been. They believe in keeping to the principles first laid down in the classic grammar books.

Eighteenth-century grammar books have persisted as a force in American life. Their rules may be archaic and seldom followed. They may be based more on the whims of a single grammarian than the real usage of any period. For many people, however, knowing them still serves as a benchmark of education and culture. Quite a few Americans still operate with grammatical attitudes that harken back to the days of the early republic, when grammar study and moral behavior were tightly entwined. For them, a command of standard grammar is more than a practical skill—it is also a virtue.

All the same, we may be entering a period when grammatical rigidity gives way to a greater appreciation of how Americans really talk. While the Internet offers sticklers unprecedented opportunities to lay down the law, it's also exposing more people than ever before to expert discussions about language and grammar. Battles that once played out mainly between specialists now take place in the public arena. Anyone with online access can join in. One result is that more people are coming around to the idea of a grammatical standard that's closer to current speech. In other words, Americans may finally be catching up with Noah Webster.

Notes

1. GRAMMAR FOR A NEW COUNTRY

1. For details of the lecture series, including the price, see John Thomas Scharf, *A History of Baltimore, City and County* (Philadelphia: Louis H. Everts, 1881), 224, 544. Money values in this chapter are based on Samuel H. Williamson, "Seven Ways to Compute the Relative Value of a U.S. Dollar Amount, 1774 to present," MeasuringWorth, http://www .measuringworth.com/uscompare/ (accessed November 19, 2012).

2. Webster recorded details of his trip in his diary for 1785, incorporated in Emily Ellsworth Fowler Ford, comp., *Notes on the Life of Noah Webster,* vol. 1 (New York, 1912), 123–45.

3. Scharf, *History of Baltimore,* 224.

4. Quotations from Webster's first lecture are taken from Noah Webster, *Dissertations on the English Language* (Boston: Isaiah Thomas & Co., 1789), his published version of the lecture series.

5. Along with grammar reform, spelling reform would remain one of Webster's most fervent causes. His 1828 dictionary featured dozens of simplified spellings, although most never caught on. Two that did were omitting the *u* in words like *honour* and *favour,* and dropping the final *k* from words like *publick* and *musick.*

6. Ford, *Notes on the Life of Noah Webster,* vol. 1, 100.

7. Quoted in Allen Walker Read, "American Projects for an Academy to Regulate Speech," *PMLA* 51 (December 1936), 1143–44.

8. John Adams to president of Congress, September 24, 1780, *The Revolutionary Diplomatic Correspondence of the United States,* vol. 4 (Washington, D.C.: Government Printing Office, 1899), 67.

9. Noah Webster, *A Grammatical Institute of the English Language, Part I* (Hartford: Hudson & Goodwin, 1783), quoted in Ford, *Notes on the Life of Noah Webster,* vol. 1, 61.

10. Charlotte Downey, introduction to Thomas Dilworth, *A New Guide to the English Tongue* [1740] (Delmar, NY: Scholars' Facsimiles & Reprints, 1978), vi.

11. Robert Lowth, *A Short Introduction to English Grammar* [1775] (Delmar, NY: Scholars' Facsimiles & Reprints, 1979), 95. Lowth did not include this rule in his first edition, but added it later.

12. Ibid., 96.

13. Ibid. Italics are Lowth's.

14. Ibid., viii.

15. Ibid., 1.

16. Dilworth, *New Guide to the English Tongue,* 99; Lowth, *Short Introduction to English Grammar,* 14.

17. Noah Webster, *A Grammatical Institute of the English Language, Part II* (Hartford: Hudson & Goodwin, 1784), 3.

18. Lowth, *Short Introduction to English Grammar,* 126.

19. Dilworth, *New Guide to the English Tongue,* 154.

20. *Freeman's Journal,* 25 April 1787, quoted in Richard J. Moss, *Noah Webster* (Boston: Twayne, 1984), 10.

21. J. Hammond Trumbull, *The Memorial History of Hartford County, Connecticut, 1633–1884,* vol. 1 (Boston: Edward L. Osgood, 1886), 632.

22. The description of Yale's food comes from Ford, *Notes on the Life of Noah Webster,* vol. 1, 22. Other descriptions of life at Yale come from Brooks Mather Kelley, *Yale: A History* (New Haven: Yale University Press, 1974), 41–42, 78–81.

23. Quoted in Ford, *Notes on the Life of Noah Webster,* vol. 1, 31.

24. Ibid., 18–19 n.

25. Ibid., 33.

26. Ibid., 42.

27. "Memoir of Noah Webster LLD," 7, quoted in E. Jennifer Monaghan, *A Common Heritage: Noah Webster's Blue-Back Speller* (Hamden, CT: Archon Books, 1983), 26.

28. Noah Webster to John Canfield, January 6, 1783, quoted in Ford, *Notes on the Life of Noah Webster,* vol. 1, 58.

29. Joel Barlow to Noah Webster, August 31, 1782, quoted in Ford, *Notes on the Life of Noah Webster,* vol. 1, 55.

30. Price from Ford, *Notes on the Life of Noah Webster,* vol. 1, 59 n. Sales figures are from Henry Steele Commager, preface to Noah Webster, *The American Spelling Book* [1831] (New York: Teacher's College, Columbia University, 1962).

31. Webster, *Grammatical Institute, Part II,* 7; Dilworth, *New Guide to the English Tongue,* 87. The second Webster quotation is from the 1800 edition, 5.

32. Webster, *Grammatical Institute, Part II,* 79.

33. Webster, *Grammatical Institute, Part II,* 1800 edition, 70–71.

34. Webster, *Grammatical Institute, Part II,* 87.

35. Noah Webster to Timothy Pickering, January 20, 1786, quoted in Ford, *Notes on the Life of Noah Webster,* vol. 1, 148 n.

36. Noah Webster Sr. to Noah Webster, July 28, 1787, quoted in Ford, *Notes on the Life of Noah Webster,* vol. 1, 174.

37. Webster, *Dissertations on the English Language,* vii–viii.

38. Ibid., 231.

39. Ibid., 286–87.

40. The amount of the loss is from Monaghan, *A Common Heritage,* 66; Noah Webster to Timothy Pickering, December 8, 1791, quoted in Ford, *Notes on the Life of Noah Webster,* vol. 1, 309.

41. Nathaniel W. Appleton to Noah Webster, January 17, 1790, quoted in Ford, *Notes on the Life of Noah Webster,* vol. 1, 278.

2. GRAMMAR FOR DIFFERENT CLASSES OF LEARNERS

1, For some discussion of this issue, see Lyda Fens-de Zeeuw, *Lindley Murray (1745–1826): Quaker and Grammarian* (Utrecht: LOT, Netherlands Graduate School of Linguistics, 2011), 81–83.

2. Lindley Murray, *Memoirs* (New York: Samuel Wood, 1827), 65. See Fens-de Zeeuw, *Lindley Murray,* 97, for Quakers in York.

3. Murray, *Memoirs,* 84; Lindley Murray to Joseph Cockfield, March 9, 1811, quoted in Fens-de Zeeuw, *Lindley Murray,* 68.

4. Murray, *Memoirs,* 86, 272.

5. Ann Tuke, Mabel Tuke, and Martha Fletcher to Lindley Murray, quoted in Allen Walker Read, "The Motivation of Lindley Murray's Grammatical Work," *Journal of English and Germanic Philology* 38 (1939), 527–28.

6. Lindley Murray, *English Grammar, Adapted to the Different Classes of Learners* (York, England: Wilson, Spence & Mawman, 1795), iii.

7. Murray, *English Grammar,* 20, 37; Robert Lowth, *A Short Introduction to English Grammar* [1775] (Delmar, NY: Scholars' Facsimiles & Reprints, 1979), 14, 29.

8. Murray, *English Grammar,* 28.

9. Ibid., 122.

10. Murray, *Memoirs,* 91.

11. Murray, *English Grammar,* 183.

12. Ibid., 208–9.

13. Ibid., 222.

14. Murray, *Memoirs,* 92.

15. Letter printed in the *Literary Magazine and American Register* 1 (January 1804), quoted in Read, "Motivation of Lindley Murray's Grammatical Work," 531–32.

16. Sales figures for England and the United States are estimates, based on what's known about numbers of editions, how large the print runs were, and how many copies sold annually. They are taken from various places, including the appendix to Charles Monaghan, *The Murrays of Murray Hill* (Brooklyn, NY: Urban History Press, 1998); Rollo LaVerne Lyman, *English Grammar in American Schools Before 1850* (Washington, D.C.: Government Printing Office, 1922), 80, 137; Murray, *Memoirs,* 262; Fens-de Zeeuw, *Lindley Murray,* 160.

17. Murray, *Memoirs,* 137.

18. Lindley Murray to John Murray, November 5, 1804, quoted in Fens-de Zeeuw, *Lindley Murray,* 200.

19. Lindley Murray, *English Exercises, Adapted to Murray's English Grammar* [1797] (York, England: Wilson & Sons, 1833), 7.

20. Lindley Murray to Jedidiah Morse, 1806, quoted in Fens-de Zeeuw, *Lindley Murray,* 199.

21. Lindley Murray to Samuel Latham Mitchill, March 26, 1804, quoted in Fens-de Zeeuw, *Lindley Murray,* 201.

22. Murray, *Memoirs,* 9. Murray says here that he attended the school at the age of six or seven, but records show that he was enrolled in 1756, when he would have been eleven. See Fens-de Zeeuw, *Lindley Murray,* 35.

23. Murray, *Memoirs,* 25.

24. Ibid., 43.

25. Monaghan argues in *The Murrays of Murray Hill* that Lindley Murray was forced to move to England, not because of his health, but because of his loyalty to the British during the Revolution. He believes that Murray was sacrificed to protect the rest of the family from retribution after the war. However, by 1783 the Treaty of Paris had granted Loyalists amnesty and Loyalist New Yorkers did not suffer much backlash. Robert Murray, who was much more openly Tory than Lindley, lived peaceably in New York for the rest of his life. Lindley Murray's poor health was unquestionably genuine. It seems reasonable to accept that as his reason for moving and for staying in Yorkshire. As his debility worsened over the years, returning to New York would have simply been too difficult.

26. Lindley Murray to Noah Webster, 1803, quoted in Emily Ellsworth Fowler Ford, comp. *Notes on the Life of Noah Webster,* vol. 1 (New York, 1912), 533.

27. Noah Webster to Joel Barlow, October 19, 1807, quoted in Ford, *Notes on the Life of Noah Webster,* vol. 2, 30.

28. Noah Webster, *A Philosophical and Practical Grammar of the English Language* (New Haven: Oliver Steele & Co., 1807), 3.

29. Ibid., 5.

30. Ibid.

31. Ibid., 13.

32. Ibid., 51, 168.

33. Ibid., 25–26, 33–34.

34. Ibid., 92.

35. Unsigned review of *A Philosophical and Practical Grammar of the English Language, Monthly Anthology and Boston Review,* May 1, 1808, 267.

36. Ibid., 275, 277.

37. Noah Webster, *A Dictionary of the English Language,* vol. 1 [1828] (London: Black, Young, and Young, 1832), xlviii–l. When Webster published the *American Dictionary of the English Language* in England, he deleted the word *American* to make the volume more palatable to English buyers. The text is unchanged.

38. Lyman, *English Grammar in American Schools,* 80–81.

39. Goold Brown, *The Institutes of English Grammar* [1823] (Delmar, NY: Scholars' Facsimiles & Reprints, 1982), x.

40. Ibid.

41. Ibid., iv.

42. Ibid., vi–vii.

43. Ibid., viii, x–xi.

44. Ibid., 38.

45. Samuel Kirkham, *English Grammar in Familiar Lectures* [1825] (Delmar, NY: Scholars' Facsimiles & Reprints, 1989), 10.

46. Ibid., 49–50.

47. Octavo books were produced by printing sixteen pages of text on one sheet of paper and folding it three times to make an eight-page section. The format sometimes implied cheapness. Elizabeth Frank, Murray's friend and secretary, states in her continuation of his memoirs that all his books were printed on good paper and with clear type (Murray, *Memoirs,* 233).

48. Murray, *Memoirs,* 101.

49. Ibid., 102.

50. Benjamin Silliman, "Travels in England, Holland, and Scotland," quoted in Murray, *Memoirs,* 146–47.

51. Andrew Reed, *Martha: A Memorial of an Only and Beloved Sister* (London: Francis Westley, 1823), 174; Daniel Alexander Payne, *Recollections of Seventy Years* [1888] (New York: Arno Press, 1968), 21.

52. C. P. Bronson, *Elocution, or Mental and Vocal Philosophy* (Louisville: Morton & Griswold, 1845), 367.

3. THE VALUE OF GRAMMAR

1. The description of Jackson's inauguration day comes from James Parton, *Life of Andrew Jackson,* vol. 3 (New York: Mason Brothers, 1888), 168–73.

2. *National Journal,* February 21, 1828, quoted in Allen Walker Read, "Could Andrew Jackson Spell?" *American Speech* 38 (October 1963), 188. Andrew Jackson's reputation as a bad speller was reinforced years later when a former supporter spread the false rumor that Jackson used the abbreviation O.K. to stand for "oll korrect." In fact, O.K. originated in the 1840s as a joke among several newspaper editors. For the full story see Allan Metcalf, *OK: The Improbable Story of America's Greatest Word* (Oxford: Oxford University Press, 2010).

3. Newspaper quotations are from Read, "Could Andrew Jackson Spell?," 191. Adams's opinion is quoted in Cyrus Townsend Brady, *The True Andrew Jackson* (Philadelphia: J. B. Lippincott, 1906), 272.

4. Brady, *True Andrew Jackson,* 190, 191.

5. Ibid., 273.

6. Ibid., 252–53.

7. Read, "Could Andrew Jackson Spell?," 192.

8. Quoted in Parton, *Life of Andrew Jackson,* vol. 3, 170.

9. David Crockett, *The Autobiography of David Crockett* [1834] (New York: Charles Scribner's Sons, 1923), 17–18.

10. James Kirke Paulding, *The Lion of the West* [1830] (Stanford, CA: Stanford University Press, 1954), 21, 27.

11. *Sketches and Eccentricities of Col. David Crockett of West Tennessee* (New York: Harper and Bros., 1837), 164.

12. Crockett, *Autobiography,* 36.

13. Ibid., 92.

14. Ibid., 17.

15. Unsigned review of *Practical Observations upon the Education of the People, North American Review,* July 1826, 53.

16. Samuel Kirkham, *English Grammar in Familiar Lectures* [1825] (Delmar, NY: Scholars' Facsimiles & Reprints, 1989), 13–14.

17. Goold Brown, *The Institutes of English Grammar* [1823] (Delmar, NY: Scholars' Facsimiles & Reprints, 1982), vi.

18. David Crockett to G. W. McLean, January 17, 1834, quoted in James Atkins Shackford, *David Crockett: The Man and the Legend,* edited by John B. Shackford (Chapel Hill: University of North Carolina Press, 1986), 265. For a detailed discussion of Crockett's genuine grammar and spelling, and the part Chilton played in correcting it, see Appendix 2 of Shackford.

19. Books that discuss female language education include Kenneth Cmiel, *Democratic Eloquence: The Fight over Popular Speech in Nineteenth-Century America* (Berkeley, Los Angeles: University of California Press, 1990); Carl F. Kaestle, *Pillars of the Republic: Common Schools and American Society, 1780–1860* (New York: Hill & Wang, 1983); Mary Kelley, *Learning to Stand and Speak: Women, Education, and Public Life in America's Republic* (Chapel Hill: University of North Carolina Press, 2006).

20. Aaron Burr to Theodosia Burr, January 8, 1794, quoted in *Correspondence of Aaron Burr and His Daughter Theodosia,* edited with a preface by Mark Van Doren (New York: S. A. Jacobs, 1929), 14.

21. Kelley, *Learning to Stand and Speak,* 67.

22. Emily Ellsworth Fowler Ford, comp., *Notes on the Life of Noah Webster,* vol. 1. (New York, 1912), 42.

23. Caleb Bingham, *The Young Lady's Accidence* [1784] (Boston: S. Lincoln, 1804), title page.

24. Benjamin Rush, "Thoughts upon Female Education" [1787], in *Essays, Literary, Moral, and Philosophical* (Philadelphia: Thomas and William Bradford, 1806), 75–77.

25. Ibid., 77.

26. Kaestle, *Pillars of the Republic*, 38; editor's notes to *David Walker's Appeal to the Coloured Citizens of the World* [1829], edited by Peter P. Hinks (University Park: The Pennsylvania State University Press, 2000), 119.

27. *Walker's Appeal*, 32.

28. Ibid., 32–33.

29. Ibid., 36.

30. As a result of the American Colonization Society's efforts, several thousand free black Americans emigrated to Liberia when it was founded in 1820.

31. *Freedom's Journal*, March 16, 1827.

32. *Freedom's Journal*, November 16, 1827.

33. *Boston Evening Transcript*, September 28, 1830, quoted in *Walker's Appeal*, 109.

34. M. L. Houser, *Abraham Lincoln, Student. His Books* (Peoria, IL: Edward J. Jacob, 1932), 9.

35. Quoted in John Locke Scripps, *Life of Abraham Lincoln* [1860] (Bloomington: Indiana University Press, 1961), 28, fn. 7.

36. Quoted in David Herbert Donald, *Lincoln* (New York: Simon & Schuster, 1995), 29.

37. Quoted in Houser, *Abraham Lincoln, Student*, 10. Houser is one of several sources for Lincoln's reading habits. Others are Scripps, *Life of Abraham Lincoln* and Albert J. Beveridge, *Abraham Lincoln, 1809–1858*, vol. 1 (Boston, New York: Houghton Mifflin, 1928).

38. Scripps, *Life of Abraham Lincoln*, 65, fn. 9. Further details of Lincoln's grammar studies come from Donald, *Lincoln* and Beveridge, *Abraham Lincoln*.

39. *New York Herald*, May 19, 1860, quoted in *Coming Age*, January 1899, 551.

40. *Atlas and Argus*, May 21, 1860; *Philadelphia Evening Journal*, May 24, 1860. Both are quoted in *North American Review*, January 1912, 738.

41. Many people have analyzed and written about Lincoln's speeches. Resources that I found useful include Kenneth Cmiel, *Democratic Eloquence;*

John Channing Briggs, *Lincoln's Speeches Reconsidered* (Baltimore: Johns Hopkins University, 2005); Paul F. Boller, *Presidential Anecdotes* (New York: Oxford University Press, 1981); Jacques Barzun, "Lincoln the Literary Genius," *Saturday Evening Post*, February 14, 1959.

4. RATIONAL GRAMMAR

1. William Bentley Fowle, *The True English Grammar*, vol. 2 (Boston: Munroe & Francis, 1829), 23–24, 27.

2. William Bentley Fowle, *The Teacher's Institute, or Familiar Hints to Young Teachers* [1847] (New York: A. S. Barnes, 1866), 119.

3. Ibid., 140.

4. Ibid., 141.

5. Ibid.

6. Fowle, *True English Grammar*, vol. 2, 9.

7. The sum involved is found in "William Bentley Fowle," *New-England Historical and Genealogical Register and Antiquarian Journal*, April 1869, 112. Relative dollar amount comes from Samuel H. Williamson, "Seven Ways to Compute the Relative Value of a U.S. Dollar Amount, 1774 to Present." MeasuringWorth. http://www.measuringworth.com/uscompare/ (accessed August 9, 2013).

8. Fowle, *Teacher's Institute*, 142–43.

9. Fowle's reforms are detailed in "William Bentley Fowle," *American Journal of Education* 10 (June 1861), 599–601.

10. Fowle, *True English Grammar*, vol. 2, 17.

11. A list appears in "William Bentley Fowle," *New-England Historical and Genealogical Register*, 116.

12. John Horne Tooke, *Epea Pteroenta* [Winged Words], *or, the Diversions of Purley*, Part I [1786] (London: J. Johnson, 1798), 341–43.

13. Ibid., 344–45.

14. *Blackwood's Edinburgh Magazine*, April 1840, 484.

15. William Bentley Fowle, *The True English Grammar*, vol. 1 (Boston: Munroe & Francis, 1827), 156.

16. Ibid., 179.

17. William S. Cardell to Thomas Jefferson, February 1820, quoted in Allen Walker Read, "American Projects for an Academy to Regulate Speech," *PMLA* 51 (December 1936), 1152.

18. William S. Cardell, *Elements of English Grammar, Deduced from*

Science and Practice, Adapted to the Capacity of Learners (New York: Bliss & White, 1826), x.

19. Ibid., 52.

20. Ibid., 20. *Thing* comes from an Old English word that can refer to a meeting or a business matter, as well as an inanimate object.

21. John Lewis, *Analytical Outlines of the English Language* (Richmond, VA: Shepherd & Pollard, 1825), 1.

22. Ibid., 17.

23. Ibid., 141, 155.

24. Unsigned review of *Analytical Outlines, North American Review,* July 1826, 109, 114; unsigned review of *Elements of English Grammar, New York Literary Gazette and American Athenaeum,* March 25, 1826, 32.

25. Unsigned review of *The True English Grammar, United States Review and Literary Gazette,* June 1827, 201; unsigned review of *Elements of English Grammar, Friend,* November 29, 1828, 49.

26. Unsigned review of *Analytical Outlines, North American Review,* July 1826, 110.

27. *United States Review and Literary Gazette,* June 1827, 202, 204–5.

28. Unsigned review of *The True English Grammar, North American Review,* October 1827, 451–52, 457.

29. Fowle, *True English Grammar,* vol. 2, 8.

30. Ibid., 25.

31. Ibid., 15–16, 33.

32. Ibid., 30.

33. Oliver Wolcott to Noah Webster, 19 Sep. 1807, quoted in Emily Ellsworth Fowler Ford, comp., *Notes on the Life of Noah Webster,* vol. 2 (New York, 1912), 27.

34. Noah Webster to Joel Barlow, October 19, 1807, quoted in Ford, *Notes on the Life of Noah Webster,* vol. 2, 30.

35. Noah Webster, *A Dictionary of the English Language* [1828], vol. 1 (London: Black, Young, and Young, 1832), vi.

36. Quoted in Ford, *Notes on the Life of Noah Webster,* vol. 2, 293.

37. Noah Webster to Thomas Dawes, July 25, 1809, quoted in Ford, *Notes on the Life of Noah Webster,* vol. 2, 70.

38. Webster, *Dictionary of the English Language,* vol. 1, vii.

39. Noah Webster to Thomas Dawes, July 25, 1809, quoted in Ford, *Notes on the Life of Noah Webster,* vol. 2, 71.

40. The numbers of new words and definitions come from Ford, *Notes on the Life of Noah Webster,* vol. 2, 309.

41. *Western Recorder,* January 20, 1829, 12; "Webster's Dictionary and Spelling Book," *Religious Intelligencer,* January 16, 1830, 544; Professor Jameson, review of *An American Dictionary of the English Language, Museum of Foreign Literature, Science and Art,* July–December 1830, 71.

42. Unsigned review of *An American Dictionary of the English Language, North American Review,* April 1829, 464, 474.

43. Noah Webster to William Chauncey Fowler, quoted in Joshua Kendall, *The Forgotten Founding Father* (New York: G. P. Putnam's Sons, 2010), 303.

44. Lyman Cobb, *A Critical Review of the Orthography of Dr. Webster's Series of Books for Systematick Instruction in the English Language* (New York: Collins & Hannay, 1831), iv.

45. Preface to Noah Webster, *An American Dictionary of the English Language* (New York: N. and J. White, 1834), iii.

46. Ford, *Notes on the Life of Noah Webster,* vol. 2, 358, fn. 1.

47. William Bentley Fowle, *Common School Grammar, Part First* (Boston: William B. Fowle & Nahum Capen, 1842), iii.

48. Peter Bullions, *The Principles of English Grammar* [1846] (New York: Pratt, Woodford, Farmer & Brace, 1854), iii, iv.

49. Ibid., 72, 119, 187.

5. GRAMMAR AND GENTILITY

1. Richard Grant White, *Words and Their Uses, Past and Present* [1870] (Boston: Houghton Mifflin, 1881), 274–75.

2. Ibid., 276.

3. Ibid., 323; Richard Grant White, *Every-Day English* (Boston: Houghton Mifflin, 1880), 277–78.

4. Ibid., 295.

5. White, *Words and Their Uses,* 7.

6. Ibid., vi.

7. Ibid., 80, 82.

8. Ibid., 18–19, 26.

9. Ibid., 24.

10. Ibid., 211.

11. Ibid., 108, 142.

12. Ibid., 265.

13. Ibid., 240.

14. Ibid., 62; William Mathews, *Words: Their Use and Abuse* [1876] (Chicago: Scott, Foresman and Co., 1898), 62. The number of books sold is from *The Dictionary of American Biography,* vol. 12 (New York: Charles Scribner's Sons, 1928–58), 406.

15. White, *Every-Day English,* 363; Mathews, *Words,* 97.

16. Edward S. Gould, *Good English, or Popular Errors in Language* [1867] (New York: W. J. Widdleton, 1870), 31; Alfred Ayres, *The Verbalist* [1881] (New York: D. Appleton & Co., 1889), 110.

17. White, *Every-Day English,* 364.

18. White, *Words and Their Uses,* 265.

19. Ibid., 86.

20. Ibid., 90, 138.

21. Gould, *Good English,* 2–3.

22. Mathews, *Words,* 116; Gould, *Good English,* 85.

23. The number of newspapers is taken from Eric Foner, *Give Me Liberty!* 2nd ed. (New York: W. W. Norton & Co., 2009), 346.

24. Henry Alford, quoted in Gould, *Good English,* 9–10; news story quoted in White, *Words and Their Uses,* 29.

25. Both articles are found in the *New York Herald,* November 10, 1869, 10.

26. Gould, *Good English,* 7; White, *Words and Their Uses,* 28, 30, 31.

27. "The English of the Newspapers," *Nation,* December 28, 1865, 814–15.

28. James Parton, *The Life of Horace Greeley, Editor of the New York Tribune* (New York: Mason Brothers, 1855), 266, 274.

29. Horace Greeley, *Recollections of a Busy Life* (New York: J. B. Ford, 1868), 84.

30. Ibid., 137.

31. Although this advice is usually attributed to Greeley, he claimed that he never said it. Several sources credit John B. L. Soule, editor of the *Terre Haute Express,* with originating the phrase, but exactly where it appeared first is unclear.

32. "Gov. Seymour as a Liar," April 9, 1868, 4.

33. "Mr. Greeley as a Gentleman," *Round Table,* April 18, 1868, 244.

34. Untitled article, *New York Times,* April 17, 1868, 4.

35. Untitled article, *New York Tribune,* April 18, 1868, 6.

36. Circulation figure is from Ruth E. Finley, *The Lady of Godey's: Sarah Josepha Hale* (Philadelphia: Lippincott, 1931), 57. Quotation is from Finley, 144.

37. Sarah Josepha Buell Hale, *Manners: Or Happy Homes and Good Society All the Year Round* [1866] (Boston: J. E. Tilton, 1868), 34, 329.

38. White, *Words and Their Uses*, 179; Mathews, *Words*, 113.

39. "Editor's Table: Grammatical Errors," *Godey's Lady's Book*, August 1857, 177; Hale, *Manners*, 37.

40. "Editor's Table: Plain Writing and Fine Writing," *Godey's Lady's Book*, September 1871, 278.

41. "Editor's Table: Euphemisms and Vulgarisms," *Godey's Lady's Book*, August 1871, 181–82; "Words under Ban," May 1871, 474.

42. Gould, *Good English*, 22; "Grammatical Errors," *Godey's Lady's Book*, August 1857, 177.

43. Walter R. Houghton et al., *American Etiquette and Rules of Politeness*, 21st ed. (Chicago: Rand McNally, 1889), 82.

44. William Swinton, *New Language Lessons: Elementary Grammar and Composition* [1877] (New York: Harper & Bros., 1885), iii.

45. Ibid., 2.

46. Thomas W. Harvey, *A Practical Grammar of the English Language* (New York: Van Antwerp, Bragg and Co., 1868), 206, 173, 179.

6. THE SCIENCE OF GRAMMAR

1. Richard Grant White, "Words and Their Uses: The Author's Humble Apology for Having Written His Book," *Galaxy*, June 1871, 786.

2. "Words and Their Uses" Part I, *College Courant*, January 19, 1870, 303.

3. Richard Grant White, *Words and Their Uses, Past and Present* [1870] (Boston: Houghton Mifflin, 1881), 23–24.

4. "Words and Their Uses" Part II, January 26, 1870, 320; Part VI, December 24, 1870, 384.

5. "Words and Their Uses" Part II, January 26, 1870, 320.

6. "Words and Their Uses," Part VIII, January 14, 1871, 13.

7. William Dwight Whitney, *Essentials of English Grammar* [1877] (Delmar, NY: Scholars' Facsimiles & Reprints, 1988), 160.

8. "Words and Their Uses" Part VII, January 7, 1871, 1.

9. "Words and Their Uses" Part IX, January 21, 1871, 25.

10. "Words and Their Uses" Part X, January 28, 1871, 38.

11. White, "Words and Their Uses," 789–90, 792.

12. Ibid., 798, 799, 800.

13. William Jones, "The Third Anniversary Discourse, delivered February 2, 1786," in *The Works of Sir William Jones*, vol. 3 (London: John Stockdale, 1807), 34.

14. The *p*/*f* alternation is part of a much broader pattern of sound changes that occurred in Germanic—the parent of English, German, Dutch, and the Scandinavian languages—after it broke away from Indo-European. This pattern is named Grimm's Law after its discoverer, Jacob Grimm of fairy tale fame.

15. Noah Webster, *A Dictionary of the English Language* [1828], vol. 1 (London: Black, Young, and Young, 1832), ix.

16. Fitzedward Hall, *Recent Exemplifications of False Philology* (New York: Scribner, Armstrong & Co., 1872), 2–3.

17. Ibid., 7–8.

18. Ibid., 31.

19. Ibid., 53.

20. Ibid., 67.

21. Ibid., 100, 112.

22. Ibid., 113.

23. "False Philology," *Old and New*, July 1873, 110; unsigned review of *Recent Exemplifications of False Philology*, *American Church Review*, October 1, 1873, 620.

24. [William D. Whitney], "Hall's 'Exemplifications of False Philology,'" *Nation*, February 15, 1873, 334, 335.

25. Richard Grant White, "Punishing a Pundit," *Galaxy*, October 1873, 439, 441.

26. Ibid., 444–45, 446.

27. Richard Grant White, "Punishing a Pundit: Conclusion," *Galaxy*, December 1873, 792.

28. Richard Grant White, "Linguistic and Literary Notes and Queries," *Galaxy*, May 1875, 670.

29. Richard Grant White, *Galaxy*, January 1874, 92, 95.

30. Richard Grant White, *Every-Day English* (Boston: Houghton Mifflin, 1880), ix.

31. Fitzedward Hall, "English Rational and Irrational," *Nineteenth Century*, September 1880, 424.

32. Whitney, *Essentials of English Grammar*, v.

33. Ibid., 3, 4.

34. This number is taken from Charlotte Downey's introduction to the facsimile edition of *Essentials of English Grammar,* 5.

35. Reed and Kellogg were not the first to think of sentence "mapping." In 1847 Stephen Watkins Clark published *A Practical Grammar: In Which Words, Phrases, and Sentences are Classified according to Their Offices, and Their Relation to Each Other* (New York: A. S. Barnes). Clark diagrams sentences using a system of circles around words and phrases, along with connecting lines. These are more difficult to interpret than Reed-Kellogg diagrams and never caught on.

36. Alonzo Reed and Brainerd Kellogg, *Higher Lessons in English* (New York: Clark & Maynard, 1878), 146, 147, 191.

37. The number of editions comes from Charlotte Downey's introduction to the facsimile edition of *Higher Lessons in English* (Delmar, NY: Scholars' Facsimiles & Reprints, 1987), 5. For some discussion of modern diagramming trends, see Kitty Burns Florey, *Sister Bernadette's Barking Dog* (Hoboken, NJ: Melville House, 2006).

7. GRAMMAR FOR A NEW CENTURY

1. The description of Theodore Roosevelt's inauguration is based on reports in "Roosevelt Hero of a Brilliant Day," *New York Times,* March 5, 1905, 1; "The Spectator," *Outlook,* March 11, 1905, 627–28; Rev. John Bancroft Devins, D.D., "Washington Welcomes a Mighty Host to Witness the Magnificent Pageant," *New York Observer,* March 9, 1905, 295–96; Frederick E. Drinker and Henry Mowbray, *Theodore Roosevelt: His Life and Work* (Washington, D.C.: National Publishing Co., 1919), 186; Nathan Miller, *Theodore Roosevelt: A Life* (New York: William Morrow and Co., 1992), 17–22.

2. *New York Times,* March 5, 1905, 1.

3. *Outlook,* March 11, 1905, 628.

4. William Bayard Hale, "'Friends and Fellow-Citizens'—Our Political Orators of All Parties and the Ways They Use to Win Us," *World's Work,* April 1912, 676.

5. Maurice Garland's introduction to Theodore Roosevelt, *Roosevelt's Writings* (New York: Macmillan, 1920), xxxiii; Irving C. Norwood, "Exit—Roosevelt, the Dominant," *Outing,* March 1909, 724.

6. A list of Theodore Roosevelt's books can be found at the National Park Service Web site for the Theodore Roosevelt Birthplace, www.nps.gov/thrb/historyculture/booksbytr.htm.

7. Lyman Abbott, "A Review of President Roosevelt's Administration," *Outlook,* February 27, 1909, 430.

8. Theodore Roosevelt, *Presidential Addresses and State Papers,* vol. 6, January 16, 1907, to October 25, 1907 (New York: The Review of Reviews, 1910), 1359; Theodore Roosevelt, "The Thraldom of Names," *Outlook,* June 19, 1909, 395.

9. Miller, *Theodore Roosevelt,* 523, 529; Hale, "Friends and Fellow-Citizens," 677.

10. Hale, "Friends and Fellow-Citizens," 678–79; Theodore Roosevelt, *Newer Roosevelt Messages,* vol. 3 (New York: Current Literature, 1919), 1075.

11. *Nick Carter Stories,* no. 121, January 2, 1915, 2.

12. William Dean Howells, *A Hazard of New Fortunes,* vol. 2 (New York: Boni & Liveright, 1889), 26.

13. George Ade, *Fables in Slang* (New York: Grosset & Dunlap, 1899), 63–74.

14. Louise Pound, "The American Dialect Society: A Historical Sketch," *Publication of the American Dialect Society* no. 17, April 1952, 5, 6.

15. "The Point of View," *Scribner's,* July 1909, 250.

16. "The Folly of Taught Grammar," *Atlantic Monthly,* February 1908, 283.

17. "Word-Coining and Slang," *Living Age,* July 13, 1907, 115, 116.

18. Ambrose Bierce, "Some Sober Words on Slang," *Cosmopolitan,* July 1907, 335.

19. Amanda Greer Kendig, "Slang," *Herald of Gospel Liberty,* May 26, 1910, 652; "Life's Black List of Slang Words," *Life,* August 1, 1912, 1525; "A Safeguard against Slang," *Youth's Companion,* March 12, 1908, 127.

20. Thomas R. Lounsbury, *The Standard of Usage in English* (New York: Harper & Brothers, 1908), vii.

21. Ibid., 2–3.

22. Ibid., 83–84.

23. Ibid., 85–86.

24. Ibid., 98, 100.

25. Unsigned review of *The Standard of Usage in English, Banker's Magazine,* June 1908, 962; "Standard Usage in English," *Independent,* July 16, 1908, 148.

26. "English by the Standards of Use and Wont," *Dial,* July 1, 1908, 16–17.

27. Leila Sprague Learned, "A Defense of Purism in Speech," *Atlantic Monthly,* May 1913, 682, 683.

28. "It's me," *Nation,* February 10, 1910, 132, 133; letter to the editor, *Nation,* February 24, 1910, 186.

29. "The Infinitive Mood," *Critic,* July 20, 1895, 45.

30. "The Infinitive Again," *Critic,* August 3, 1895, 80.

31. "The Split Infinitive Again," *Critic,* August 24, 1895, 121.

32. "How to Not Read," *Critic,* January 1900, 33.

33. Lounsbury, *The Standard of Usage,* 248.

34. Ibid., 267, 268.

35. "Correct Speaking and Writing," *Ladies' Home Journal,* March 1903, 45; May 1903, 39.

36. E. B. White, "Letter from the East," *New Yorker,* July 27, 1957, 36.

37. William Strunk, Jr., *The Elements of Style* (Geneva, NY: Press of W.P. Humphrey, 1918), "Introductory." All quotations are from the online edition of the book found on www.bartleby.com/141/.

38. White, "Letter from the East," 36.

39. Strunk, *Elements,* "Elementary Rules of Usage," rule 1; "Elementary Principles of Composition," rule 11.

40. Strunk, *Elements,* "Elementary Principles of Composition," rules 12, 13, 18.

41. E. B. White to Allen Strunk, quoted in Mark Garvey, *Stylized* (New York: Touchstone, 2009), 12.

42. White, "Letter from the East," 36.

43. Ibid., 36, 43.

44. E. B. White to Jack Case, November 3, 1958, quoted in Garvey, *Stylized,* 70.

45. William Strunk, Jr., *The Elements of Style,* with revisions, an introduction and a new chapter on writing by E. B. White (New York: Macmillan, 1959), 52–53.

46. Ibid., 69–70.

47. Ibid., 46, 48.

48. Ibid., x–xi, 33.

49. E. B. White to Jack Case, December 17, 1958, quoted in Garvey, *Stylized*, 101.

50. Ibid., 102.

51. John T. Frederick, "Speaking of Books," *Rotarian*, September 1959, 37; untitled review, *Analysts Journal*, November 1959, 101–2.

52. Charles Poore, "Books of the Times," *New York Times*, June 9, 1959, 35.

53. Untitled review, *New Yorker*, June 20, 1959, 119.

54. The sales figure is taken from Garvey, *Stylized*, 84.

55. Strunk, *Elements*, rule 11; letter quoted in Garvey, *Stylized*, 118–19.

56. Letters quoted in Garvey, *Stylized*, 137, 202.

8. THE PERSISTENCE OF GRAMMAR

1. Details of the press release are taken from David Skinner, *The Story of Ain't: America, Its Language, and the Most Controversial Dictionary Ever Published* (New York: Harper, 2012), 10–11, and Herbert C. Morton, *The Story of* Webster's Third: *Philip Gove's Controversial Dictionary and Its Critics* (Cambridge: Cambridge University Press, 1994), 166–68.

2. McCandlish Phillips, "Webster Soups Up Its Big Dictionary," *New York Times*, September 7, 1961. Most of the newspaper and magazine articles addressing the *Webster's Third* controversy that appeared between 1961 and 1962, including most of those cited here, are collected in James Sledd and Wilma R. Ebbitt, *Dictionaries and That Dictionary: A Casebook on the Aims of Lexicographers and the Targets of Reviewers* (Chicago: Scott, Foresman, 1962).

3. "It Ain't Necessarily Uncouth," *Chicago Daily News*, September 9, 1961.

4. "The Death of Meaning," *Toronto Globe and Mail*, September 8, 1961.

5. "It 'Ain't' Good," *Sunday Star*, September 10, 1961.

6. *New York Times*, November 30, 1961; *Richmond News Leader*, January 3, 1962, 22; *National Review*, February 13, 1962, 98.

7. "Webster's New Word Book," *New York Times*, October 12, 1961.

8. "A Non-Word Deluge," *Life*, October 27, 1961, 4; "Say It 'Ain't' So," *Science*, November 10, 1961, 1493.

9. Wilson Follett, "Sabotage in Springfield," *Atlantic*, January 1962, 73–77.

10. Sydney J. Harris, "Good English Ain't What We Thought," *Chicago Daily News,* October 20, 1961.

11. *The English Language Arts,* prepared by the Commission on the English Curriculum of the National Council of Teachers of English (New York: Appleton-Century-Crofts, 1952), 277, 278.

12. Philip B. Gove, "Linguistic Advances and Lexicography," *Word Study,* October 1961, 8.

13. Philip Gove to G. & C. Merriam Company, February 12, 1946, quoted in Morton, *The Story of* Webster's Third, 34. Gove discusses his view that different speaking styles are valid for different speakers, depending on their social situation, in Brooks Atkinson, "Webster Editor Disputes Critics; Says New Dictionary Is Sound," *New York Times,* March 1, 1962.

14. Philip B. Gove, "A Letter to the Editor of *The New York Times,*" *New York Times,* November 5, 1961.

15. Philip B. Gove, "A Letter to the Editor of *Life Magazine,*" *Life,* November 17, 1961, 13.

16. Roy H. Copperud, "English as It's Used Belongs in Dictionary," *Editor & Publisher,* November 25, 1961, 44.

17. "Dictionary Dithers," *America,* November 18, 1961, 236; "On New Words and New Meanings," St. Louis *Post Dispatch,* December 17, 1961; "The Latest Word," *Reporter,* April 12, 1962, 14.

18. Bergen Evans, "But What's a Dictionary For?" *Atlantic,* May 1962, 58.

19. Ibid., 59.

20. Ibid., 62.

21. Bergen Evans, "Noah Webster Had the Same Troubles," *New York Times Magazine,* May 1962, 77.

22. Dwight MacDonald, "The String Untuned," *New Yorker,* March 10, 1962, 130.

23. Ibid., 150.

24. Ibid., 159.

25. William Allan Neilson, editor-in-chief, *Webster's New International Dictionary of the English Language,* 2nd ed. (Springfield, MA: 1934), v, 1. Sledd's article is quoted in Morton, *The Story of* Webster's Third, 211.

26. *Springfield Union,* February 19, 1962, quoted in Morton, *The Story of* Webster's Third, 223.

27. Percentages are taken from Thomas J. Creswell, *Usage in Dictionaries*

and Dictionaries of Usage, Publication of the American Dialect Society (Tuscaloosa: University of Alabama Press, 1975), 28.

28. "Dr. Philip B. Gove, 70, Is Dead; Editor of the Webster's Third," *New York Times,* November 17, 1972, 50.

29. Patricia T. O'Conner, *Woe Is I* (New York: Riverhead Books, 1996), 10; Bryan A. Garner, *Garner's Modern American Usage* (Oxford: Oxford University Press, 2003), 470.

30. O'Conner, *Woe Is I,* 183; Mignon Fogarty, QuickandDirtyTips.com, http://www.quickanddirtytips.com/education/grammar/ending-a -sentence-with-a-preposition (accessed April 15, 2014); Garner, *Modern American Usage,* 633.

31. For some discussion of this issue, see Geoffrey K. Pullum, "Economist Still Chicken: Botches Sentence rather than Split Infinitive," *Language Log,* June 11, 2013, http://languagelog.ldc.upenn.edu/nll/?p =4680.

32. "Happy Birthday, Strunk and White," *New York Times* online, April 24, 2009, http://roomfordebate.blogs.nytimes.com/2009/04/24/ happy-birthday-strunk-and-white/ (accessed February 4, 2014).

33. Geoffrey K. Pullum, "The Land of the Free and *The Elements of Style*," *English Today* 102, June 2010, 34, 35, 43.

34. Michael Bulley, "Defending Strunk and White," *English Today* 104, December 2010, 57, 58.

35. Ryan Bloom, "Inescapably, You're Judged by Your Language," *New Yorker* online, May 29, 2012, http://www.newyorker.com/online/blogs/ books/2012/05/language-wars-descriptivists.html; "Lynne Truss Has a Grammatical Axe to Grind," *Telegraph,* January 5, 2014, http://www .telegraph.co.uk/journalists/lynne-truss/10547372/Lynne-Truss-has-a -grammatical-axe-to-grind.html.

36. Jonathon Owen, "Lynne Truss and Chicken Little," *Arrant Pedantry,* January 13, 2014, http://www.arrantpedantry.com/2014/01/13/lynne-truss -and-chicken-little/; Geoffrey K. Pullum, "Not Cricket," *Chronicle of Higher Education,* January 28, 2014, http://chronicle.com/blogs/lin guafranca/2014/01/28/not-cricket/.

37. Jonathon Owen, "What Descriptivism Is and Isn't," June 4, 2012, http://www.arrantpedantry.com/2012/06/04/what-descriptivism-is-and-isnt/.

Bibliography

Ayres, Alfred. *The Verbalist* [1881]. New York: D. Appleton, 1889.

Barzun, Jacques. "Lincoln the Literary Genius." *Saturday Evening Post*, February 14, 1959, 30, 62–64.

Beveridge, Albert J. *Abraham Lincoln, 1809–1858*. 2 vols. Boston, New York: Houghton Mifflin, 1928.

Boller, Paul F. *Presidential Anecdotes*. New York: Oxford University Press, 1981.

Booraem, Hendrik. *Young Hickory: The Making of Andrew Jackson*. Dallas: Taylor, 2001.

Brady, Cyrus Townsend. *The True Andrew Jackson*. Philadelphia: J. B. Lippincott, 1906.

Briggs, John Channing. *Lincoln's Speeches Reconsidered*. Baltimore: Johns Hopkins University, 2005.

Brown, Goold. *The Institutes of English Grammar* [1823]. Delmar, NY: Scholars' Facsimiles & Reprints, 1982.

Bullions, Peter. *The Principles of English Grammar* [1846]. New York: Pratt, Woodford, Farmer & Brace, 1854.

Cardell, William S. *Elements of English Grammar, Deduced from Science and Practice, Adapted to the Capacity of Learners*. New York: Bliss & White, 1826.

Cmiel, Kenneth. *Democratic Eloquence: The Fight over Popular Speech in Nineteenth-Century America*. Berkeley, Los Angeles: University of California Press, 1990.

Cobb, Lyman. *A Critical Review of the Orthography of Dr. Webster's Series of Books for Systematick Instruction in the English Language*. New York: Collins & Hannay, 1831.

Coyle, Lee. *George Ade.* New York: Twayne, 1964.

Crockett, David. *The Autobiography of David Crockett* [1834]. New York: Charles Scribner's Sons, 1923.

Derks, Scott, and Tony Smith. *The Value of a Dollar: Colonial Era to the Civil War, 1600–1865.* Millerton, NY: Grey House, 2005.

Dilworth, Thomas. *A New Guide to the English Tongue* [1740]. Delmar, NY: Scholars' Facsimiles & Reprints, 1978.

Donald, David Herbert. *Lincoln.* New York: Simon & Schuster, 1995.

Evans, Bergen. "Noah Webster Had the Same Troubles." *New York Times Magazine,* May 13, 1962, 11, 77, 79, 80.

Fens-de Zeeuw, Lyda. *Lindley Murray (1745–1826): Quaker and Grammarian.* Utrecht: LOT, Netherlands Graduate School of Linguistics, 2011.

Finegan, Edward. *Attitudes Toward English Usage: The History of a War of Words.* New York: Teachers College Press, 1980.

Finley, Ruth E. *The Lady of Godey's: Sarah Josepha Hale.* Philadelphia: Lippincott, 1931.

Foner, Eric. *Give Me Liberty!* 2nd ed. New York: W. W. Norton & Co., 2009.

Ford, Emily Ellsworth Fowler, comp. *Notes on the Life of Noah Webster.* Edited by Emily Ellsworth Ford Skeel. 2 vols. New York, 1912.

Fowle, William Bentley. *Common School Grammar, Part First.* Boston: William B. Fowle & Nahum Capen, 1842.

———. *The Teacher's Institute, or Familiar Hints to Young Teachers* [1847]. New York: A. S. Barnes, 1866.

———. *The True English Grammar.* 2 vols. Boston: Munroe & Francis, 1827–1829.

Fox, Anthony. *Linguistic Reconstruction: An Introduction to Theory and Method.* Oxford: Oxford University Press, 1995.

Gould, Edward S. *Good English, or Popular Errors in Language* [1867]. New York: W. J. Widdleton, 1870.

Gove, Philip Babcock, ed.-in-chief. *Webster's Third New International Dictionary of the English Language, Unabridged.* Springfield, MA: G. & C. Merriam Company, 1961.

Greeley, Horace. *Recollections of a Busy Life.* New York: J. B. Ford, 1868.

Hale, Sarah Josepha Buell. *Manners: Or Happy Homes and Good Society All the Year Round* [1866]. Boston: J. E. Tilton, 1868.

Hall, Fitzedward. *Recent Exemplifications of False Philology.* New York: Scribner, Armstrong & Co., 1872.

Harvey, Thomas W. *A Practical Grammar of the English Language*. New York: Van Antwerp, Bragg and Co., 1868.

Heidler, David S., and Jeanne T. Heidler. *Daily Life in the Early American Republic, 1790–1820: Creating a New Nation*. Westport, CT: Greenwood Press, 2004.

Houser, M. L. *Abraham Lincoln, Student. His Books*. Peoria, IL: Edward J. Jacob, 1932.

Howe, Daniel Walker. *Making the American Self: Jonathan Edwards to Abraham Lincoln*. Cambridge, MA: Harvard University Press, 1997.

Kaestle, Carl F. *Pillars of the Republic: Common Schools and American Society, 1780–1860*. New York: Hill & Wang, 1983.

Kelley, Brooks Mather. *Yale: A History*. New Haven: Yale University Press, 1974.

Kelley, Mary. *Learning to Stand and Speak: Women, Education, and Public Life in America's Republic*. Chapel Hill: University of North Carolina Press, 2006.

Kellog, Allyn S. *Memorials of Elder John White and of His Descendants*. Hartford: Cask, Lockwood and Co., 1860.

Kendall, Joshua. *The Forgotten Founding Father*. New York: G. P. Putnam's Sons, 2010.

Kirkham, Samuel. *English Grammar in Familiar Lectures* [1825]. Delmar, NY: Scholars' Facsimiles & Reprints, 1989.

Lewis, John. *Analytical Outlines of the English Language*. Richmond, VA: Shepherd & Pollard, 1825.

Lounsbury, Thomas R. *The Standard of Usage in English*. New York: Harper & Brothers, 1908.

Lowth, Robert. *A Short Introduction to English Grammar* [1775]. Delmar, NY: Scholars' Facsimiles & Reprints, 1979.

Lyman, Rollo LaVerne. *English Grammar in American Schools Before 1850*. Washington, D.C.: Government Printing Office, 1922.

Mathews, William. *Words: Their Use and Abuse* [1876]. Chicago: Scott, Foresman and Co., 1898.

Mencken, H. L. *The American Language*. 4th ed. [1936]. New York: Alfred A. Knopf, 2000.

Micklethwait, David. *Noah Webster and the American Dictionary*. Jefferson, NC: McFarland & Co., 2000.

Miller, Nathan. *Theodore Roosevelt: A Life*. New York: William Morrow and Co., 1992.

Monaghan, Charles. *The Murrays of Murray Hill*. Brooklyn, NY: Urban History Press, 1998.

Monaghan, E. Jennifer. *A Common Heritage: Noah Webster's Blue-Back Speller*. Hamden, CT: Archon Books, 1983.

———. *Learning to Read and Write in Colonial America*. Amherst: University of Massachusetts Press, 2005.

Morton, Herbert C. *The Story of* Webster's Third: *Philip Gove's Controversial Dictionary and Its Critics*. Cambridge: Cambridge University Press, 1994.

Moss, Richard J. *Noah Webster*. Boston: Twayne, 1984.

Murray, Lindley. *English Exercises, Adapted to Murray's English Grammar* [1797]. York, England: Wilson & Sons, 1833.

———. *English Grammar, Adapted to the Different Classes of Learners*. [1824]. Delmar, NY: Scholars' Facsimiles & Reprints, 1981.

———. *English Grammar, Adapted to the Different Classes of Learners*. York, England: Wilson, Spence & Mawman, 1795.

Murray, Lindley. *Memoirs*. With a preface and a continuation of the memoirs by Elizabeth Frank. New York: Samuel Wood, 1827.

Murray, Sarah E. *In the Olden Time: A Short History of the Descendants of John Murray the Good*. New York: Stettiner, Lambert & Co., 1894.

Nye, Russel Blaine. *Society and Culture in America, 1830–1860*. New York: Harper & Row, 1974.

Osterweis, Rollin G. *Three Centuries of New Haven, 1638–1938*. New Haven: Yale University Press, 1953.

Parton, James. *Life of Andrew Jackson*. 3 vols. New York: Mason Brothers, 1888.

———. *The Life of Horace Greeley, Editor of the New York Tribune*. New York: Mason Brothers, 1855.

Pound, Louise. "The American Dialect Society: A Historical Sketch." *Publication of the American Dialect Society* no. 17, April 1952, 3–28.

Read, Allen Walker. "American Projects for an Academy to Regulate Speech." *PMLA* 51 (December 1936): 1141–79.

———. "Could Andrew Jackson Spell?" *American Speech* 38 (October 1963): 188–95.

———. "The Motivation of Lindley Murray's Grammatical Work." *Journal of English and Germanic Philology* 38 (1939): 525–39.

Reed, Alonzo, and Brainerd Kellogg. *Higher Lessons in English*. New

York: Clark & Maynard, 1878. Reynolds, David S. *Waking Giant: America in the Age of Jackson.* New York: HarperCollins, 2008.

Rush, Benjamin. "Thoughts upon Female Education" [1787]. In *Essays, Literary, Moral, and Philosophical.* Philadelphia: Thomas and William Bradford, 1806.

Scharf, John Thomas. *A History of Baltimore, City and County.* Philadelphia: Louis H. Everts, 1881.

Schweiger, Beth Barton. "A Social History of English Grammar in the Early United States." *Journal of the Early Republic* 30 (Winter 2010): 533–55.

Scripps, John Locke. *Life of Abraham Lincoln* [1860]. Bloomington: Indiana University Press, 1961.

Shackford, James Atkins. *David Crockett: The Man and the Legend.* Edited by John B. Shackford. Chapel Hill: University of North Carolina Press, 1986.

Skinner, David. *The Story of Ain't: America, Its Language, and the Most Controversial Dictionary Ever Published.* New York: Harper, 2012.

Sledd, James, and Wilma R. Ebbitt. *Dictionaries and That Dictionary: A Casebook on the Aims of Lexicographers and the Targets of Reviewers.* Chicago: Scott, Foresman, 1962.

Strunk, William, Jr. *The Elements of Style.* Geneva, NY: Press of W.P. Humphrey, 1918. Online edition, www.bartleby.com/141/.

———. *The Elements of Style.* With revisions, an introduction and a new chapter on writing by E. B. White. New York: Macmillan, 1959.

Swinton, William. *New Language Lessons: Elementary Grammar and Composition* [1877]. New York: Harper & Bros., 1885.

Tieken-Boon van Ostade, Ingrid. *The Bishop's Grammar: Robert Lowth and the Rise of Prescriptivism in English.* Oxford: Oxford University Press, 2011.

Trumbull, J. Hammond. *The Memorial History of Hartford County, Connecticut, 1633–1884.* 2 vols. Boston: Edward L. Osgood, 1886.

Walker, David. *David Walker's Appeal to the Coloured Citizens of the World* [1829]. Edited and with a new introduction and annotations by Peter P. Hinks. University Park: The Pennsylvania State University Press, 2000.

Webster, Noah. *The American Spelling Book* [1831]. New York: Teacher's College, Columbia University, 1962.

Webster, Noah. *A Dictionary of the English Language* [1828]. 2 vols. London: Black, Young, and Young, 1832.

———. *Dissertations on the English Language.* Boston: Isaiah Thomas & Co., 1789.

———. *A Grammatical Institute of the English Language, Part II.* Hartford: Hudson & Goodwin, 1784.

———. *A Grammatical Institute of the English Language, Part II.* 6th ed. [1800]. Delmar, NY: Scholars' Facsimiles & Reprints, 1980.

———. *A Philosophical and Practical Grammar of the English Language.* New Haven: Oliver Steele & Co., 1807.

White, E. B. "Letter from the East." *New Yorker,* July 27, 1957, 35–36, 42–44.

White, Richard Grant. *Every-Day English.* Boston: Houghton Mifflin, 1880.

———. *Words and Their Uses, Past and Present* [1870]. Boston: Houghton Mifflin, 1881.

———. "Words and Their Uses: The Author's Humble Apology for Having Written His Book." *Galaxy,* June 1871, 786–800.

Whitney, William Dwight. *Essentials of English Grammar* [1877]. Delmar, NY: Scholars' Facsimiles & Reprints, 1988.

"William Bentley Fowle." *American Journal of Education* 10 (June 1861): 597–610.

———. *New-England Historical and Genealogical Register and Antiquarian Journal,* April 1869, 109–118.

Williams, Talcott. "Lincoln the Reader." *American Review of Reviews,* February 1920, 193–96.

Williamson, Samuel H. "Seven Ways to Compute the Relative Value of a U.S. Dollar Amount, 1774 to Present." MeasuringWorth. http://www.measuringworth.com/uscompare/.

Wilson, Douglas L. "What Jefferson and Lincoln Read." *Atlantic,* January 1991, 51–57, 60–62.

Woods, William F. "The Evolution of Nineteenth-Century Grammar Teaching." *Rhetoric Review* 5 (Autumn 1986): 4–20.

"Words and Their Uses," Parts I–X. *College Courant,* November 19, 1870–January 28, 1871.

Index

a, 63–64, 68

A.B.C. school, 103

Academy of Natural Sciences, 120

Academy of Philadelphia, 57

accent, American, 11

accusative, 18. *See also* objective case

ACS. *See* American Colonization Society

active voice, 241

Adams, John, 12

Adams, John Quincy, 81–82

Ade, George, 218–19, 222

adjectives, 63

adverbs, 63, 206

African Americans, 97–102, 154. *See also* free blacks

agent, 122

ain't, 244–47, 249, 251, 252, 259, 261, 264

Allison, Patrick, 6

America, 258

American Academy of Language, 11, 124

American Colonization Society (ACS), 99–100, 278n30

American Dialect Society, 219–20, 232

American Dictionary of the English Language (Webster, Noah), 66, 129–38, 243

abridgment of, 138–41

for English market, 136, 275n37

price and copies, 136, 138

American Ethnological Society, 262

American Etiquette and Rules of Politeness, 171

American Heritage Dictionary, 263–64

American language

accent, 11

British language compared to, 2, 8–13, 28, 135

dialects, 38, 93

idiom, 2, 31, 93

uniform national language, 8, 38

American Philological Association, 186

American Spelling Book (Webster, Noah), 133

Americanisms, 61, 135

The American Magazine, 35–36

The American Minerva, 39, 60

The American Spelling Book (Webster, Noah), 30

Amherst College, 132

among, with *whom,* 109

an, 63–64, 68

The Analysts Journal, 240

Analytical Outlines of the English Language (Lewis), 125–27

Anglo-Saxon (Old English)
  unvarnished, 159
  verbs, 180–81, 230
  words from, 37, 38, 62, 119, 121, 125
aphorisms, 48
*An Appeal to Coloured Citizens of the
  World* (Walker, D.), 97–101
Appleton, Nathaniel, 38
Aristotle, 120
Arnold, Benedict, 33
Arrant Pedantry blog, 269
articles, before names, 33
as
  as follows, 64, 68
  like/as, 4, 152–53
Associated Press, 268
Atheneaum, 193
Atlantic, 221, 227, 249, 258
Atlas and Argus, 108
attributes, 63
Aurora, 39
Ayres, Alfred, 157, 204

Barlow, Joel, 28, 35, 61, 130
be. See to be
Belles-Lettres Society, 115
between you and I, 1
Bible, 7
  examples from, 48
  King James Bible, 14, 132
  reading, 94, 102
  as source, 132, 134
  Webster's Bible, Common Version,
    133
  Wycliffe's translation of, 230
Bierce, Ambrose, 221–22
Bingham, Caleb, 95, 113, 114
biweekly, 261, 262
blab schools, 104
blackboards, 116
Blackstone, William, 102

Blackwood's, 121
Blair, Francis P., 83
blog posts, 177, 266–69
Bloom, Ryan, 268
Book Society, 21
Boston Latin School, 114, 116
Boston Palladium, 260
Bradford, William, 21
*A Brief History of Epidemic and
  Pestilential Diseases* (Webster,
  Noah), 60–61
British language, 2, 8–13, 28, 135
Brown, Goold, 69–73, 91, 92
Buckminster, Joseph, 25–26
Bulley, Michael, 267
Bullions, Peter, 142
bully pulpit, 213
Burr, Aaron, 94
Burr, Theodosia, 94
Bush, Sarah, 104

canebrake, tales from, 85, 88
Cardell, William, 124–27
Carnegie, Andrew, 155
carpetbaggers, 154
case. *See also* nominative case
  dative, 47, 204
  definition of, 47, 122
  genitive, 18, 47
  noun, 18, 203–4
  objective, 18, 19, 32, 72
  vocative, 204
Case, Jack, 237, 239–40
casual speech, 15, 212, 216, 219
Channing, William Ellery, 115
Chaucer, Geoffrey, 120, 181, 183, 185,
  204
Chicago Daily News, 244, 250
Chilton, Thomas, 92
Chronicle of Higher Education, 269
Clark, Stephen Watkins, 285n35

Cobb, Lyman, 137–38

Coleridge, Samuel, 194

College Courant, 175–85, 223, 226, 246

colloquial style, 109, 169, 212, 217

commands, 19

Commentaries on the Law of England (Blackstone), 102

Common School Grammar (Fowle), 141

common schools, 81, 95

comparative linguistics, 190

comparisons
    comparatives, 71
    phrases, 204
    subject of missing verb in, 13

A Compendious Dictionary of the English Language (Webster, Noah), 61, 129

composition, 142, 235, 238–39, 241

conjunctions, 63, 121

connectives, 63

Constitution, 35, 39

Converse, Sherman, 135, 138

Copperud, Roy H., 257–58

copyright laws, 6, 53, 140

corduroy roads, 34

Cornish, Samuel, 101

corporal punishment, 117

country words and phrases, 88

A Critical Review of the Orthography of Dr. Webster's Series of Books for Systematick Instruction in the English Language (Cobb), 137–38

The Critic, 228–29

Crockett, David, 84–89, 92–93, 212, 216

Daily Whig, 163

dame school, 112

Darwin, Charles, 185

dative case, 47, 204

Davy Crockett's Almanack, 85

Day, Benjamin, 160

deprecate, depreciate, 261–62

descriptive linguists, 251–52, 269

Dialect Notes, 219, 232

The Dial, 202

diary clubs, 222–23

Dickens, Charles, 76

Dictionary of American Regional English, 220

Dictionary of the English Language (Johnson), 61, 138

different than, different from, 238, 247, 250

Dilworth, Thomas
    criticism of, 19, 28
    influence of, 22, 30–31, 104
    A New Guide to the English Tongue, 13, 15
    practice verses, 20

dime novels, 216–17

direct objects, 18

Dissertations on the English Language (Webster, Noah), 36–39, 65, 141

Dodson, Stephen, 266

double negatives, 3, 32, 47, 66
    ban on, 13, 68, 71, 153, 191
    examples of, 32, 217, 265

Douglas, Stephen, 107

Dracula (Stoker), 266

dress, 150

drunk, 180–81

due to, 227, 235, 250

Editor & Publisher, 257

Elements of English Grammar (Cardell), 124–25

Elements of Useful Knowledge (Webster, Noah), 61

The Elements of Style (Strunk), 232–42, 265–67

elevated style, 14, 15, 17, 109, 221

English Grammar, Adapted to the Different Classes of Learners (Murray, L.), 41, 45–55, 63–64, 70–72, 74–75, 77, 232, 233
  abridged version of, 51, 113
  dominance of, 106
  improvement on, 142
  memorization of, 98, 172
  subtitle of, 92
English Grammar in Familiar Lectures (Kirkham), 73–74, 91, 106
English language. *See also* Anglo-Saxon
  bad, 37–38, 203, 220, 252
  command of, 3, 7
  family of, 189
  good, 37, 203, 228, 252, 266
  Latin compared to, 9–10, 18–19, 33, 36–38, 46–47, 123, 265
  Webster, Noah, lectures on, 5–10, 33, 34
English market, 136, 275n37
errors, grammar, 105, 231
Essentials of English Grammar (Whitney, W.), 202–4
etiquette books, 170–71
etymology, 17–18, 119, 131, 139, 172, 224. *See also* parts of speech
euphemisms, 132, 149, 169
Evans, Bergen, 258–60
Evening Post, 60
everybody
  plural pronouns with, 250
  they with, 235
Every-Day English (White, R.), 144, 147, 156, 157, 201, 204
everyone, 227, 239
"Excelsior" (Longfellow), 4
experience, 194

fables, 20
  slang, 218, 222
false syntax, 15, 32, 62, 72, 148, 179

father/pater, 189
Federalists, 39, 132
female, 168, 182
Female Monitorial School, 117
feminized words, 170
finalize, 247, 256, 258, 259, 260
Fogarty, Mignon, 265–66
Follett, Wilson, 249–50
form (level of scholarly achievement), 113
Fourier, Charles, 164
Fourierism, 164
Fowle, William Bentley, 111–18, 269
  Common School Grammar, 141
  The Teacher's Institute, 113, 116
  The True English Grammar, 112, 118, 121–23, 127–29
Fowler, William, 137
Franklin, Benjamin, 13, 26, 57
Franklin Institute, 120
free blacks, 80, 97–99, 101, 278n30
Freedom's Journal, 100–101
Freeman's Journal, 21
French orthography, 29
from, 119–20, 123, 190
  different than, different from, 238, 247, 250
frontier idiom, 93
future tense, 16–17, 37

The Galaxy, 147, 175, 177, 183, 197, 200–201, 253, 267
Garner, Bryan, 265
gender, 16, 168. *See also* women
genitive case, 18, 47
gentleman, gents, 149, 156–57
Germanic languages, 189–90, 284n14
Gerry, Elbridge, 82
Gilded Age, 154
Godey, Louis, 166
Godey's Lady's Book, 166–70, 267

Good English, or Popular Errors in Language (Gould), 157, 158, 161

Goodrich, Chauncey, 139–40

Gospel of Luke, 19

Gould, Edward S., 157, 158, 159, 161

Gove, Philip B., 243–44, 253–57, 261–64, 268

grammar
definition of, 16, 31, 90, 120, 121, 252
purpose of, 15–16, 127
rules, 1, 4, 109, 269

grammar books
memorization of, 2–3, 17, 31, 114
popularity of, 7, 90–91
style of, 62

Grammatical Institute of the English Language (Webster, Noah), 5, 52
Part I, 12, 29–30
Part II, 19, 30–33, 35, 55, 63, 141
Part III, 22, 30

grammatical resolution, 19

Grantism, 154

Greek language, 47, 90, 187–88

Greeley, Horace, 163–66, 282n31

Green, Duff, 83

Greene, Lynn M., 107

Greenleaf, James, 36

Grimm, Jacob, 284n14

Grimm's Law, 284n14

Hale, Sarah Josepha, 166–70

Hall, Fitzedward, 192–202, 204, 205, 207, 269

Hamilton, Alexander, 39

Hanks, Nancy, 102

Harper's, 177, 204, 223, 250

Harris, Sydney, 250

Harrison, William Henry, 163

Hartford Convention, 132

Harvard, 13, 81, 82, 114, 219

Harvey, Thomas, 172–73

hat in ring, 214

A Hazard of New Fortunes (Howells), 217–18

Higher Lessons in English (Reed, Alonzo, and Kellogg), 205–7

Home, Henry, 32

Hooker, Thomas, 21

hopefully, 1, 238, 268

Horne Tooke, John
criticism of, 127–28
theories of, 61, 73, 111, 124, 126, 131, 190
Winged Words, or The Diversions of Purley, 37, 62, 64, 118–21, 125

Howells, William Dean, 217–18

hypercorrection, 48

I
I instead of *me* after preposition, 4
I seen, I done, 179–80
It is I, 10, 31, 47, 153, 265
It is I compared to *It is me*, 10, 31
between you and I, 1
you and me, you and I, 231

imperative mood, 19

The Importance of Being Earnest (Wilde), 266

indicative mood, 19

Indo-European languages, 188–90

The Institutes of English Grammar (Brown), 69–73, 91

International Phonetic Alphabet, 253

Internet, 177, 270. *See also* blog posts

Irish immigrants, 157–58

irregardless, 247, 249, 251, 256–57

It is I
It is me compared to, 10, 31
use of, 47, 153, 265

It is me
  I am it compared to, 181
  It is I compared to, 10, 31
  It's me, 89, 227–28, 265
  use of, 32, 55, 65, 66, 122, 123, 173,
    206–7, 227

Jackson, Andrew, 79–84, 89, 93, 99, 134,
    210, 212, 276n2
Jackson, Rachel, 82
Jay, John, 39
Jefferson, Thomas, 79, 99, 124
jeopardize, 150–51, 199, 207
Johnson, Samuel, 61, 138, 194, 255
Jones, William, 187–90
joy riding, 220

Kellogg, Brainerd, 205–7
Kennedy, John F., 251
The Kentucky Preceptor, 105
King James Bible, 14, 132
Kirkham, Samuel, 69, 73–74, 91, 92, 106

The Ladies' Home Journal, 231
lady, 156–57
Language and the Study of Language
    (Whitney, W.), 186
languages. *See also specific languages*
  evolution of, 9, 11, 148, 151, 225, 240
  relationships, 189–90
Latin
  English language compared to, 9–10,
    18–19, 33, 36–38, 46–47, 123, 265
  English-style plurals with, 65
  Greek, Sanskrit and, 187–88
  study of, 90, 104, 112
  use of, 241–42
Learned, Leila Sprague, 227
lend, loan, 231
Lessons in Elocution (Scott), 105
Lewis, John, 125–27

lexicography, 254
life, 135
Life magazine, 249, 256–57
like
  as and, 4, 152–53
  embedded clauses introduced by,
    250
Lincoln, Abraham, 102–10, 146
Lincoln, Thomas, 102–3
Lindley, Mary, 56
Lindley, Thomas, 56
linguistic science, 173
linguistics, 190, 207, 251–54
The Lion of the West (Paulding), 85–86
The Living Age, 221
loan, lend, 231
Log Cabin, 163
logic, 148–49, 178, 180, 182, 200
Longfellow, Henry Wadsworth, 4
Lounsbury, Thomas, 175–86, 191, 204,
    246, 252
  The Standard of Usage in English,
    223–27, 229–31
low expressions, 49, 87, 222
low words, 61
Lowth, Robert
  criticism of, 37, 120
  influence of, 30, 31–33, 45, 47, 63, 74,
    141
  on noun forms, 19
  on sentence parsing, 19–20
  *A Short Introduction to English
    Grammar*, 13–15, 16, 46, 64, 173
lyceum movement, 120
Lyceum of Natural History, 120

MacDonald, Dwight, 260–63, 268
Madison, James, 26, 79, 99
male, 168
malefactors of great wealth, 213–14
a man, replaced with *one*, 152

Manners: Or, Happy Homes and Good Society All the Year Round (Hale), 168
maps, 116
"Mary had a little lamb" (Hale), 166
Mathews, William, 156, 159
McKinley, William, 209
me. See also It is me
   I instead of *me* after preposition, 4
   you and me, you and I, 231
Merriam, Charles, 140–41
Merriam, George, 140–41
Merriam Company, 243, 248, 255, 264
Merriam-Webster Dictionary, 141
Milton, John, 14, 71
Mitchill, Samuel Latham, 54–55
Modern Language Notes, 202
modifiers, 63
   them as noun modifier, 158
monitorial system, 115–17
Monroe, James, 79
mood, 19
moral instruction, 20, 105. *See also* virtue and grammar
Morse, Jedidiah, 54
Murray, Hannah Dobson, 41–42, 58
Murray, John, 53–54, 56
Murray, Lindley
   criticism of, 69–71, 120, 122, 144
   English Grammar, 41, 45–55, 63–64, 70–72, 74–75, 77, 92, 98, 106, 113, 142, 172, 232, 233
   family history and career of, 55–61, 75, 274n22, 274n25
   influence of, 76–77, 104, 113, 120, 129, 141, 231, 235
   poor health of, 41–42, 44, 58–59, 75, 275n25
   The Power of Religion on the Mind, 43–44
   Webster, Noah, and, 60, 63–68
Murray, Robert, 55–58, 275n25

names
   articles before, 33
   noun labels as, 63
A Narrative of the Life of David Crockett of the State of Tennessee (Crockett), 88–89, 92–93
National Council of Teachers of English, 252
National Journal, 81–82
The Nation, 162, 177, 196, 198, 227–28
nauseous, 261
Neilson, William Allan, 262
New Language Lessons (Swinton), 172
New Testament, 13, 20
New York Herald, 108, 161
New York Literary Gazette, 126
New York Times Book Review, 265
New York Times Magazine, 260
New York Tribune, 163, 165
The New Yorker, 233, 236–37, 241, 260, 263, 268
The New York Times, 147, 161, 209
   reviews in, 165, 240, 244–45, 247–48, 255–56, 258–59, 264–65
A New Guide to the English Tongue (Dilworth), 13, 15
newspapers, 160–65
Nicholas Nickleby (Dickens), 76
The Nineteenth Century magazine, 201
nominative case
   after *to be,* 47, 71, 109, 265
   after comparatives, 71
   noun, 19, 46, 72
   pronouns, 171, 204
   subjects in, 18
   after verbs and prepositions, 48
none, 266
nonstandard forms
   examples of, 87–89, 122, 247, 249
   pronouns, 48
   study of, 219–21

North American Review, 90, 127, 136

noun

    case, 18, 203–4

    definition of, 17–18, 46, 71, 106, 121, 123, 125, 172, 203

    examples of proper, 33

    forms, 19

    irregular, 144

    labels as agent or object, 122

    labels as names, 63

    nominative case, 19, 46, 72

    noun declension, 18

    possessive, 19, 46, 72

    preposition-noun combinations, 47

    them as noun modifier, 158

objective case

    direct objects in, 18

    for pronouns, 19, 32

    use of, 72

objects

    direct, 18

    noun labels, 122

    of prepositions, 18

obnoxious, 150

obsolete words, 49

O'Conner, Patricia, 265–66

octavo books, 75, 276n47

offensive words and phrases, 133, 134, 149

O.K., 276n2

Old English. *See* Anglo-Saxon

Old Testament, 131

one, a man replaced with, 152

Origin of Species (Darwin), 185

orthography, 17, 172

    Americanization from French, 29

The Outlook, 213, 214

overblown words, 86

over-genteel or pompous words, 156

overlong sentences, 49

Owen, Jonathon, 269

Oxford English Dictionary, 119, 202

pants, 149, 156, 207, 221

Paradise Lost (Milton), 14

part from, part with, 202

participles, 72

    past, 179–80

Parton, James, 263–64

parts of speech

    definition of, 17–18, 46, 105, 123, 125

    discussion of, 63, 71–72, 126

    outlining of, 46–47, 62

passive sentences, 241

passive verbs, 266

past participles, 179–80

pater/father, 189

patriotism, 91, 95

Paulding, James K., 85–86

Payne, Daniel, 77

penny press, 160–63

Perkins, Nathan, 22

perspicuity, 49, 71

p/f, 189–90, 284n14

Philadelphia Evening Journal, 108

Phillips, McCandlish, 244

Philological Society, 35–36

philology, 35, 176, 186, 207, 225

A Philosophical and Practical Grammar of the English Language (Webster, Noah), 62, 65–68, 111, 123, 128, 136, 141

Pickering, Timothy, 33, 38

plagiarism, 45, 67, 70, 73

pleasing style, 50

plurals

    Latin with English-style, 65

    pronouns with *everybody,* 250

poems, 3–4

Poore, Charles, 240–41

possessives
  in genitive case, 18
  noun, 19, 46, 72
  's, 19, 64–65, 68, 241
Post Dispatch, 258
potential mood, 19
The Power of Religion on the Mind
  (Murray, L.), 43–44
*A Practical Grammar of the English
  Language* (Harvey), 172–73
prayers, 20
precision, 49, 71, 142
prepositions
  classification of, 121
  I instead of *me* after, 4
  nominative case after verbs and, 48
  objects of, 18
  preposition-noun combinations, 47
  preposition-stranding, 14, 31, 47,
    49–50
  sentence-final, 14, 49–50, 173, 265
Primary School Committee, 115–17
Princeton, 81, 90
The Principles of English Grammar
  (Bullions), 142
private learners, 72, 92
progressives, 73
pronouns
  after *to be,* 1, 32
  classification of, 46
  in conjoined phrases, 48
  everybody with plural, 250
  nominative case, 171, 204
  nonstandard, 48
  objective case for, 19, 32
  sexist, 48
  as substitutes, 63
pronunciation, 17, 62, 248, 253, 258
propriety, 49, 71, 142
prosody, 17, 62, 172
provincialisms, 74

Psalter, 13, 20
public schools, 90, 97, 101–2, 117
Pullum, Geoffrey, 266–67, 269
purity, 49, 71, 142, 191

Quakers, 41–45, 52, 56, 58, 97, 233
question-and-response format, 31

rational grammarians, 111, 185, 191, 269
*Recent Exemplifications of False
  Philology* (Hall), 192–96, 200, 204
Reed, Alonzo, 205–7
Reed, Andrew, 76
regionalisms, 89, 93
  examples of, 109, 217, 220
  expressions, 86
  variation, 74
Reporter, 258
Revolutionary War, 10, 24–26, 33,
  55–56, 58
Richmond News Leader, 245
The Rights of All, 101
The Riverside Shakespeare (White, R.),
  147
Rockefeller, John D., 155
Roosevelt, Theodore, 209–16
The Rotarian, 240
The Round Table, 164
Royal American Magazine, 12
rule of three, 103
Rush, Benjamin, 96

's, 19, 64–65, 68, 241
Salon.com, 268
Sanskrit, 186–88, 192
science
  linguistic, 173
  principles, 185
  promotion of, 120–21
  teaching, 116
Science magazine, 244, 249

scientist, 200, 225

Scott, William, 105

Scribner's, 213, 220

Second Great Awakening, 131

sentences

   diagramming, 20, 206–7, 285*n*35

   overlong, 49

   parsing, 19–20, 32, 48, 62, 70, 71–72,
      91, 116, 125, 203, 207

   passive, 241

   sentence-final preposition, 14, 49–50,
      173, 265

   structure, 20, 62

Seward, William, 108–9

sexist pronouns, 48

Seymour, Horatio, 164, 165

Shakespeare, William, 147, 180–81, 183,
   228

shall

   shall/should, 254

   shall/will, 16–17, 37–38, 110, 152–53,
      158, 173, 226, 240

   with third person, 109

   use of, 171, 191, 265

shibboleths, 4, 265

*A Short Introduction to English
   Grammar* (Lowth), 13–15, 16, 46,
   64, 173

should/shall, 254

Silliman, Benjamin, 76

Simplified Spelling Board, 204, 213

*Sketches and Eccentricities of Col. David
   Crockett of West Tennessee*
   (Crockett), 86

Sketches of the History of Man (Home),
   32

slang

   examples of, 161, 235, 247

   fables, 218, 222

   use of, 160, 171, 211–13, 216–22, 232,
      246, 248, 252

slavery, 75, 97–99, 101, 107, 164

Sledd, James, 262–63

Smithson, James, 120

Smithsonian Institution, 120

Snowden, Samuel, 98

Soule, John B. L., 282*n*31

speech. *See also* parts of speech

   casual, 15, 212, 216, 219

   natural habits of, 144

   stage western, 87

   verbal critics on, 142, 156

   written language compared to, 17

spelling, 17

   misspellings, 89, 92–93, 235

   reform, 9, 38, 137–39, 271*n*5

   simplified, 61, 89, 213

split infinitives

   debate on, 171, 200, 228–30, 240, 265

   examples of, 1, 13

stage western speech, 87

The Standard of Usage in English
   (Lounsbury), 223–27, 229–31

statements, 19

Steele, John, 21

Steele, Mercy, 21

Stevenson, Howard, 236

Stiles, Ezra, 23

Stoker, Bram, 266

Story, Joseph, 80, 84

Stowe, Harriet Beecher, 76

structural linguists, 251, 262

Strunk, William, Jr., 232–42, 265–67

style guides, 41, 49, 207, 242, 265

subjects

   of missing verb in comparisons, 13

   in nominative case, 18

subjunctive mood, 19

substandard label, 246–47, 252

substantive, 17. *See also* noun

substitutes, 63

Sun newspaper, 160–61

Sunday Star, 244, 245, 246

Swinton, William, 172

synonyms, 49, 149, 151, 168, 261

A Synopsis of Words in Twenty Languages
(Webster, Noah), 131–33

syntax, 172
definition of, 47
false, 15, 32, 62, 72, 148, 179
issues, 122, 125

Taft, William, 214–15

"tall talk," western, 85–87

The Teacher's Institute (Fowle), 113, 116

The Telegraph, 268

tense
future, 16–17, 37
verbs, 19, 37

than
different than, different from, 238, 247,
250
then and, 94

thee, 16, 17, 65

them, as noun modifier, 158

then, than, 94

they
with *everybody,* 235
with singular antecedent, 47–48,
152–53

thing, 125, 280*n*20

thou
thee and, 16, 17, 65
use of, 72

to
due to, 227, 235, 250
verb separated from, 171, 173, 230
to whom, 204

to be
in Greek, Latin and Sanskrit, 187–88
nominative case after, 47, 71, 109, 265
pronouns after, 1, 32
unless you be, unless you are, 109

Toronto Globe and Mail, 245

The Travels of Cyrus, 57

Treaty of Paris, 275*n*25

Trinity Lane School, 44, 48

trousers, 149, 221

The True English Grammar (Fowle), 112,
118, 121–23, 127–29

Truss, Lynne, 268

Twain, Mark, 154, 217

Uncle Tom's Cabin (Stowe), 76

United States Telegraph, 82, 83

unless you be, unless you are, 109

Usage Panel, 263–64

Vanderbilt, Cornelius, 155

verbal critics, 142, 156, 225

The Verbalist (Ayres), 157, 204

verbs
Anglo-Saxon, 180–81, 230
classification of, 62–63
comparisons and subject of missing,
13
conjugation, 19
definition of, 46, 71, 123
mood, 19
new, 135
nominative case after prepositions
and, 48
passive, 266
to separated from, 171, 173, 230
tense, 19, 37
unfamiliar forms, 16

villain, 163

virtue and grammar, 2, 20, 50, 91, 170,
250–51, 270

vocative case, 204

voting rights, 80, 154

Walker, David, 97–101

Walker, Edward, 101–2

War of 1812, 80, 83, 132

was, with *you,* 65–66, 89

Washington, George, 24, 26, 39, 79

The Washington Post, 268

Webster, John, 20–21

Webster, Noah. *See also Grammatical Institute of the English Language*

American Dictionary of the English Language, 66, 129–41, 243, 275n37

American Spelling Book, 133

The American Minerva, 39, 60

The American Spelling Book, 30, 133

A Brief History of Epidemic and Pestilential Diseases, 60–61

A Compendious Dictionary of the English Language, 61, 129

Connecticut school of, 27, 94–95

criticism of, 69

Dissertations, 36–39, 65, 141

Elements of Useful Knowledge, 61

English language lectures of, 5–10, 33, 34

essays by, 6

family history and career of, 20–39, 140

influence of, 73, 104, 109–10, 270

Murray, L., and, 60, 63–68

A Philosophical and Practical Grammar, 62, 65–68, 111, 123, 128, 136, 141

spelling reform and, 9, 38, 137–39, 271n5

Synopsis, 131–33

theories of, 2, 6, 122, 151, 159, 179, 184, 190–91, 207, 223

Webster, Noah (father), 21, 22, 35

Webster, Rebecca, 35, 36, 133

Webster, William, 133

Webster's Bible, Common Version, 133

Webster's Second, 243, 245–48, 254, 256–63

Webster's Third New International Dictionary, 243–64, 268–69

Western Recorder, 136

western "tall talk," 85–87

Westminster Assembly's "Shorter Catechism," 112

which, compared to *whose,* 13

White, E. B., 233, 236–42, 251, 252

White, John, 146

White, Richard Grant

criticism of, 178–86, 191–200, 205, 227

Every-Day English, 144, 147, 156, 157, 201, 204

in *The Galaxy,* 147, 175, 177, 183, 197, 200–201, 253, 267

The Riverside Shakespeare, 147

theories of, 143–53, 155, 158, 161–62, 169, 170, 203, 265, 268–69

Words and Their Uses, 143–45, 147–53, 178, 186, 194, 196–99, 201, 204

Whitney, Josiah, 185

Whitney, William Dwight, 175–86, 191

Essentials of English Grammar, 202–4

review by, 196–97, 246

who

with nonhumans, 47, 65

use of, 65

Who did she or *you speak to?,* 55, 65, 122, 184, 252, 269

whom compared to, 10, 31–32 37–38, 268

whom

among with, 109

incorrect use of, 171

who compared to, 10, 31–32 37–38, 268

to whom, 204

whose

with nonhumans, 47, 194

which compared to, 13

Wilberforce, William, 75

Wilde, Oscar, 266

will

    will/shall, 16–17, 37–38, 110, 152–53, 158, 173, 226, 240

    will/would, 254

Williams, Ralph Olmsted, 201–2

Wills, Garry, 245

Wilson, Woodrow, 215

Winged Words, or The Diversions of Purley (Horne Tooke), 37, 62, 64, 118–21, 125

Winning of the West (Roosevelt), 213

Woe Is I (O'Conner), 265

Wolcott, Oliver, 129–30

women, education of, 91, 93–97, 116, 167–68. *See also female; lady*

Women's Rights Convention, 152

Worcester, Joseph, 138–39, 141

Word Study, 253–54

words

    from Anglo-Saxon, 37, 38, 62, 119, 121, 125

    bizarre combinations, 161

    country words and phrases, 88

    feminized, 170

    histories, 176, 179, 184, 189–91

    low, 61

    misuse of, 148–53, 178, 235, 238–39

    new, 11, 150–51, 158–59, 169, 247–48, 258, 260

    obsolete, 49

    offensive words and phrases, 133, 134, 149

    origins, 65, 74, 111, 119–20, 123, 124, 131–32, 134

    overblown, 86

    over-genteel or pompous, 156

    pairs, 169, 189

    primary and secondary classes, 62–63

    with similar meanings, 159

Words and Their Uses (White, R.), 143–45, 147–53

    comments on, 178, 186, 194, 196–99, 201

    popularity of, 204

Words: Their Use and Abuse (Mathews), 156

would/will, 254

written language, 17

Wycliffe, John, 230

Yagoda, Ben, 266

Yale, 13, 21, 22–25, 55

ye, 16

you

    use of, 65, 72

    was with, 65–66, 89

    ye and, 16

    between you and I, 1

    you and me, you and I, 231

Young Kate (Lewis), 125

The Young Lady's Accidence (Bingham), 95, 113, 114